创新型人才跨境电子商务专业

跨境
电子商务双语教程

陈竹韵　朱丽娜◎主编

蔡雯钰　胡豪　黄翔　张梦瑶◎副主编

电子工业出版社

Publishing House of Electronics Industry

北京·BEIJING

内容简介

本书为国内领先的英汉对照的跨境电子商务（简称"跨境电商"）专业教材，共 8 章，主要内容包括跨境电商绪论、跨境电商网上开店与选品、跨境电商产品发布与管理、跨境电商网络营销与策划、跨境电商物流与海外仓、跨境电商通关实务、跨境电商支付与结算、跨境电商客户服务。

本书既可供国内大学生和社会上有一定英文基础、想学习跨境电商相关知识与技能的读者使用，也可供"一带一路"沿线国家的留学生和国外感兴趣的读者使用。

编者提供全套的数字化中英文对照练习、答案和视频材料。

图书在版编目（CIP）数据

跨境电子商务双语教程 / 陈竹韵，朱丽娜主编 . —北京：电子工业出版社，2023.3

ISBN 978-7-121-44908-6

Ⅰ . ①跨… Ⅱ . ①陈… ②朱… Ⅲ . ①电子商务 – 双语教学 – 高等职业教育 – 教材 Ⅳ . ① F713.36

中国国家版本馆 CIP 数据核字（2023）第 015364 号

责任编辑：袁桂春 特约编辑：张燕虹
印　　刷：北京七彩京通数码快印有限公司
装　　订：北京七彩京通数码快印有限公司
出版发行：电子工业出版社
　　　　　北京市海淀区万寿路 173 信箱　　邮编：100036
开　　本：787×1 092　1/16　印张：12.75　字数：425 千字
版　　次：2023 年 3 月第 1 版
印　　次：2025 年 7 月第 4 次印刷
定　　价：68.00 元

凡所购买电子工业出版社图书有缺损问题，请向购买书店调换。若书店售缺，请与本社发行部联系，联系及邮购电话：（010）88254888，88258888。

质量投诉请发邮件至 zlts@phei.com.cn，盗版侵权举报请发邮件至 dbqq@phei.com.cn。

本书咨询联系方式：（010）88254199，sjb@phei.com.cn。

Preface
前　言

More than 2,000 years ago, the Ancient Silk Road, starting from Chang'an, connected the Eurasian continent and became an important economic and cultural link between the East and the West. Today, China's cross-border E-commerce traders set up a silk road on the Internet, which made it possible to "buy globally and sell globally". This new E-road effectively promotes the trade among China and countries along "the Belt and Road" with the integration of technology, capital, goods and personnel driven by information flow. Thus, a new pattern of digital globalization, which is with open values, inclusiveness, balance and win-win strategy, is constructed by sharing high quality resources. The industry survey found that cross-border E-commerce enterprises are in urgent need of international, high-skilled and inter-disciplinary talents who can speak foreign languages, understand international trade rules and network technologies. In September, 2016, our author group was the first in China to teach cross-border E-commerce courses using the mode of Sino-foreign cooperation. Our group went abroad to teach in August, 2018. Consequently, we have obtained some teaching achievements both at home and abroad, and have accumulated valuable experience for the preparation of this book.

In 2019, the Ministry of Education decided to make cross-border E-commerce an independent major for higher education enrollment. With the popularization of online teaching around the world, not only school students and social students in China, but also more and more international students and overseas students are actively joining in this industry. This book was written to meet the needs of these learners.

This bilingual book has eight chapters. Chapter 1 briefly introduces the development experiences of cross-border E-commerce, global mainstream E-commerce platforms, talent demand, new technology application and

2000 多年前，古丝绸之路从长安出发，连接欧亚大陆，成为东西方经济文化的重要纽带。今天，中国的跨境电商搭建起一条网上丝绸之路，使"全球买、全球卖"成为可能，有效推动中国与"一带一路"沿线各国以信息流带动技术流、资金流、物资流和人才流的交融，推进优质资源有序流动和共享共用，构建"开放、包容、均衡、共赢"的数字全球化新格局。行业调研发现，跨境电商企业急需会外语、懂国际贸易规则和网络技术的国际化、高技能、复合型人才。2016 年 9 月，编写团队在国内首次采用中外合作的模式教授跨境电商课程。2018 年 8 月，团队赴境外教学，在国内外获得了一些教学成果，为本书编写积累了宝贵的经验。

2019 年，教育部确定将跨境电商作为大学的独立专业招生。随着全球网络教学的普及，不仅是中国在校生和社会生正在加入这个行业，越来越多的留学生和境外学习者也正在加入这个行业。本书的编写正是为了满足这些学习者的需求。

这本双语书共 8 章。第 1 章简要介绍跨境电商的发展历程、全球主流电商平台和人才需求、新技术应用等行业背景。第 2 ～ 8

other background information in this industry. The contents of Chapters 2 to 8 are organized according to the working process of cross-border E-commerce. They introduce online shop opening and product selection, posting and management, online marketing and planning, logistics and overseas warehouses, customs clearance practices, payment and settlement, customer service, etc.

After learning this book, Chinese learners or foreigners who want to improve their English communication skills can understand what cross-border E-commerce is, how to find the right products in China, and how to sell goods at the right price by using the right marketing strategy on the right platform, and then send goods to global customers at the right time. If this book is used as a textbook, it is recommended that the total class hours be 56-60, including 4 class hours for the first chapter and 6-8 class hours for the other chapters. It can also be adjusted to reduce or increase class hours according to teaching needs.

The main features of this book are as follows:

1. Timeliness, integrity and scientific nature of the system

The authors are experts from this industry or teachers teach this course at school, who have all been engaged in bilingual teaching of cross-border E-commerce for many years. According to the students' learning rules and operation procedures, the authors not only summarize the common features of Alibaba, AliExpress, Amazon, eBay, Shopee, Lazada and other platforms, but also refine the characteristics of each platform to carry out business according to the E-commerce ecological environment in different countries.

2. The effectiveness, practicability and diversity of the contents

This book designs the character image of Xiaowei, a beginner of cross-border E-commerce, to arrange the teaching contents, and simulates the working process of the character entering the cross-border E-commerce field as the main line. Each chapter is subdivided into different sections of knowledge points and skill points for a topic. It may improve students' knowledge and skills, and cultivate their

章，按跨境电商的工作流程系统地介绍网上开店与选品、产品刊登与管理、网络营销与策划、物流与海外仓、通关实务、支付与结算、客户服务等。

学习完本书，想提高英语交流能力的中国学习者或外籍人士能够理解跨境电商是什么，如何在中国找到合适的产品，在合适的平台，通过合适的营销方案，将产品以合适的价格，在合适的时间送到全球顾客手中。如作为教材，建议总学时为56～60学时，其中第1章为4学时，其他章为6～8学时，也可视教学需要酌情减少或增加课时。

本书主要有以下特点：

1. 体系的及时性、完整性、科学性

编者均为从事多年跨境电商双语教学的学校教师或行业专家。根据学生的学习规律和操作流程，他们既总结了阿里巴巴国际站、速卖通、亚马逊、eBay、Shopee、Lazada等平台的共性，又提炼了每个平台的特点，按照不同国家电商生态环境开展业务。

2. 内容的有效性、实用性、多样性

本书设计了跨境电商初学者小薇的人物形象来编排教学内容，以模拟该人物进入跨境电商领域的工作流程为主线。每章都针对一个主题细分出不同板块的知识点和技能点，在提高学生知识、技能的同时，培育学生多元文化

international literacy of multicultural communication.

3. The humanization, hierarchy and interaction of the structure

In order to help learner understanding, all teaching contents and exercises are in the form of Chinese and English. Each chapter completes one major task, which is embedded with the requirements of knowledge, skills and qualities.

4. The digital, flexible and real-time resources

This book provides a globally registered teaching resource pack providing video, PPT, cases, question bank and answers, various examination papers, recommended simulation software, etc. The author can regularly communicate with readers and provide answers on the Internet, and all materials will be updated in real time, and teaching can be conducted flexibly according to the needs of teachers.

The framework of this book, Chapter 1 and Chapter 8 are in charged by Zhuyun Chen from Zhejiang Institute of Mechanical & Eleltrical Engineering, which is the construction unit of National Demonstration Higher Vocational Colleges and High-level Vocational Colleges with Chinese characteristics (A Level). Mengyao Zhang is in charge of Chapter 2, Hao Hu is in charge of Chapter 3 and Chapter 4, Xiang Huang is in charge of Chapter 5, Wenjue Cai is in charge of Chapter 6, Zhuyun Chen and Jing Yi are in charge of Chapter 7. Dongxu Sui carefully proofread the manuscrip of this book. Thanks to the guidence and valuable suggestions to this book provided by business experts Lina Zhu and Jingquan Zheng from Zhejiang International Trade Digital Technology Co., Ltd., and Hangzhou Hongyu Education Technology Co., Ltd., and Senior Advisor of College-Enterprise Collaboration Zhiping Yin from Alibaba Taobao Education. Rachel Liu, director of overseas department of Box Hill Institute in Australia, led a team of foreign experts to provide guidance.

The rapid development of cross-border E-commerce is inseparable from the strong support of Chinese government

沟通的国际化素养。

3. 结构的人性化、层次性、互动性

为了帮助学习者理解，所有教学内容和习题都以中英文对照的形式出现。每章完成1项大工作任务，内嵌知识、技能、素养的要求。

4. 资源的数字化、弹性化、实时化

本书配套提供可全球登录的教学资源包：提供视频、PPT、案例、题库和答案、各类试卷、推荐模拟软件等。作者可定期在网上与读者交流和提供答疑，所有资料实时更新，也可按教师需求自由组合进行教学。

本书由国家示范性高等职业院校、中国特色高水平高职学校建设单位（A档）浙江机电职业技术学院的陈竹韵负责编写框架和第1章、第8章，张梦瑶负责编写第2章，胡豪负责编写第3章、第4章，黄翔负责编写第5章，蔡雯珏负责编写第6章，陈竹韵和易静负责第7章。隋东旭对本书做了细致的审校工作。感谢浙江国贸数字科技有限公司和杭州黉宇教育科技有限公司的企业专家朱丽娜、郑经全，阿里巴巴淘宝教育校企合作高级专家殷志平为本书编写提供指导并提出宝贵建议。澳大利亚博士山学院海外部主任 Rachel Liu 率领外籍专家团队提供指导。

跨境电商事业的迅猛地发展，离不开中国政府部门的大力支持，

departments, the selfless work of obscure cross-border E-commerce practitioners, and the continuous exploration of college teachers, who have provided a large number of professional talents for the society. These together form a thriving ecosystem that benefits consumers around the world. The authors would like to thank the China (Hangzhou) Cross-border E-commerce Comprehensive Pilot Zone and its subordinate parks for their strong support.

The development of big data, artificial intelligence, 5G, VR, block-chain and other technologies will continue to transform this young industry. Thanks to this era of great changes and opportunities. We will always keep our original intention and keep moving forward.

In the process of writing this book, we strive for perfection, but due to the limitation of the level, some errors are inevitable, please forgive us and point them out. If you have any questions, please contact us by E-mail 940856915@qq.com.

默默无闻的跨境电商从业者的忘我工作,以及高校教师们的不断探索,他们为社会输送大量的专业人才。这些共同形成了整个欣欣向荣且能造福于全球消费者的生态圈。编者感谢中国(杭州)跨境电商综合试验区及下属园区的大力支持。

大数据、人工智能、5G、VR、区块链等技术的发展必将不断变革这个年轻的行业。感谢这个伟大变革和充满机会的时代,我们将永保初心、不断前行。

在本书编写过程中,我们力求完美,但因水平所限难免有所疏漏,敬请包涵并指正,如有问题请发邮件至 940856915@qq.com。

Contents
目　录

Chapter 1
第 1 章

An Introduction to Cross-Border E-Commerce
跨境电商绪论

Lead-in case

Xiaowei is a freshman in a vocational college. In her hometown, there are lots of small or medium-sized factories making products such as socks, shoes, T-shirts, ties, towels, pans, fabrics and other goods. They are facing the reality of shrinking demands from offline market, rising labour and material costs, out-of-date manufacturing process. Nearly half of the offline shops are facing great challenges. Most of those factories tend to sell their products to the overseas market and change their traditional sales channels to online platforms to survive. Therefore, she is very interested in cross-border E-commerce. However, she has no idea of the whole big picture of this industry. By learning this chapter, you and Xiaowei will understand the opportunities in the cross-border E-commerce market, and design a career plan to embrace the new digital economic era.

Learning objectives

1. Objectives of knowledge

(1) To master the definition, classification and development of cross-border E-commerce.

(2) To master the global cross-border E-commerce mainstream platforms and their characteristics.

(3) To understand the relevant positions and requirements of cross-border E-commerce industry, and the direction of professional development.

(4) To understand the application and prospects of new technologies such as big data, 5G, VR in the industry.

2. Objectives of skills

(1) To use foreign language for cross-cultural business communication and to use computer software for daily business correspondence and other documents.

(2) To carry out online and offline research activities, collect and summarize information based on the questions.

案例导入

小薇是高职一年级的新生。她的家乡有许多中小型工厂生产袜子、鞋子、T恤、领带、毛巾、平底锅、布料和其他商品。然而，它们面临着线下市场需求萎缩、劳动力和材料成本上升、制造工艺过时的现实问题。近一半的线下商店面临着巨大的挑战。为了生存，大部分工厂准备将产品的传统销售渠道改为网络平台销往海外市场。因此，她对跨境电子商务非常感兴趣。但是，她对这个行业的基本情况一无所知。通过本章学习，你将与小薇一起初步了解当前跨境电商市场面临的机会，设计职业规划来拥抱数字经济新时代。

学习目标

1. 知识目标

（1）掌握跨境电商的定义、分类和发展历程。

（2）掌握全球跨境电商主流平台和各电商平台特点。

（3）了解跨境电商行业相关岗位和要求，职业发展方向。

（4）了解大数据、5G、VR 等新技术在行业的应用和前景。

2. 技能目标

（1）能用外语进行跨文化商务沟通，用计算机软件处理日常业务函电等文件。

（2）能根据提出的问题，开展线上线下调研活动，对信息进行梳理和汇总。

(3) To objectively analyze one's own characteristics and find one's own career development direction related to cross-border E-commerce.

(4) To quickly acquire new skills in line with changes in the times and innovate in the field of work.

3．Objectives of qualities

(1) To have a patient, detailed and rigorous work style.

(2) To have the spirit of abiding by laws and regulations related to foreign trade and self-discipline.

(3) To have good leadership in communication and coordination, decision-making, analysis and judgment, motivation, etc.

(4) To have a long-lasting interest in and change in new knowledge and skills.

1.1 Overview of Cross-Border E-Commerce

1.1.1 Concept and Characteristics of Cross-Border E-Commerce

The development of Internet technology has broken the traditional five-ring links of international trade among domestic producers, domestic traders, foreign distributors, foreign retailers and the terminal consumers. The intermediary link of cross-border E-commerce has been greatly shortened. Domestic producers can directly trade with consumers to realize the exchange flows of information, cash and logistics. 2014 is called the first year of cross-border E-commerce. After several years of the surge in the overseas purchasing (i.e. "purchasing foreign products online") market, on August 1, 2014, the General Administration of Customs issued announcements No. 56 and 57, namely *Notice on the Supervision of Inbound and Outbound Goods and Articles Related to Cross-Border Trade E-Commerce* and *Notice on the Addition of Customs Supervision Mode Code*. The government approved the cross-border E-commerce mode for the first time. China formally entered the period of explosion and rapid growth of cross-border E-commerce.

Cross-border E-commerce refers to an international business activity in which the transaction entities from

（3）能客观分析自身的特质，寻找与跨境电商相关的职业发展方向。

（4）能快速根据时代变化掌握新技能，在工作领域进行技术创新。

3．素质目标

（1）具有耐心、细致、严谨的工作作风。

（2）具有遵守外贸相关法律法规和自律精神。

（3）具有良好的沟通与协调、决策、分析与判断、激励等领导力。

（4）对新知识、新技能具有持久的学习兴趣和变革力。

1.1 跨境电商概述

1.1.1 跨境电商的概念和特点

互联网技术的发展打破了传统的国内生产商、国内贸易商、国外分销商、国外零售商、终端消费者的五环国际贸易链路。跨境电商将贸易链路的中介环节大大缩短。国内生产商可以直接与终端消费者交易，实现信息流、资金流和物流的交换。2014年被称为跨境电商元年。海外代购（即"海淘"）市场历经数年的激增后，2014年8月1日，海关总署发布了56、57号公告，即《关于跨境贸易电商进出境货物、物品有关监管事宜的公告》和《关于增列海关监管方式代码的公告》。政府层面首次认可了跨境电商的模式。中国正式进入跨境电商的爆发和快速增长期。

跨境电商是指不同关境的交易主体，通过跨境电商平台达成

different customs borders conduct transactions, make payments and settlements through cross-border E-commerce platforms, and deliver commodities and complete transactions through cross-border logistics.

Cross-border E-commerce is divided into cross-border import E-commerce and cross-border export E-commerce. Cross-border import E-commerce imports products from overseas into China to meet the needs of domestic consumers. In order to ensure the quality and quantity of imported products, at present most cross-border import E-commerce platforms in China, such as yMatou, Tmall Global, NetEase Kaola, Suning Cloud Merchants, Shunfeng Haitao and other self-purchasing platforms. Cross-border export E-commerce exports goods made in China to foreign countries, mainly small and medium-sized sellers stationed on third-party E-commerce platforms, such as Alibaba, AliExpress, DHgate, Lightinthebox, Made-in-China, etc. Sellers edit the image of goods into electronic information such as pictures, keywords, commodity descriptions, and upload them to the platform, publish on the Internet for sale. After the transaction is conducted with buyers, the goods are transported to the buyers by international courier.

Cross-border E-commerce exhibits the following characteristics:

(1) Global: Internet is a borderless media with global and non-centralized characteristics. Compared with traditional transaction approaches, cross-border E-commerce is a borderless transaction, which does not have the geographic factors of traditional transactions. Internet users can have the maximum sharing of information across national boundaries to provide products and services to the market.

(2) Intangible: The development of invisible networks enables products and services to be transmitted in the forms of data, sound and images.

(3) Anonymous: Due to the non-centralized and global nature of cross-border E-commerce, it is difficult to directly identify the identity and geographic location of cross-border E-commerce users except by using technical means, which leads to the asymmetry between freedom and responsibility.

交易、进行支付结算，并通过跨境物流送达商品、完成交易的一种国际商业活动。

跨境电商分为跨境进口电商和跨境出口电商。跨境进口电商将海外的产品进口到中国，满足国内消费者需求。为确保进口产品的供应品质和数量，目前国内大多数跨境进口电商平台，如洋码头、天猫国际、网易考拉、苏宁云商海购、顺丰海淘以及其他自采自营平台。跨境出口电商是将中国制造的商品出口到国外，以入驻到第三方电商平台的中小卖家为主，如阿里巴巴国际站、速卖通、敦煌网、兰亭集势、中国制造网等。卖家们把商品编辑成图片、关键词、商品描述等电子信息上传至平台，发布至互联网上进行销售，与买家达成交易后，通过国际快递将商品运输到买家手上。

跨境电商呈现以下特征：

（1）全球性：网络是一个没有边界的媒介体，具有全球性和非中心化的特征。与传统的交易方式相比，跨境电商是一种无边界交易，并不存在传统交易所具有的地理因素。互联网用户可以最大限度地跨国界共享信息，向市场提供产品和服务。

（2）无形性：网络的发展使产品与服务以数据、声音和图像的方式传输。

（3）匿名性：由于跨境电商的非中心化和全球性的特性，除运用技术手段外，很难直接识别跨境电商用户的身份和其所处的地理位置，导致自由与责任的不对称。

(4) Instantaneous: For Internet, the speed of transmission is independent of geographic distance. Regardless of space-time distance, cross-border E-commerce sends and receives information almost at the same time, breaking the space-time barrier of international trade.

(5) Paperless: In cross-border E-commerce, the process of sending and receiving information from computers replaces paper transaction files, making transactions paperless.

(6) Rapidly evolving: The iteration of technology, and the upgrade of consumer experience will rapidly promote the transformation of cross-border E-commerce mode. National laws and regulations of platform must keep up with the fast changing pace.

1.1.2　Classification of Cross-Border E-Commerce

Cross-border E-commerce can be divided into B2B, B2C, C2C, M2C and other E-commerce modes by business model, and the details are as follows:

B2B = Business to Business, both the supplier and the demander of E-commerce transactions are merchants (or enterprises or companies), who use the E-commerce platform to complete the process of publishing supply and demand information, making and confirming orders, payment process and issuance, transmission and receipt of bills, determine distribution plans and monitor the distribution process, including Alibaba, Made-in-China, Global Resource Network, DHgate, etc.

B2C = Business to Customer, enterprises provide online shopping and online payment platforms for terminal customers through the Internet, including Tmall Global, NetEase Kaola, Amazon, etc.

C2C = Consumer to Consumer, by providing an online trading platform for buyers and sellers, realize the transactions between individual sellers and buyers, or exchange the second-hand idle goods, including eBay, Etsy, etc.

M2C = Manufacturer to Customer, which is the cross-border E-commerce mode directly from the production

（4）即时性：对于网络而言，传输的速度和地理距离无关。无论时空距离如何，跨境电商的发送信息与接收信息几乎是同时的，打破国际贸易的时空阻隔。

（5）无纸化：在跨境电商中，计算机的信息发送和接收过程记录取代了纸质交易文件，交易实现无纸化。

（6）快速演进：技术的迭代、消费体验的升级会快速推进跨境电商模式的转变。国家法律法规和平台的监管也必须跟上快速变化的节奏。

1.1.2　跨境电商分类

跨境电商按商业模式可分为B2B、B2C、C2C、M2C 等电子商务模式，具体如下：

B2B = Business to Business，进行电商交易的供需双方都是商家 (或企业、公司)，使用电商平台，完成发布供求信息，订货及确认订货，支付过程及票据的签发、传送和接收，确定配送方案并监控配送过程等交易过程，包括阿里巴巴国际站，中国制造网、环球资源网、敦煌网等。

B2C = Business to Customer，企业通过互联网为终端消费者提供网上购物和在线支付的购物平台，包括天猫国际、网易考拉、亚马逊等。

C2C = Consumer to Consumer，通过为买卖双方提供一个在线交易平台，实现个人卖家与买家之间的交易，或交换二手闲置货品，包括 eBay、Etsy 等。

M2C = Manufacturer to Customer，从生产企业直接到消费

enterprise to the consumer. From analyzing consumer needs, development, production and retail of products, specialists of production enterprise strictly check each link, reducing the length of supply chain to the shortest, and realizing the minimum waste of value chain. At present, more and more manufacturing enterprises are entering the platform, which also forces the middlemen to transform their business mode.

Independent stations, with more and more businesses stationed on the platform, fierce competition makes sellers difficult to obtain traffic flow. Sellers can create their own Shopify and other similar cross-border E-commerce platforms, which can create private traffic flow, brand, flexible marketing and operating methods, and also bring more technical challenges.

1.1.3 Development Experiences of Cross-Border E-Commerce

Global cross-border E-commerce has been booming all over the world since Amazon started to sell books in 1995. Amazon's Black Five, Alibaba's Double 11, Jingdong's 6 · 18 and other shopping festivals have made their sales turnover on the rise. E-commerce companies have outperformed offline physical shops. In 2020, lots of world famous companies went bankrupt due to a variety of factors, including MUJI U.S. companies, well-known U.S. retailers Ascena and Brooks Brothers, Victoria's Secret U.K., and Debenhams in Britain. However, Alibaba, Jingdong (注：简写为 JD) and other companies have become comprehensive conglomerates including E-commerce, payment, logistics, health and education industries.

In recent years, the number of Internet users worldwide has grown continuously. According to the statistics of the International Telecommunication Union, the total number of Internet users reached 4.1 billion in 2019, an increase of 5.3% year on year. The global percentage of netizens increased from 16.8% in 2005 to 53.6% in 2019; from 2005 to 2019, the number of netizens increased by an average of 10% annually. Among these, 86.6% of people in well-

者个人的跨境电商模式。从分析消费者需求、产品的研发、生产到零售，生产企业对每个环节都由专人严格把关，把供应链长度减到最短，实现价值链的最小浪费。目前，越来越多的制造企业入驻平台，也迫使中间商转型。

独立站，随着平台入驻的商家越来越多，竞争日益激烈，流量的获取越来越难。商家创建属于自己的 Shopify 等类似跨境电商平台，能够为商家创造私域流量、品牌，以及灵活的营销与运营方式，也带来更多的技术挑战。

1.1.3 跨境电商发展历程

全球跨境电商自亚马逊于 1995 年经营书籍开始，在世界各国蓬勃发展。亚马逊的黑五、阿里巴巴的双十一、京东 6 · 18 等购物节销售额节节攀升。电商公司的经营业绩超过了线下实体商店。2020 年，由于各种因素，许多世界知名公司破产，包括无印良品美国公司、美国知名零售商 Ascena 和布鲁克斯兄弟、维秘的英国公司、英国德本汉姆等。然而，阿里巴巴、京东等公司却已发展成包含电商、支付、物流、健康、教育等的综合性互联网集团。

近年来，全球互联网用户的数量继续增长。据国际电信联盟的统计数据，2019 年全球网民总数达到 41 亿人，同比增长 5.3%。全球网民比例从 2005 年的 16.8% 上升到 2019 年的 53.6%；2005 年到 2019 年，网民数量平均每年增长 10%。其中，发达国家 86.6% 的人使用互联

developed countries use the Internet; only 19.1% in the least developed countries. According to the data from E-Marketer, the global online retail sales and their share of global retail sales increased year by year from 2017 to 2019 (Figure 1-1). In 2019, global online retail sales were $3.5 trillion, accounting for 14% of global retail sales. E-Marketer predicts that the global online retail sales and their share will continue to grow steadily. It is estimated that by 2023, the global online retail sales will reach $6.5 trillion, accounting for 22% of global retail sales.

网；最不发达国家只有 19.1%。根据 E-Marketer 数据，2017 年至 2019 年，全球在线零售额及其占全球零售额的比重逐年上升（图 1-1）。2019 年，全球网络零售额为 3.5 万亿美元，占全球零售额的 14%。E-Marketer 预测，全球在线零售额及其份额将继续保持稳定增长。据估计，到 2023 年，全球网络零售额将达到 6.5 万亿美元，占全球零售额的 22%。

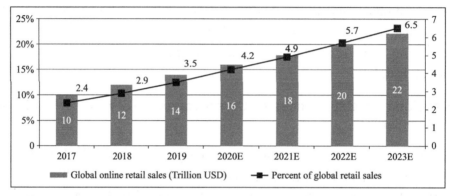

Figure 1-1　2017-2023 Global Online Retail Sales Statistics and Forecast

Resource: E-Marketer, Foreword Industry Research Institute

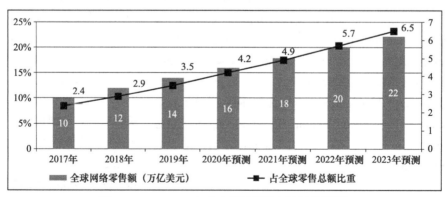

图 1-1　2017-2023 年全球网络零售额统计及预测

资料来源：网络营销者，前瞻产业研究院

From a regional perspective, Asia-Pacific region remained as the pioneer and main force in the global E-commerce market in 2019 (Figure 1-2). Since Asia-Pacific region became the world's largest online retail market in 2013, its average annual growth rate has remained above 20%.

从区域角度来看，2019 年亚太地区仍是全球电商市场的先遣和主力部队（图 1-2）。自 2013 年亚太地区成为全球最大的在线零售市场以来，其年均增长率一直保持在 20% 以上。

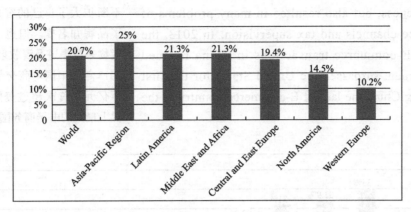

Figure1-2　TOP6 Growth Rate of Online Retail Sales in Various Regions of the World in 2019

Resource: E-Marketer, Foreword Industry Research Institute

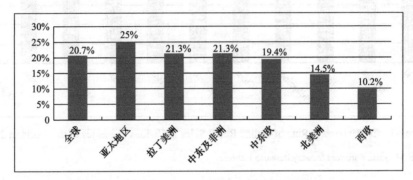

图 1-2　2019 年全球前六的地区的网络零售增长率

资料来源：网络营销者，前瞻产业研究院

E-Marketer statistics (Figure 1-2) show that in 2019, online retail sales in Asia-Pacific region grew by 25%, 4.3 percentage points higher than the global average level, which was also, higher than in other regions. E-Marketer statistics (Figure 1-3) show that six of the top 10 countries in the global online retail growth are from Asia-Pacific region, including R.O. Korea, Indonesia, Malaysia, China, Philippines and India.

The history of cross-border E-commerce in China is very short and can be divided into the following stages:

Initiation period (before 2014): Starting in 2005, with the improvement of people's living standards, overseas Chinese students bought goods and mailed to their relatives and friends. Gradually, by posting information on social websites, they constantly expanded their customer groups, increase

E-Marketer 的统计数据（图1-2）显示，2019 年亚太地区在线零售额增长率达到25%，比全球平均水平高出 4.3 个百分点，也高于其他地区。在全球网络零售增长排名前十的国家中，有六个国家来自亚太地区，分别是韩国、印度尼西亚、马来西亚、中国、菲律宾和印度。

我国跨境电商发展时间很短，大体可分为以下几个阶段：

萌芽期（2014 年以前）：从 2005 年开始，随着人民生活水平的提高，出国留学人员为亲戚朋友代购商品后邮寄。渐渐地，他们通过在社交网站上发布信息，

brand awareness, but also resulted in many problems of goods source channels and tax supervision. In 2013, the volume of E-commerce transactions in China reached 10 trillion Yuan, surpassed the United States for the first time, making China the largest E-commerce country in the world.

不断扩大了自己的客户群，提高了品牌知名度，但也产生了不少货物来源渠道及税收监管的问题。2013年，中国电商交易额达到10万亿元，首次超过美国，成为世界上最大的电子商务国家。

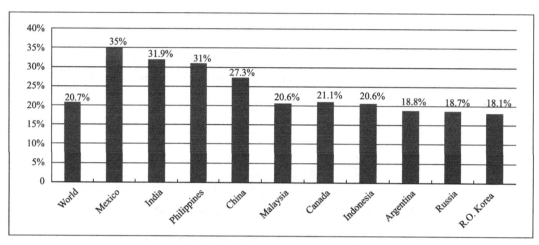

Figure1-3　Top10 Growth Rate of Online Retail Sales in Various Countries of the World in 2019

Resource: E-Marketer, Foreword Industry Research Institute

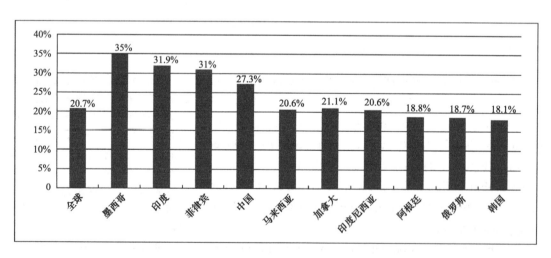

图 1-3　2019 年全球排名前十的国家的网络零售增长率

资料来源：网络营销者，前瞻产业研究院

Start-up period (2014-2017): In 2014, with announcements No. 56 and No. 57 of the General Administration of Customs defining the legitimate status of cross-border E-commerce

启动期（2014—2017 年）：2014年，海关总署发布的56、57 号公告明确了跨境电商的合法地位并

and incorporating supervision, Tmall Global, NetEase Kaola, Small Red Book, yMatou and other platforms have been established successively, and more and more consumers choose to purchase overseas products in formal platforms.

Cross-border E-commerce in Zhejiang province has developed rapidly and made a breakthrough, becoming a new growth point of Zhejiang's export trade. Relying on the favorable E-commerce development environment and abundant market commodity resources, the State Council approved the establishment of China (Hangzhou) cross-border E-commerce comprehensive pilot area (hereinafter referred to as the comprehensive pilot area) on March 7, 2015. In January 2016, Standing Committee of the State Council decided to promote the experience of Hangzhou cross-border E-commerce comprehensive pilot area.

纳入监管，天猫国际、网易考拉海购、小红书、洋码头等平台相继成立，越来越多的消费者选择在正规平台购买海外产品。

浙江省跨境电商发展迅速并取得突破性进展，成为浙江新的外贸出口增长点。依托良好的电商发展环境和丰富的市场商品资源，2015 年 3 月 7 日，国 务 院同意设立中国（杭州）跨境电商综合试验区（以下简称综合试验区）。2016 年 1 月，国务院常务会议决定推广杭州跨境电商综合试验区经验。

Knowledge Extension: The Comprehensive Pilot Area of Hangzhou

The comprehensive pilot area of Hangzhou achieves the integration of information flow, capital flow and goods flow for cross-border E-commerce through the construction of "six systems and two platforms", namely, information sharing system, financial service system, intelligent logistics system, E-commerce integrity system, statistical monitoring system and risk control system, online comprehensive service platform and offline comprehensive park platform. Thus, business liberalization, facilitation and standardization are realized.

知识拓展：杭州跨境电商综合试验区

杭州跨境电商综合试验区通过构建信息共享体系、金融服务体系、智能物流体系、电商诚信体系、统计监测体系和风险防控体系，以及线上综合服务平台和线下综合园区平台这"六体系两平台"，完成跨境电商信息流、资金流、货物流的"三流合一"，实现跨境电商自由化、便利化、规范化发展。

High-speed development period (after 2018): The national incentive and supervision policies are improving increasingly, and the pilot cities for cross-border E-commerce are expanding in China. By December 2020, China has established 105 cross-border E-commerce comprehensive pilot areas covering 30 provinces (districts and municipalities directly under the Central Government), forming a pattern of development of domestic and overseas linkage and mutual economic development between East and West. A new pattern of dual-cycle development with domestic circulation as the main factor and mutual promotion

高速发展期（2018 年之后）：国家激励和监管政策日益完善，跨境电商试点城市在中国不断扩大。到 2020 年 12 月，中国已建立 105 个跨境电商综合试验区，地域范围覆盖 30 个省（区、直辖市），形成了陆海内外联动、东西双向经济互促的发展格局。一个以国内循环为主、国内外互促的

between foreign and domestic circulation is being formed, which lays a foundation for promoting the stable, sustainable and high-speed development of China's economy.

双循环发展的新格局正在形成，为推动我国经济稳定、持续、高速发展奠定了基础。

1.1.4 Development Prospects of Cross-Border E-Commerce

1.1.4 跨境电商发展前景

1. Southeast Asia market has a bright future

On November 15, 2020, the 10 ASEAN countries, China, Japan, R.O. Korea, Australia and New Zealand signed *Regional Comprehensive Economic Partnership* (RCEP). It is expected that the Southeast Asian market will have a bright future. Lazada and Shopee platforms will certainly play an important role. There will be a significant increase in the number of sellers and buyers, as well as a considerable purchasing population base and purchasing power. At present, Alibaba and Tencent in China have laid out the market and have joined the two platforms one after another. It is believed that the Southeast Asian market will become the main cross-border E-commerce market in the world in the next few years.

2. OEM enterprises register international brand and go overseas through multi-channels

1. 东南亚市场前景广阔

2020 年 11 月 15 日，东盟十国加上中国、日本、韩国、澳大利亚及新西兰签署了《区域全面经济伙伴关系协定》（RCEP）。预计东南亚市场具有广阔的未来前景。Lazada 和 Shopee 平台必有作为。卖家和买家的数量明显增加，购买人口基数和购买力相当可观。目前，中国阿里巴巴和腾讯纷纷布局该市场并已入股这两大平台。相信在未来几年，东南亚市场将成为全球跨境电商主要市场。

2. OEM（Original Equipment Manufacture，原始设备制造商，其基本含义指定牌生产合作，俗称"贴牌"或"代工"）企业注册国际品牌并多渠道出海

By directly facing overseas consumers, the original factory-type cross-border E-commerce sellers are no longer satisfied with the traditional OEM model, and realize the importance of cultivating brands and channels. Through direct or indirect investment in overseas enterprises, these enterprises independently register companies or register their own brand international trademarks. Through video website, Google search, online exhibition, social sharing and other modes, enterprises can enhance brand awareness, increase browsing volume, conversion rate and average transaction price.

原工厂型的跨境电商卖家直接面对境外消费者，不再满足于传统的 OEM 模式，并意识到了培养品牌和渠道的重要性。这些企业通过直接或间接投资境外企业，独立注册公司或注册自有品牌的国际商标。企业通过视频网站、谷歌搜索、线上展会、社交分享等模式，增强品牌认知度，提高浏览量、转化率和客单价。

Knowledge Extension: *Regional Comprehensive Economic Partnership*（RCEP）

知识拓展：《区域全面经济伙伴关系协定》（RCEP）

RCEP aims to establish a free trade agreement with a unified market by reducing tariffs and non-tariff barriers.

RCEP 旨在通过降低关税和非关税壁垒建立统一市场的自由贸

After the RCEP is reached, it will cover more than 29% of the world's population, more than 30% of GDP and about 28% of global trade volume, making it the largest and the most potential free trade area in the world. More than 90% of the goods trade in the region will achieve zero tariff after the agreement comes into force, which makes the RCEP hopeful to fulfill all the goods trade liberalization commitments in a short time.

易协定。RCEP 达成后，将覆盖全球 29% 以上的人口、30% 以上的 GDP 和 28% 左右的全球贸易额，成为全球最大、具潜力的自由贸易区域。该协定生效后，该地区 90% 以上的货物贸易将实现零关税，这使 RCEP 有望在短时间内兑现所有货物贸易自由化承诺。

3．Independent stations will lead the market

As more and more sellers enter the cross-border E-commerce platforms, the costs for traffic flow and order acquisition are increasing, and the profit growth space is limited. Independent stations are platforms where sellers build their own websites to show their products and attract customers to place orders. Unlike cross-border E-commerce platforms, independent stations can establish a better brand image and directly sell products to customers. At present, sellers with high quality, strong brand influence or complex technology may incorporate independent stations into operational planning.

3．独立站将引领市场

随着跨境电商平台入驻的商家越来越多，流量和订单的获取成本越来越高，利润增长空间有限。独立站是指店家自己建一个网站来展示自己的产品，并让客户购买、下单的平台。独立站与跨境电商平台不同，能较好地树立品牌形象，直接把产品销售给客户。现阶段，自身品质较高、品牌影响力较强或技术较复杂的卖家，可将独立站纳入商业规划。

1.2   The Choice of Mainstream Cross-Border E-Commerce Platforms

1.2.1   Market Distribution of International E-Commerce Platforms

Cross-border E-commerce platforms are created by Internet companies and have formed their own dominant markets in the global political and economic environment for more than a decade.

North America generally refers to the United States, Canada, Greenland and other regions. It is the most economically developed continent in the world. Its total GDP and per capita GDP surpassed those of the European Union. In the cross-border E-commerce markets of the United States and Canada, there are two famous E-business platforms, Amazon and eBay. Etsy mainly sells art works, clothing, jewelry and other decorative items.

1.2   跨境电商主流平台选择

1.2.1   国际电商平台市场分布

跨境电商平台是由互联网公司创立的，在 10 余年的全球政治和经济环境中形成了各自的主导市场。

北美洲通常指美国、加拿大和格陵兰岛等地区。它是世界上经济最发达的大洲。其 GDP 总量和人均 GDP 均超越欧盟。美国和加拿大的跨境电商市场，有亚马逊和 eBay 两大跨境电商平台。Etsy 主要销售艺术品、服装、珠宝和其他装饰物品。

As a gathering place of well-developed countries, Europe has many superior cross-border E-commerce platforms in many countries or sub-regions. Cdiscount is currently France's first large-scale cross-border E-commerce platform, belonging to Casino Group, one of France's largest super merchants, which is similar to online wholesale shops. Bol.com is the largest E-commerce platform in Belgium, the Netherlands and Luxembourg with over 7.5 million active users and 16,000 sellers. It is an E-commerce retailer of books, toys and electronic products covering more than 20 categories and more than 15 million different products. Binga is mainly for middle and high-end people in Europe. It sells bedding and linen fabrics, decorations, wall art works, clocks, lights, candles, jewelry and other products.

The African E-commerce market is facing tremendous opportunities for growth. According to the prediction given by McKinsey, online shopping in Africa will account for 10% of total retail sales in 2025 and will grow at an annual rate of 40% in the next decade. According to the statistics from Alibaba, in 2019, the import volume of African commodities increased by 98%, the number of buyers increased by 64%, the volume of African export commodities on the platform increased by 69%, and cross-border E-commerce became a new highlight of trade between China and Africa. Jumia, founded in 2012 and known as the African Amazon, now has more than 4 million consumers, and Kilimall currently receives more than 10,000 orders per day.

On the Alibaba platform, goods from "the Belt and Road" countries continuously are welcomed by Chinese consumers. The total commodity sales of countries along "the Belt and Road" that have entered China through Tmall Global have been growing rapidly. The year-on-year growth in 2018 was 120%, almost doubled that number in 2017. Cainiao Logistics built a backbone network of global intelligent logistics, forming six eHubs in Hangzhou, Hong Kong, Kuala Lumpur, Dubai, Moscow and Liege, promoting second-level customs clearance and giving small and medium-sized enterprises the world's currency rights.

On the AliExpress platform, in 2018, the number of

欧洲作为发达国家的聚集地，存在不少国家或子区域的优势跨境电商平台。Cdiscount 目前是法国第一大跨境电商平台，隶属于法国最大超商之一 Casino Group 集团，类似在线批发商城。Bol.com 是比利时、荷兰、卢森堡地区最大的电商平台，拥有超过 750 万名活跃用户、1.6 万个卖家。它是书籍、玩具和电子产品电商零售商，涉及 20 多个品类，超 1500 万种不同的产品。Binga 以面向欧洲中高端人群为主。它销售床上用品和亚麻织物、装饰物、墙面艺术品、钟表、灯具、蜡烛、首饰饰品类等各类产品。

非洲电商市场迎来巨大发展机遇。据麦肯锡预测，2025 年非洲网上购物将占零售总额的 10%，且在未来 10 年里，非洲网络零售额将以每年 40% 的速度增长。据阿里巴巴统计数据，2019 年度非洲商品的进口成交额同比增长 98%，购买商品的买家数增长 64%，平台上非洲出口商品成交额增长 69%，跨境电商成为中非之间新的贸易亮点。2012 年成立的 Jumia 被誉为"非洲的亚马逊"，现拥有 400 多万名消费者，Kilimall 目前日均订单量超过 1 万单。

在阿里巴巴平台上，"一带一路"国家商品持续受到中国消费者欢迎。通过天猫国际进入中国的"一带一路"沿线国家商品总销售额持续快速增长。2018 年同比增长 120%，与 2017 年相比几乎翻倍。菜鸟物流建设全球智能物流骨干网，在杭州、香港、吉隆坡、迪拜、莫斯科、列日形成 6个 eHub，推动秒级通关，令全球中小企业拥有世界通货权。

在速卖通平台上，2018 年"一

buyers in the countries along "the Belt and Road" accounted for 56%, and consumers in the countries along the line created 57% of orders and 49% of transactions. Lazada, the largest E-commerce company in Southeast Asia, has become a bridge between Chinese businesses and 560 million consumers in Southeast Asia. With Lazada's overseas warehouses, the logistics timeliness in many countries in Southeast Asia has been reduced from one week to 72 hours.

1.2.2　Global E-Commerce Platforms

Among the global E-commerce platforms, Alibaba, AliExpress in China and Amazon, eBay in the United States have high reputation.

Knowledge Extension: Alibaba Technology Co., Ltd.

It is a company founded in Hangzhou, Zhejiang province in 1999 by 18 people led by Yun Ma, a former English teacher. On September 19, 2014, Alibaba Group was officially listed on the New York Stock Exchange, creating the largest IPO record in history with the stock code of "Baba".

Alibaba Group operates a number of businesses related to the Internet and builds a huge business ecosystem. Its main businesses includes Taobao, Tmall, Juhuasuan, Alibaba, AliExpress, 1688, Ali Mom, Alibaba Cloud Computing, Ant Financial Service, Cainiao Logistics and so on.

Established in 1999, Alibaba is the first business sector of Alibaba Group, which has now become the world's leading B2B E-commerce platform for cross-border trade. The platform uses digitized pattern technology and products to reconstruct the full link of cross-border trade, accurately match the business needs of both buyers and sellers of cross-border trade, and provide them with digital marketing, trading, finance and supply chain services. It has over 150 million registered members and publishes 300,000 cross-border purchasing requirements on the platform every day. It

带一路"沿线国家买家数占比达 56%，沿线国家消费者创造了 57% 的订单量和 49% 的交易额。东南亚最大电商 Lazada 则成为中国商家和东南亚 5.6 亿名消费者之间的桥梁。借助 Lazada 海外仓，东南亚多国的物流时效从 1 周缩短到 72 小时必达。

1.2.2　全球性电商平台

在全球性电商平台中，中国的阿里巴巴国际站、速卖通和美国的亚马逊、eBay 具有较高的知名度。

知识拓展：阿里巴巴网络技术有限公司

阿里巴巴是于 1999 年由原英语教师马云带领的 18 人在浙江杭州创立的公司。2014 年 9 月 19 日，阿里巴巴在纽约证券交易所正式挂牌上市，创造了历史上最大的 IPO 纪录，股票代码为 "Baba"。阿里巴巴经营多项与互联网相关的业务，构建了庞大的商业生态系，其主营业务包括淘宝网、天猫、聚划算、阿里巴巴国际站、速卖通、1688、阿里妈妈、阿里云、蚂蚁金服、菜鸟物流等。

阿里巴巴国际站成立于 1999 年，是阿里巴巴集团的第一个业务板块，现已成为全球领先的跨境贸易 B2B 电商平台。该平台以数字化格局技术与产品，重构跨境贸易全链路，精准匹配跨境贸易买卖双方业务需求，为其提供数字化营销、交易、金融及供应链服务。它拥有 1.5 亿多名注册会员，每天在平台上发布 30 万笔跨境采购需求。

provides a full range of online services and tools for small and medium-sized enterprises, such as one-stop shop decoration, product display, marketing promotion, business negotiation and shop management, to help enterprises reduce costs and efficiently open international market.

它为中小企业提供一站式的店铺装修、产品展示、营销推广、生意洽谈及店铺管理等全系列线上服务和工具，帮助企业降低成本、高效率地开拓国际市场。

Established in 2010, AliExpress is China's largest cross-border export B2C platform, and also the number one website for electronics companies in Russia and Spain. It is called the "International Taobao" by many sellers. Buyers on it are from over more than 220 countries and regions, covering 30 first-level industry categories such as clothing, 3C, home appliances, accessories, etc. AliExpress offers online car sales service in Russia, where customers can place orders directly on the platform, pay an advance payment, and pick up a car by making a final payment at a designated offline shop.

阿里速卖通成立于 2010 年，是中国最大的跨境出口 B2C 平台，同时也是在俄罗斯、西班牙排名第一的电商网站。它被广大卖家称为"国际版淘宝"。其平台买家范围已经遍及 220 多个国家和地区，覆盖服装服饰、3C、家居用品、饰品等共 30 个一级行业类目。阿里速卖通在俄罗斯推出在线售车服务，顾客可以直接在平台上下单，支付预付款，到指定线下门店支付尾款即可提车。

Amazon, founded in 1995, is the largest online E-commerce company in the United States. It is located in Seattle, Washington. It currently has 18 sites, including US, Canada, Mexico, UK, Germany, China and Japan, etc. The platform is one of the earliest companies to start E-commerce on the network, from the book sales business to the online retailer with the largest variety of goods in the world and the second largest Internet enterprise in the world. 35.4% of Amazon users are from North America regions, 31.8% are from European regions, and 24.1% are from Asia-Pacific regions. In March 2020, the platform ranked first among that year's top 500 global brand values. Amazon features: (1) High access requirements, strict rules, vendors' business qualifications will be extremely strictly reviewed, and sellers' operations are also strictly required. (2) Focus on logistics and after-sales services, mainly using FBA automatic shipping mode. (3) Value products and ignore shops, products uploaded by sellers must meet Amazon's requirements, and fake sellers will be severely punished.

亚马逊成立于 1995 年，是美国最大的一家网络电商公司。它位于华盛顿州的西雅图，目前有美国站、加拿大站、墨西哥站、英国站、德国站、中国站、日本站等 18 个站点。该平台是网络上最早开始经营电子商务的公司之一，从销售书籍到成为全球商品品种最多的网上零售商和全球第二大互联网企业。亚马逊的 35.4% 用户来自北美地区、31.8% 的用户来自欧洲地区、24.1% 的用户来自亚太地区。2020 年 3 月，该平台位列 2020 年全球品牌价值 500 强第 1 名。亚马逊的特点：（1）门槛高，规则严格，对卖家的企业资质会进行极其严格的审核。对卖家的运营也严格要求。（2）注重物流和售后服务，主要采用 FBA 自发货物流模式。（3）重产品，轻店铺。卖家上传的产品必须符合亚马逊的要求，假货卖家将受到严厉的惩罚。

eBay was founded as an auction website at the most beginning in 1995, but now it retains auction in its sales model, which is a feature that distinguishes eBay from other platforms. The seller sets the starting price and online time of the commodity, when the auction ends, the highest bidding price is the final price, and the buyer with the highest bidding price is the winning bidder of the commodity. The advantages of the eBay platform are: (1) Lower access requirements for opening eBay shops than Amazon, but more formalities. (2) eBay shops are free, but you have to pay for publishing products. (3) eBay has a long audit cycle, no more than 10 items can be listed at first, and only auction is allowed, sales can be made more only after the credit is accumulated. (4) Professional customer service, communicate via phone or Internet.

1.2.3　Regional E-Commerce Platforms

Shopee, founded in Singapore in 2015, is the mainstream platform in Southeast Asia such as Malaysia, Thailand, Taiwan of China, Indonesia, Vietnam and Philippines. Shopee deals in consumer electronics, home appliances, beauty and health care products, maternal and child products, clothing and fitness equipment. Shopee Community has over 30 million media fans, 7 million active sellers and more than 8,000 employees in Southeast Asia and China. It is the fastest growing platform in Southeast Asia, and the firstly preferred platform for the export of China's products.

Established in 2012, Lazada, with key target markets in Indonesia, Malaysia, Philippines and Thailand, is currently one of the largest E-commerce platforms in Southeast Asia, spending only 2.75 years from its inception to its valuation of $1 billion. In 2016, Ali invested and acquired 51% of its equity. In 2019, Lazada officially became the IOC's official partner in Southeast Asia. Lazada's self-built logistics network has over 30 warehousing centers in 17 cities in Southeast Asia. It

eBay 在 1995 年创立之初是一个拍卖网站，现在的销售模式中仍保留拍卖，这是 eBay 区别于其他平台的特点。卖家设定商品的起拍价和在线时间，拍卖结束时的最高竞拍价就是最终金额，出价最高的买家客户为该商品的中标者。EBay 平台的优点有：（1）相较于在亚马逊开店，eBay 开店的门槛较低，但手续相对比较多。（2）eBay 开店是免费的，但发布产品必须付钱。（3）eBay 的审核周期时间很长，刚开始不能多于 10 个商品，并且只可以拍卖，累积信用后之后才可以越卖越多。（4）有专业客服，可通过电话或互联网进行沟通交流。

1.2.3　区域性电商平台

虾皮（Shopee）于 2015 年在新加坡成立，是东南亚地区的马来西亚、泰国、中国台湾地区、印度尼西亚、越南及菲律宾的主流平台。Shopee 经营电子消费品、家居用品、美容保健、母婴用品、服饰及健身器材等。Shopee 社群媒体粉丝数量超过 3000 万人，拥有超过 700 万个活跃卖家，员工超过 8000 人，遍布东南亚及中国。它是东南亚发展最快，也是中国产品出口的首选平台。

Lazada 于 2012 年成立，主要目标市场有印度尼西亚、马来西亚、菲律宾及泰国，目前是东南亚最大电商平台之一，从成立到估值达 10 亿美元仅花 2.75 年。2016 年，阿里巴巴投资并取得了它 51% 的股权。2019 年，Lazada 正式成为国际奥委会在东南亚地区的官方合作伙伴。Lazada 自建物流网络，在东南亚 17

establishes self-operated warehouses, sorting centers and electronic technology facilities in various countries, works with partner networks to achieve cross-border and "last kilometer" logistics capabilities, and substantially reduces the expensive freight costs incurred by poor infrastructure in some parts of Southeast Asia.

Russia has the largest online customers in Europe, it borders China, and has convenient logistics and transportation. It is an important market for "the Belt and Road". The main platforms are as follows: (1) Lamoda: headquartered in Moscow, the group is the leading online platform in fashion and lifestyle in Russia and the CIS countries, as well as a frequent winner of industry awards. Lamoda offers over 4 million products from 3,000 international and local brands of clothing, shoes, accessories, cosmetics and perfumes; its logistics network Lamoda LM Express in Russia, Ukraine, Belarus and Kazakhstan, and more than 150 cities provides courier services. (2) Wildberries: founded in 2004; it is the online sales platform for shoes, clothing and accessories in Russia, sells about 100,000 shoes, clothing and brand accessories, provides a nationwide freight-free courier service, and it is the first power in Russia to provide unconditional free delivery business. (3) Yandex is not only a search engine enterprise in Russia, but also provides omni-channel marketing services such as news, maps and encyclopaedias, E-mail boxes, and Internet advertising related to E-commerce. YandexMarket has developed residential channels for Chinese sellers, who can use its service to build their own logistics channels to ship goods and improve transportation efficiency.

Africa is a market dominated by mobile terminals, and online shopping has become the engine of trade growth in Africa, mainly including: (1) Zando, founded in 2012 by Rocket Internet, is South Africa's largest online clothing shop. Zando is a subsidiary of Jumia Group, which has branches in many countries in Africa, specializing in footwear, clothing,

个城市拥有 30 多个仓储中心，在各国建立自营仓库、分拣中心和电子科技设施，配合合作伙伴网络，实现跨境及"最后一公里"物流能力，大幅降低东南亚部分地区因基础设施落后而产生的昂贵运费。

俄罗斯拥有欧洲最大的在线客户，国土与中国接壤，物流运输方便。它是"一带一路"的重要市场。俄罗斯主要平台有以下几家：（1）Lamoda：集团总部位于莫斯科，是俄罗斯和独联体国家时尚和生活方式领域的领先在线平台，也是行业奖项的常客。Lamoda 提供超过400 万种产品，来自 3000 个国际和本地品牌的服装、鞋子、配饰、化妆品和香水；物流网络 Lamoda LM Express 在俄罗斯、乌克兰、白俄罗斯和哈萨克斯坦的 150 多个城市提供快递服务。（2）Wildberries：成立于 2004 年，是俄罗斯本土的鞋服及饰品在线销售平台，销售有约 10 万款鞋类、服装以及品牌配件等，还提供全国免运费快递服务，也是俄罗斯第一家提供无条件免费送货的电商。（3）Yandex 不仅是俄罗斯的搜索引擎企业，还提供与电商相关的新闻、地图和百科全书、电子邮箱、互联网广告等全渠道营销服务。YandexMarket 已对中国卖家开发入驻渠道，卖家可使用YandexMarket 平台自建物流渠道发货，提高运输效率。

非洲是以手机终端为主的市场，网络购物已成为非洲贸易增长的引擎，主要有：（1）Zando，由 Rocket Internet 公司创立于 2012年，是南非最大的线上服装店。Zando 是 Jumia 集团的子公司，在

home appliances and beauty products. (2) Takealot is a well-known online shopping website in South Africa, formerly Take2, which was officially launched in June 2011 after being acquired by Tiger Global Management Company and Kim Reid. The platform mainly sells books, electronic products, horticultural products, maternal and child products, etc. (3) Konga, Nigeria's most visited shopping website, was founded in July 2012 by Sim Shagaya. Originally focused on baby, beauty products and personal care products, Konga has been expanded to fashions, small items and household products.

1.3　Cross-Border E-Commerce Career Planning

Local governments in China actively promote the construction of cross-border E-commerce comprehensive pilot areas. Professionals are urgently needed for the development of a series of ecospheres, such as platforms, sellers, supply chains, finance, etc. in the cross-border E-commerce industry. Especially in the current special situation, when shopping is conducted by clicking the mouse by using fingers instead of walking, the contradiction between supply and demand of cross-border E-commerce human resource is prominent.

1.3.1　Analysis of Cross-Border E-Commerce Job Posts

From the initial cross-border E-commerce specialist, cross-border E-commerce jobs are gradually divided into operation, promotion, customer service, art designing and other job posts according to the employment demand. In the future, with the changes of the times, job posts related to big data analysis, artificial intelligence, VR and other new technologies will be increased, and some posts with low technical content will be eliminated.

Some companies call operation promotion a post, engaged in sales work. Some enterprises will separate the posts of operation and promotion. The main job of the operation post is to operate the products on the platform.

非洲多个国家都设立分公司，主营鞋类、服装、家居用品和美容产品等。（2）Takealot 是南非知名的在线购物网站，前身是 Take2，老虎全球管理公司和 Kim Reid 收购 Take2 后，于 2011 年 6 月正式上线。该平台主要销售书籍、电子产品、园艺用品、母婴用品等。（3）Konga，是尼日利亚访问量最高的购物网站，由 Sim Shagaya 成立于 2012 年 7 月。Konga 原专注于婴儿、美容和个人护理类商品，现已扩充至时装、小件商品、家用产品。

1.3　跨境电商职业生涯规划

我国各地政府积极推动跨境电商综合试验区的建设。从事跨境电商行业的平台、卖家、供应链、金融等一系列生态圈的发展急需专业人才。尤其是在当前用手指代替或鼠标代替外出进行购物的特殊环境下，跨境电商的人才需求矛盾突出。

1.3.1　跨境电商从业岗位分析

跨境电商从业岗位从最初的跨境电商专员，逐渐按用工需求分化为运营、推广、客服、美工等岗位。未来会随着时代的变迁而增加与大数据分析、人工智能、VR 等新技术相岗位，也会淘汰一些技术含量较低的岗位。

有些公司将运营推广称为一个岗位，从事销售类工作。有些企业将运营与推广分岗。运营岗的主要工作就是运营平台上面的产品。通

Through the information of the platform, a series of data analysis, keyword change, promotion planning and other marketing means are carried out to promote the transaction. Promotion post is not to promote the products on the platform, but to promote the company's products through short videos, search, sharing and other social media outside the platform, which is a bit similar to the domestic self-media operation.

The main work of customer service post is to handle pre-sale product research and pricing, inquiry reply and tracking during sales, after-sales evaluation, dispute handling and customer maintenance, etc. Who can use minority languages or have working experiences are more welcomed.

Graphic Designer's post is responsible for shooting and processing pictures and videos. Different platforms have different requirements. Amazon platform will have higher requirements for pictures and relatively give higher payments.

Live broadcasting can enhance brand awareness and directly attract customer attention to product recognition, increase the viscosity and quantity of fans, and promote the order completion by answering questions, displaying product, distributing coupon and booting order quantity, etc.

Logistics posts can utilize platform and other online and offline resources to seek the optimal services such as postal parcels, commercial couriers, international special lines of railways or highways, and overseas warehouses for cross-border E commcrcc logistics.

The above posts vary according to the size of the company. Some small and medium-sized companies have fewer posts, which requires a post with various functions, for example, an operation post also involves customer service, art design, logistics and other works.

1.3.2 Required Skills for Cross-Border E-Commerce Positions

The positions of cross-border E-commerce have different focus, but the basic characteristics of the job posts in this industry can be summarized as "foreign language + international trade + network technology". The analysis is as follows:

过平台的信息、一系列的数据分析、关键词修改、促销策划等营销手段促成交易。推广岗，不是在平台上推销产品，而是通过平台以外的短视频、搜索、分享等社交媒体，将公司的产品推广出去，有点类似于国内自媒体运营。

客服岗位的主要工作是处理售前产品的调研与定价、销售过程中的询盘回复与跟踪、售后评价、纠纷处理与客户维护等。会小语种或具有客服经验的人更受欢迎。

美工岗负责专门拍摄、处理图片和视频。不同平台有不同要求。亚马逊平台对图片的要求就会比较高，相对薪资会高一些。

直播岗通过网络直播向客户种草产品、回答粉丝问题、展示产品、发放优惠券、引导下单等，增强品牌知名度，使顾客更加直观地认识商品，增加粉丝的黏度及数量，促进下单成交。

物流岗能利用平台及其他线上线下资源，寻求最优化的跨境电商物流的邮政小包、商业快递、铁路或公路国际专线，海外仓等服务。

以上岗位因公司规模而不同。一些中小型公司设置的岗位较少，这就要求一岗多能，如运营岗兼做客服、美工、物流等工作。

1.3.2 跨境电商岗位必备技能

跨境电商各岗位的侧重不同，但该行业岗位的基本特征可归纳为"外语＋国际贸易＋网络技术"。分析如下：

1. Be proficient in multiple foreign languages

Fluency in English listening, speaking, reading and writing is required for doing cross-border E-commerce business. Operating posts generally require CET-4, while customer service or copywriting posts require more than CET-6, with a few requiring TEM-4 or TEM-8. If you are going to open a certain national market, the ability to minority languages shall be required. The languages in greater demand are Japanese, French, German, Spanish, Italian, etc.

2. Be familiar with international trade rules

Be able to organize the process of import and export of commodities according to the requirements of customers in a team way; have the ability to abide by and apply related intellectual property rights of commodities, access rules of various countries for import and export of commodities and other laws and regulations; have the ability to conduct consumer behavior and market research in international target markets; have the ability to conduct overall research and establish high performance-price ratio of international logistics and customs declaration; have the ability to memorize all kinds of expense and tax policies of target market and carry out price accounting.

3. Learn the new rules of platform technology

Competition among platforms is becoming fiercer than ever. Rules for opening shops, marketing, logistics and collecting money are changing increasingly, and network technologies are emerging endlessly. Sellers must open shops and upload products according to E-commerce platform requirements, and display products in the form of picture, video or VR in various target markets. This requires employees to constantly learn the rules of the platform, and meet the requirements of the platform or social media for new technology photography and post-processing. In addition, because of the increasingly fierce competition among shops on E-commerce platforms, how to build independent stations has become a new essential skill. Commodity analysis selections, product push, personalized interfaces, etc. require data support, and may require skills such as Python language and artificial intelligence.

1．熟练掌握多门外语

从事跨境电商要求具有流利的英语听、说、读、写表达能力。运营岗一般要求达到大学英语四级，客服或文案岗要求则比较高，要求达到六级以上，少数会要求英语专四或专八。如果你要打开一个特定的国家市场，则会要求具有小语种能力。需求量比较大的语种为日语、法语、德语、西班牙语、意大利语等。

2．熟悉国际贸易规则

能采用团队协作的方式按照客户的要求组织商品进出口流程；具有遵守和应用相关商品知识产权、各国进出口各种商品的准入规则等法律法规的能力；具有调查国际目标市场的消费行为与市场的能力；具有统筹调研并确立高性价比的国际物流与报关报检的能力；具有熟记目标市场的各种费用税收政策并进行价格核算的能力等。

3．学习平台技术新规则

各平台竞争越来越激烈。开店、营销、物流和收款规则越来越多变，网络技术层出不穷。卖家必须按电商平台要求开店、上传产品，将产品以图片、视频或VR的形式在各目标市场展现。这就要求从业人员不断学习平台规则，能按平台或社交媒体要求进行新技术摄影及后期处理等。此外，因电商平台的店铺竞争越来越激烈，如何建独立站成为新必备技能。商品分析选品、产品推送、个性化界面等需要数据支撑，可能需要掌握Python语言、人工智能等技能。

1.3.3 The Path of Cross-Border E-Commerce Career Development

Cross-border E-commerce industry can be developed in four dimensions: technology, platform, management and entrepreneurship. Fresh hands can focus on one dimension to further cultivate for long-term career development instead of short-sighted and frequent job-hopping.

1．The dimension of technology

It is suitable for operation, promotion, data analysis, customer service, logistics and other posts. After 2-3 years of training, it can take on the post of data analysis manager, operation manager, logistics manager of cross-border E-commerce in a department, and finally even the technical director of a shop.

2．The dimension of platform

Multi-platform expansion, such as the primary operation post that used to operate AliExpress, can expand horizontally to Amazon, Lazada, Shopee, eBay and other platforms in the same or different target markets, to be a rare talent for enterprises, as well as to become an operation manager to take on heavy responsibilities.

3．The dimension of management

If an employee is not good at technology, but good at discovering flashpoints of different personnel, then he can use various incentives to bring each person's strengths into play, and arise the strength of the team to attack different markets, he can also grow from the primary operationer to the operation manager, the operation director, and the person in charge of the company.

4．The dimension of entrepreneurship

Cross-border E-commerce business model can be simple or complex, small-scale or large-scale. If you do not like to work in other people's enterprises, you can discover overseas market opportunities, open shops independently or in partnership to start a business, control wealth and time freely and continuously expand the team after a certain scale of operation, to achieve your own life goals.

1.3.3 跨境电商职业发展路径

跨境电商行业可以分技术、平台、管理和创业四个维度进行发展。新人可以专注于一个维度进行深耕，以获得长久的职业发展，而不是眼光短浅、频繁跳槽。

1．技术维度

该维度适合运营、推广、数据分析、客服、物流等岗位。经过2～3年的锻炼，可以从初级进阶到中级，胜任一个部门跨境电商数据分析经理、运营经理、物流经理等岗位，最终成为一个店铺的技术负责人。

2．平台维度

多平台拓展，比如原来仅运营阿里速卖通的初级运营岗，可以一个岗位横向拓展，延展到相同或不同目标市场的亚马逊、Lazada、Shopee、eBay等平台，成为企业不可多得的人才，同样也可以承担运营经理的重任。

3．管理维度

如果从业人员不擅长技术，而善于发现不同人员的闪光点，则可利用各种激励手段发挥每个人的长处，调动团队的力量去攻下不同的市场，也可从运营初级开始，逐渐成长为运营经理、运营总监、公司负责人。

4．创业维度

跨境电商商业模式既可简单也可复杂，既可小规模也可大规模。如果不喜欢在他人的企业打工，则可发掘海外市场机会，独立或合伙开店铺创业，财富与时间自由支配，在经营达到一定规模后不断壮大队伍，实现自己的人生理想。

1.4　The Application of New Cross-Border E-Commerce Technologies

Cross-border E-commerce is an industry with continuous iteration of technology. Every day, countless scientific researchers are carrying out technology research and development to meet or even create the needs of consumers.

1.4.1　The Application of Big Data Analysis in Cross-Border E-Commerce

Big data has changed the former business logic, benefiting more people and improving the overall efficiency of society. As a seller, if you don't communicate with customers face to face or go abroad, it is difficult to accurately predict which goods will be hot or unsatisfactory in which countries? What are the customers' needs? What kind of goods would be preferred? At what time, in what way and where do customers go shopping? What are consumers' preferences for the price, quality and expectations of the goods? What is the trend in sales? What are the comments and suggestions for commodities? Big data makes sellers' expectation for all these possible.

Cross-border E-commerce platforms collect customer search, browsing, favorite, sharing and order information to provide customers with more expected services. With the same cross-border E-commerce platform, each customer will see a different interface when they open it, because the platform precisely pushes each customer a customized interface and selected goods. Big data also provides factory-customized C2M services, and Alibaba's Rhinoceros Intelligent Project achieves a 15-day delivery target.

In addition to E-commerce platforms, when customers search web pages, watch live broadcasts and videos, and share social media, those goods that have been searched and browsed on the commercial platforms will pop up the relevant commodity page to push and induce orders. Internet companies form a mechanism of data co-construction,

1.4　跨境电商新技术的应用

跨境电商是一个技术不断迭代的行业。每天都有无数科研人员在进行技术研发以满足甚至创造消费者的需求。

1.4.1　大数据分析在跨境电商的应用

大数据改变了原有商业逻辑，使更多的人受益，提高社会整体工作效率。作为卖家，如果不与顾客面对面地沟通或走出国门，则很难精确预测哪些商品在哪些国家是热门款或滞销款，顾客有哪些需求，喜欢什么样的商品，消费者通常在什么时间用什么样的方式去哪里逛，消费者对商品的价格、品质、期望偏好有哪些，销量的变化趋势是什么样的，对商品有什么评价和建议。大数据让这些卖家的期望成为可能。

跨境电商平台收集顾客的搜索、浏览、收藏、分享及下单信息，为顾客提供更符合预期的服务。同一个跨境电商平台，每位顾客打开后看到的界面都不一样，因为平台给每位顾客精准推送定制化界面和可供选择的商品。大数据还可提供工厂直接按客户定制的 C2M 服务，阿里巴巴的"犀牛智造"项目实现下单 15 天交货的目标。

除电商平台外，顾客在搜索网页、观看网络直播和视频、分享社交媒体时，那些曾经在电商平台上搜索浏览过的商品，会跳出相关商品页面推送，诱导下单。互联网公司之间形成一个数据共

sharing and mutual benefit, which is quietly changing the development of online business ecology.

Big data also serves the society by collecting information. In the new retail era, online business platforms have been integrated with offline physical shops to form complementary business circles supported by data, such as Ali, Jingdong, Suning, etc. Based on the big data statistics and customers' demand predicting, goods can be delivered to shops or distribution points nearer to offline customers in advance, which greatly reduces the waiting time and improves customers' satisfaction level.

1.4.2 The Application of 5G Technology in Cross-Border E-Commerce

2G technology has brought SMS communication, 3G has brought social networks, 4G has brought video social networking, and 5G has brought more space for imagination. The speed for downloading of 5G can theoretically reach 4.5Gbit/s, and a movie can be downloaded nearly in a second. Although currently the communication technology development and network speed in Southeast Asia are relatively slow, its growth rate is higher than that in the well-developed countries. It may jump directly to 5G, crossing PC to mobile.

The 5G era has transformed the original pictorial visual communication of tangible goods into high-definition and smooth video form, bringing more direct sensory experience to cross-border E-commerce. Supported by 5G network, consumers can experience product information in a multi-dimensional way through voice, text, video and other means, to achieve real-time interaction between people and people, people and things, objects and objects, to query more accurate logistics dynamics in real time. Especially the assembly and simple maintenance of complex commodities such as home appliances or mechanical products, they improve consumers' original static shopping service experience. In the future, cross-border E-commerce may transit from tangible goods to intangible goods such as education, medical care, travel, entertainment and so on.

建、共享和互赢机制，正无声地改变着线上商业生态的发展。

大数据还通过收集到的信息为社会服务。新零售时代线上的电商平台已与线下实体店合为一体，以数据为支撑形成互补的商业圈，例如阿里、京东、苏宁等。依据大数据统计及预测客户需求，可提前将商品配送到离线下客户较近的店铺或配送点，大大缩短到货时间，提高客户满意度。

1.4.2 5G 技术在跨境电商的应用

2G 技术带来了短信沟通，3G 带来了社交网络，4G 带来了视频社交，5G 带来更大的想象空间。5G 的下载速度理论上可以达到 4.5Gbit/s，约一秒钟能下载一部电影。虽然目前东南亚地区的通信技术发展和网络速度相对比较慢，但其增量要比发达国家市场的增量高，可能直接跳到 5G，跨过 PC 端到了移动端。

5G 时代将原本图片式的有形商品单维视觉传达转变为高清流畅的视频形式，给跨境电商带来更直接的感官体验。消费者在 5G 网络支持下，通过语音、文字、视频等多种方式交流，可多维体验产品信息，实现人与人、人与物、物与物的实时互动，实时查询更精准的物流动态。特别是复杂商品如家居用品或机械类产品的组装和简单维修保养，改善了消费者的原本静态购物服务体验。未来，跨境电商可能由有形商品过渡到教育、医疗、旅行、娱乐等无形商品。

1.4.3　The Application of Artificial Intelligence in Cross-Border E-Commerce

Artificial intelligence has three key elements: data mining, natural language processing, and machine learning. The application of artificial intelligence in cross-border E-commerce mainly reflects in four aspects: marketing planning, enterprise management, supply chain management and customer service. Artificial intelligence helps consumers upgrade their user experience while innovating cross-border E-commerce work modes and improving efficiency. Currently, Artificial intelligence has been widely used in: (1) Intelligent assistants and chat robots to answer customers'questions in real time; (2) Automatic operation and management of warehousing and distribution; (3) Predicting customer preferences and recommendation through data analysis combined with recommendation algorithms.

Alibaba launches TmallGenie and Ali Assistants. Customer service chat robots handle about 95% of consulting business, including voice and text consulting. Cainiao network artificial intelligence calculates the most effective logistics routes, reduces vehicle usage by at least 10%, and reduces driving distance by at least 30%. Amazon and eBay help platforms and E-commerce companies formulate targeted marketing strategies by improving the performance of their algorithms. Letian, Japan's largest E-commerce website, uses artificial intelligence technology to analyze hundreds of millions of products, enhance machine learning, predict customer behavior and recommend sales.

With the rapid development of artificial intelligence, Internet sellers can analyze and stimulate consumer behavior more effectively, and the automatic customer service system of each platform can greatly reduce the labor costs of sellers. With the help of artificial intelligence, sellers can process and analyze consumers' purchasing desire, habits, abilities and other data in real time more quickly, so as to formulate and optimize sales plans and prices, reduce operating costs, create consumers'

1.4.3　人工智能在跨境电商的应用

人工智能有三个关键要素：数据挖掘、自然语言处理及机器学习。人工智能在跨境电商领域的应用主要体现在营销策划、企业管理、供应链管理和客户服务四个方面。人工智能在创新跨境电商工作模式和效率的同时，还帮助消费者实现用户体验升级。当前，人工智能已普遍应用在：（1）智能助理和聊天机器人，实时回答客户的问题；（2）仓储配送的自动化运行和管理；（3）通过数据分析，结合推荐算法预测客户偏好并推荐商品。

阿里巴巴推出天猫精灵和阿里助手。客服聊天机器人处理约95%的咨询业务，包括语音及文字咨询。菜鸟网络人工智能计算最有效的物流路线，减少车辆使用量至少10%，行驶距离至少减少30%。亚马逊和eBay通过提升算法的性能帮助平台和电商企业制定针对性的营销策略。日本最大的电商网站乐天利用人工智能技术分析上亿种产品，强化机器学习，预测客户行为并进行推荐销售。

人工智能的快速发展，让互联网卖家更有效地分析和刺激消费者行为，各平台的自动客服系统大大降低了卖家的人工成本。在人工智能帮助下，卖家能更快地对消费者的购买欲望、习惯、能力等数据进行实时处理和分析，制定并优化销售方案和价格，减少运营成本，从而创造消费者购买需求并提高转化率。此外，线

purchasing needs and improve conversion rates. In addition, new things such as unmanned retailing, unmanned driving and unmanned storage in offline physical shops make more jobs replaced by machines in the future and also bring more challenges for humankind.

1.4.4 The Application of Virtual Reality in Cross-Border E-Commerce

Virtual reality is currently the ultimate application form of multimedia technology. It integrates the rapidly developing wisdom of computer software and hardware, sensing, robots, artificial intelligence and behavioral psychology. It mainly depends on the development of key technologies such as three-dimensional real-time graphics display, location tracking, touch and smell sensor technology, artificial intelligence, high-speed computing and parallel computing technology, and human behavior researches. People wear special sensor devices such as stereo glasses, data gloves, etc, which makes it seems like that they are in a sensory world with three-dimensional vision, hearing, touch and even smell, which gives people a sense of immersion in the environment and interaction with it.

Cross-border E-commerce can greatly enhance the security of customers in the purchase process through open and visual means, and it can present the shopping environment and goods more truly. In April 2016, Taobao launched a new way of shopping called Buy+. Customers use VR technology to break through the time and space limitations and really go shopping at anywhere and anytime. For example, if a customer wants to buy a sofa, with VR technology, he will no longer worry about the sofa's style, size and whether its color matches the environment or not. Customers wear VR glasses to "put" the sofa directly at home with a clear view of size and color. Overseas VR purchasing will become a trend in the future. Cooperate directly with overseas purchasing agents to open cross-border E-commerce platforms, and use auxiliary sensors and computer graphics systems to generate interactive 3D shopping environment locally. Although the customers are not in the shopping scenes, through the

下实体店的无人零售、无人驾驶、无人仓储等新兴事物，使未来更多的工作被机器代替，也给人类带来了更多挑战。

1.4.4 虚拟现实在跨境电商的应用

虚拟现实是目前多媒体技术的终极应用形式。它集成计算机软硬件、传感、机器人、人工智能及行为心理学等科学领域飞速发展的智慧，主要依赖三维实时图形显示、定位跟踪、触觉及嗅觉传感技术、人工智能、高速计算与并行计算技术及人的行为学研究等多项关键技术的发展。人们戴上立体眼镜、数据手套等特制的传感设备，似乎置身于一个具有三维的视觉、听觉、触觉甚至嗅觉的感官世界，从而给人以环境沉浸感，并且与这个环境实现互动。

跨境电商通过开放、可视化手段能大大加强顾客在购买过程中的安全感，能更加真实地呈现购物环境和商品。2016年4月，淘宝推出了一种叫做Buy+的全新购物方式。顾客利用VR技术突破时间和空间的局限，真正随时随地地逛商场。比如，顾客想购买一张沙发，有了VR技术，他不用担心沙发款式和尺寸是否合适，颜色是否与环境吻合。顾客带上VR眼镜，便可将沙发直接"放"在家里，尺寸和颜色一目了然。VR海外购将成为未来的一股潮流。与海外的代购商直接合作开启跨境电商的平台，利用辅助传感器、计算机图形系统，在本

transmission of the shopping scene pictures and wearing VR glasses, they can step into overseas shops and go shopping for the products they like. On March 26, 2020, the Joint Defense and Control Mechanism of the State Council held a press conference. Shaofeng Xie, a spokesman for the Ministry of Industry and Information, said that a 5G+VR panoramic virtual shopping guide cloud platform was created in the field of commerce. Users can browse cloud shelves and windows at any time by using their mobile phones, which can achieve 360 degree panoramic view, 720 degree no dead corner shopping experience. This technology has been used in nearly 100 commercial enterprises in Beijing, Guangdong, Chongqing, Jiangsu and Jiangxi, etc. In the Internet+ era, the technological revolution has made the "immersive" shopping experience an irreversible trend.

地生成可以交互的三维购物环境。虽然顾客人不在购物现场，但是通过购物现场画面的传输，佩戴 VR 眼镜就能一步迈进海外店面，实景逛街选择心仪的产品。2020 年 3 月 26 日，国务院联防联控机制召开新闻发布会。工业和信息化部新闻发言人谢少锋表示在电商领域打造了 5G+VR 的全景虚拟购物导购云平台。用户利用手机就可随时浏览云货架、云橱窗，可实现 360°全景、720°无死角购物体验。该技术已经在北京、广东、重庆、江苏、江西等近百家商业企业中推广应用。互联网+时代，技术革命使"身临其境"的购物体验成为不可逆转的时代潮流。

New words

1. cross-border E-commerce 跨境电子商务
2. comprehensive pilot area 综合试验区
3. General Administration of Customs 海关总署
4. browsing volume 浏览量
5. conversion rate 转化率
6. average transaction price 客单价
7. consumer behaviour 消费者行为
8. social media 社交媒体
9. live broadcast E-commerce　直播电商
10. big data 大数据
11. customer's needs 客户需求
12. artificial intelligence 人工智能
13. data mining 数据挖掘
14. virtual reality 虚拟现实

Chapter 2

Cross-Border E-Commerce Online Shop Opening and Product Selection

第2章 跨境电商网上开店与选品

Lead-in case

Xiaowei has had a preliminary understanding of the development mode, different categories of cross-border E-commerce, as well as the major E-commerce platforms. Faced with the rapid development of cross-border E-commerce industry, Xiaowei decides to register a cross-border E-commerce company first and open shops to sell products on several mainstream platforms. Through this chapter, you and Xiaowei will have a preliminary understanding of the registration process and relevant policies of cross-border E-commerce companies, the selection of cross-border E-commerce platforms and the store registration process, as well as how to select products based on data analysis.

Learning objectives

1. Objectives of knowledge

(1) To master the registration process and relevant policies of cross-border E-commerce companies.

(2) To master the selection of major global cross-border E-commerce platforms and the process of opening shops.

(3) To understand the selection standards and channels of cross-border E-commerce products.

(4) To master the data analysis in cross-border E-commerce product selection.

2. Objectives of skills

(1) Be able to complete the registration of cross-border E-commerce companies.

(2) Be able to complete the registration of shops on AliExpress, Amazon and other third-party cross-border E-commerce platforms.

(3) Be able to use data analysis in cross-border E-commerce product selection according to the market.

案例导入

小薇已经初步了解了跨境电商的发展模式、不同分类，以及各大主流电子商务平台。面对跨境电商产业快速发展的趋势，小薇决定先注册一家跨境电商公司，同时还将选择几个主流平台开设店铺售卖产品。通过本章学习，你将与小薇一起初步了解当前跨境电商公司的注册流程和相关政策、跨境电商平台的选择和店铺注册流程，以及如何利用数据分析工具进行选品。

学习目标

1. 知识目标

（1）掌握跨境电商公司注册流程和相关政策。

（2）掌握全球跨境电商主流平台的选择及开设店铺的流程。

（3）熟悉跨境电商产品的选择标准和选择渠道。

（4）掌握跨境电商数据化选品方法。

2. 技能目标

（1）能完成跨境电商公司注册。

（2）能完成速卖通、亚马逊等跨境电商第三方平台店铺的注册。

（3）能根据市场进行跨境电商数据化选品。

3．Objectives of qualities

(1) To have a patient, meticulous and rigorous work style.

(2) To have the spirit of abiding by laws and regulations related to foreign trade.

(3) To have the professional ethics of honesty and trustworthiness.

(4) To have a long-lasting interest in and change in new knowledge and skills.

2.1　Overview of Cross-Border E-Commerce Company Registration

2.1.1　Cross-Border E-Commerce Company Registration Process

First of all, cross-border E-commerce sellers need to register a company. When applying for opening shops on various platforms, the company information such as business license will be needed. It is suggested to choose limited liability companies as the type of company registration. Because this type of company is easier to get approved when the platform reviews the application for admission.

The materials required for company registration are: ① company registered address; ② company name, registered capital, business scope (must include import and export business), the proportion of shareholders; ③ ID card and mobile phone number of the legal person, shareholders, supervisor, financial manager, etc.

After the above materials are prepared, submit an application for name verification to the Local Administration for Market Regulation. Generally, the business license will be issued within 5-10 working days after approval.

After the business license is issued, the company needs to go to the designated point to apply for the company's official seal, financial seal, contract seal, legal representative seal, and invoice seal, and immediately after that, it will be arranged for bank account opening. Cross-border E-commerce companies need to apply for opening a U.S. dollar account.

After the account opening is completed, cross-border

3．素质目标

（1）具有耐心、细致、严谨的工作作风。

（2）具有遵守外贸相关法律法规和自律精神。

（3）具有诚实守信的职业道德。

（4）具有对新知识、新技能持久的学习兴趣和变革力。

2.1　跨境电商公司注册概述

2.1.1　跨境电商公司注册流程

跨境电商卖家首先需要注册一家公司。在各大平台申请店铺入驻时，都会用到公司的营业执照等信息。公司注册类型建议选择有限责任公司。这种类型的公司在平台审核入驻申请时比较容易通过。

公司注册所需的资料有：① 公司注册地址；② 公司名称、注册资金、经营范围（必须包括进出口业务）、股东占股比例情况；③ 法人、股东、监事、财务经理等人的身份证信息及手机号码。

上述资料准备好之后，向当地市场监督管理局提交申请核名。一般在 5 ～ 10 个工作日核名通过后，下发营业执照。

下发营业执照以后，公司需要到指定刻章点办理公司公章、财务章、合同章、法人代表章、发票章，紧接着安排银行开户。跨境电商公司在开户时需申请开立一个美元账户。

开户完成后，跨境电商公司

E-commerce companies need to apply to the local customs for the registration of foreign trade operators. Without the registration, they will not be able to obtain the relevant qualifications. Since cross-border E-commerce companies have the right to declare imports and exports, they must apply for a declaration registration certificate as well. At the same time, they need to apply to the customs for encrypted transmission, declare transmission ID, legal person card, and operator card.

Finally, the registration of the cross-border E-commerce company has been completed and foreign trade businesses can be carried out.

2.1.2 Policies on Registration of Cross-Border E-Commerce Companies

On December 10, 2018, the General Administration of Customs promulgated the *Announcement on the Supervision of Cross-Border E-Commerce Retail Import and Export Commodities* (GACC Announcement No.194 of 2018). The announcement pointed out that cross-border E-commerce companies, logistics companies, payment companies and other companies involved in cross-border E-commerce business should register with the local customs in accordance with the relevant regulations; overseas cross-border E-commerce companies should entrust a domestic agent to register with the customs office where the agent is located.

On December 29, 2018, the General Administration of Customs promulgated the *Announcement of the General Administration of Customs on Matters Concerning the Administration of Customs Registration of Cross-Border E-Commerce Enterprises* (GACC Announcement No. 219 of 2018). The announcement pointed out that cross-border E-commerce payment enterprises and logistics enterprises should obtain relevant qualification certificates in accordance with the General Administration of Customs Announcement No. 194 of 2018, and submit relevant qualification certificates

需要向当地海关申请对外贸易经营者备案。如果没有做备案，则不能取得相关资质。由于跨境电商公司有进出口报关权，因此还需向海关申请取得报关登记证。同时，它们需要向海关申请办理加密传输方式，申报传输 ID、法人卡，以及操作人员卡。

至此，跨境电商公司注册完成，可以正常开展对外贸易业务。

2.1.2 跨境电商公司注册相关政策

2018 年 12 月 10 日，海关总署颁布了《关于跨境电子商务零售进出口商品有关监管事宜的公告》（海关总署公告〔2018〕194 号）。该公告指出，跨境电子商务平台公司、物流公司、支付公司等参与跨境电子商务零售进口业务的公司，应当依据海关报关单位注册登记管理相关规定，向所在地海关办理注册登记；境外跨境电子商务公司应委托境内代理人向该代理人所在地海关办理注册登记。

2018 年 12 月 29 日，海关总署颁布了《海关总署关于跨境电子商务企业海关注册登记管理有关事宜的公告》（海关总署公告〔2018〕219 号）。该公告指出，跨境电子商务支付企业、物流企业应当按照海关总署 2018 年第 194 号公告的规定取得相关资质证书，并按照主管部门相关规定，在办理海关注册登记手续时提交相关

when handling customs registration procedures in accordance with relevant regulations.

2.1.3　Issues Need to Pay Attention on Registration of Cross-Border E-Commerce Companies

Generally speaking, transactions are completed through cross-border E-commerce platforms, and goods need to be delivered through cross-border E-commerce logistics after payment. Companies providing these services need to have cross-border E-commerce filing qualifications. Whether a cross-border E-commerce company can register successfully to carry out foreign trade business depends on whether the filing can be passed. The filing procedures are complicated, and many companies fail to file due to incomplete materials preparation and unqualified subject.

The requirements for cross-border E-commerce filing procedures are as follows: ① the subject needs to be a domestic registered company, and an overseas company needs to find a domestic company to act as its agent; ② the company needs to have import and export rights; ③ E-commerce companies need to have an online shop.

The materials required for cross-border E-commerce filing qualification are: ① business license; ② official seal; ③ ID card of the legal person; ④ online shop website.

The filing of cross-border E-commerce requires not only corporate filing, but also commodity filing. After completing the filing, the company can obtain the following qualifications: ① to open a shop on the cross-border E-commerce platform; ② to complete filing in the customs department; ③ to complete filing in the inspection and quarantine department.

2.2　Cross-Border E-Commerce Platform Selection and Shop Registration

2.2.1　Cross-Border E-Commerce Platform Selection

1．Alibaba

Founded in 1999, Alibaba platform is the first business sector of Alibaba Group and has now become the world's leading cross-border B2B E-commerce platform. Alibaba

资质证书。

2.1.3　跨境电商公司注册需注意的问题

一般来讲，通过电商平台达成交易，进行支付结算之后需要通过跨境电商物流将商品送达。完成这些业务的公司就需要具有跨境电商备案资质。跨境电商公司能否注册成功开展对外贸易业务，重点在于备案能否通过。备案手续复杂，很多公司因为资料准备不齐全、主体资格不符合等原因导致备案失败。

跨境电商备案办理的主体资格条件有：① 备案公司需要为境内注册公司，境外公司需要找境内企业代理业务；② 公司需要有进出口权；③ 电商类公司需要有网上商店。

跨境电商备案所需材料有：① 公司营业执照；② 公章；③ 法人身份证；④ 网上商店网址。

办理跨境电商备案不仅需要进行公司备案，还需要进行商品备案。办理完成备案后，公司可获得的资质有：① 跨境电商平台开店；② 海关部门备案；③ 检验检疫部门备案。

2.2　跨境电商平台选择与店铺注册

2.2.1　跨境电商平台选择

1．阿里巴巴国际站

阿里巴巴国际站平台成立于 1999 年，是阿里巴巴集团的第一个业务板块，现已成为全球领先

platform provides export marketing promotion service, which helps small and medium-sized enterprises to expand international trade. Based on the world's leading inter-enterprise E-commerce website, Alibaba trade platform, it promotes suppliers' enterprises and products, and then obtains trade opportunities and orders. At the same time, it is one of the preferred online platforms for export companies to expand international trade.

Alibaba (Figure 2-1) provides one-stop store decoration, product display, marketing and promotion, business negotiation and shop management, a full range of online services and tools, to help enterprises reduce costs, efficiently open up the large foreign trade market.

的跨境贸易 B2B 电子商务平台。阿里巴巴国际站平台提供出口营销推广服务，帮助中小企业拓展国际贸易。它基于全球领先的企业间电商网站阿里巴巴国际站贸易平台，推广供应商的企业和产品，进而获得贸易商机和订单。同时，它也是出口企业拓展国际贸易的首选网络平台之一。

阿里巴巴国际站平台（图2-1）提供一站式的店铺装修、产品展示、营销推广、生意洽谈及店铺管理等全系列线上服务和工具，帮助企业降低成本、高效率地开拓外贸大市场。

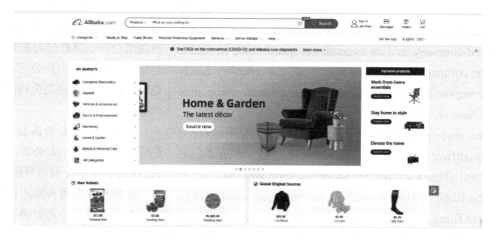

Figure 2-1   Homepage of Alibaba
图 2-1   阿里巴巴国际站首页

At present, Alibaba logistics has covered more than 200 countries and regions around the world, and will resonate with ecological partners to redefine global freight standards through digitalization. The "door-to-door" service is one of the key directions: the goods are transported from the factory to the domestic port, declares, enters the overseas port by sea, land or air, clears customs, pays taxes, and finally completes the final delivery.

目前，阿里巴巴国际站物流已覆盖全球 200 多个国家和地区，并与生态合作伙伴产生共鸣，通过数字化重新定义全球货运标准。"门到门"服务能力是重点方向之一：货物从工厂拉到境内港口、报关，通过海陆空进入境外港口，清关、完税，最后完成末端配送。

2. AliExpress

AliExpress is an online trading platform created by Alibaba Group for the global market, which is called "the international version of Taobao" by majority of sellers. On this platform, sellers can sell products to almost any country they can think of. Since 2010, after more than 10 years of rapid development, AliExpress has owned 44 categories and 18 language sites. It is the only cross-border E-commerce export B2C retail platform in China that covers all the countries and regions of "the Belt and Road", and its business covers more than 230 countries and regions around the world.

The access requirements of AliExpress (Figure 2-2) is not high, which can meet the desire of many small enterprises to do export business. Moreover, the transaction process is simple, the order generation, delivery, receiving, payment and other processes between the buyer and the seller are all completed online. There is a wide variety of goods on AliExpress platform, while the price is low. The products on AliExpress platform have a strong competitive advantage in price, therefore, compared with traditional international trade business, they have a strong market competitive advantage.

Therefore, AliExpress is mainly aimed at emerging markets, and its main consumer groups are low and middle-end buyers from developing countries and relatively backward countries.

2. 速卖通

速卖通是阿里巴巴集团旗下面向全球市场打造的在线交易平台,被广大卖家称为"国际版淘宝"。在这个平台上,卖家可以把商品卖到他们可以想到的几乎任何国家。从 2010 年开始,经过 10 多年的飞速发展,速卖通已拥有 44 个品类、18 个语种站点。它是中国唯一覆盖"一带一路"全部国家和地区的跨境电商出口 B2C 零售平台,其业务遍及全球 230 多个国家和地区。

速卖通平台(图 2-2)入驻门槛不高,能够满足众多小企业做出口业务的愿望。而且,交易流程简单,买卖双方的订单生成、发货、收货、支付等流程全部在线上完成。速卖通平台上的商品品种繁多,同时价格低廉。速卖通平台上的商品具有较强的价格竞争优势,与传统国际贸易业务相比,具有较强的市场竞争优势。

因此,速卖通主要针对新兴市场,来自发展中国家和相对落后国家的中低端买家是其主要消费群体。

Figure 2-2   Homepage of AliExpress

图 2-2   速卖通首页

3．Amazon

Founded in 1995, Amazon is the largest online E-commerce company in the United States. Its headquarter is located in Seattle, Washington. It is one of the first companies to start E-commerce. Amazon started to just sell books online, and now it has become the world's largest online retailer and the world's second largest Internet company (Figure 2-3). Amazon has a total of 18 sites around the world, a logistics system composed of 109 operation centers across the world. Its logistics distribution covers 185 countries and regions, and more than 285 million active users worldwide.

3．亚马逊

亚马逊成立于 1995 年，是美国最大的网络电子商务公司。其总部位于华盛顿州的西雅图。它是最早开始经营电子商务的公司之一。亚马逊一开始只经营网上书籍销售业务，现在已成为全球商品品种最多的网上零售商和全球第二大互联网企业（图 2-3）。亚马逊在全球共有 18 个站点，拥有由跨越全球的 109 个运营中心组成的物流体系，物流配送覆盖 185 个国家和地区，全球活跃用户超过 2.85 亿人。

Figure 2-3　Homepage of Amazon Platform

图 2-3　亚马逊平台首页

Amazon prioritizes goods over shops, and each product sold on its platform has only one detail page. "Fulfillment by Amazon" (FBA) is an important service it provides. Sellers only need to send goods to the local Amazon fulfillment center, and Amazon will provide services such as product picking, packaging, delivery, customer service, and return and exchange. Therefore, sellers only need to focus on how to improve product quality and build brands, and Amazon platform provides fast and convenient logistics services, which provides strong support for sellers.

亚马逊重商品、轻店铺，在其平台上销售的每件商品都只有一个详情页面。"亚马逊物流"（FBA）是其提供的一项重要服务，卖家只需要将商品发送到当地的亚马逊运营中心，亚马逊就会提供商品的拣货、包装、配送、客服及退换货等服务。因此，卖家只需要专注于如何提升商品质量和打造品牌，由亚马逊平台提供快捷方便的物流服务，这为卖家提供了强大的支持后盾。

Compared with AliExpress, Amazon has higher access requirements, and most sellers registered on it are large brands or strong sellers.

4．eBay

Founded in 1995 and headquartered in Silicon Valley of California, eBay Group is the world's largest C2C platform. eBay is an online auction and shopping website that allows people all over the world to buy and sell goods online. It has 380 million overseas buyers, 152 million active users, and more than 800 million products published by individuals or businesses worldwide. Its local site covers 38 countries and regions around the world (Figure 2-4). eBay has strict requirements on sellers, providing high quality goods with competitive price.

与速卖通相比，亚马逊入驻门槛较高，入驻的多为大品牌或实力雄厚的大卖家。

4．eBay

eBay 集团成立于 1995 年，其总部位于美国加利福尼亚州硅谷，是全球最大的 C2C 平台。eBay 是一个可以让全球民众上网买卖物品的线上拍卖及购物网站。它在全球范围内拥有 3.8 亿个海外买家，1.52 亿名活跃用户，以及 8 亿多件由个人或商家刊登的商品。其本地站点覆盖了全球 38 个国家和地区（图 2-4）。eBay 对卖家的要求非常严格，提供高质量的产品和具有竞争力的价格。

Figure 2-4　Homepage of eBay Platform
图 2-4　eBay 平台首页

Sellers can sell goods on the eBay platform in two ways: one is auction, and the other is a buyout price. The auction mode is the most typical feature of this platform. Generally, sellers start an auction by setting the starting price and online time for the item, and then see who can bid the highest amount when the auction ends. The highest bidder wins the item. On the eBay platform, second-hand goods transactions account for a large proportion.

卖家可以通过两种方式在 eBay 平台上销售商品：一种是拍卖，另一种是一口价。拍卖方式是这个平台的最大特色。一般，卖家通过设定商品的起拍价及在线时间开始拍卖，然后看结束时谁的竞拍金额最高。最高者获得拍卖物品。在 eBay 平台上，二手货交易占较大比例。

5．Shopee

Founded in Singapore in 2015, Shopee is an E-commerce platform in Southeast Asia and Taiwan of China. In just a few years, Shopee has developed rapidly. At present, the platform has 7 million active sellers and the number of social media fans exceeds 30 million. In 2018, Shopee GMV reached $10.3 billion, a year-on-year increase of 149.9%. The number of App downloads exceeded 200 million, making it the preferred platform for domestic products to export to Southeast Asia (Figure 2-5).

5．Shopee（虾皮）

Shopee 于 2015 年成立于新加坡，是东南亚及中国台湾的电商平台。在短短几年内，Shopee 发展迅猛。目前，该平台已拥有 700 万个活跃卖家，社交媒体粉丝数量超过 3 000 万个。2018 年，Shopee GMV 达到 103 亿美元，同比增长 149.9%，App 下载量超过 2 亿，是国货出海东南亚首选平台（图 2-5）。

Figure 2-5　Homepage of Shopee

图 2-5　Shopee 首页

Shopee attaches great importance to the function of "chatting" with consumers. It has the potential to open up the E-commerce social platform market in Southeast Asia and Taiwan of China. Buyers can bargain directly with sellers and ask about the product timely. It emphasizes that buyers and sellers understand the interactive nature of communication timely. Getting close to users increases the pre-sale purchase rate, reduces the chargeback rate and dispute rate, and increases the repeat purchase rate as well.

In terms of logistics, Shopee provides self-established logistics called "SLS" (Shopee Logistics Service) to solve multi-site operation problems in a one-stop manner and track the order throughout the entire process. In terms of pre-sale and after-sale service, the minority-language scheme brings great convenience to both buyers and sellers, which not only

Shopee 很注重与消费者"聊"的功能，具有打开东南亚及中国台湾这个电商社交平台市场的发展潜力。用户可以直接向卖家进行砍价和能及时问问到产品的情况，强调买卖双方及时了解沟通的交互属性。与用户贴近不仅可以提升售前购买率，降低退单率及纠纷率，也提升了重复购买率。

在物流方面，Shopee 提供自建物流 SLS，一站式解决多站点运营难题，全程追踪订单流程；在售前和售后服务方面，小语种语言方案给买卖双方带来了极大便利，不仅降低了卖家运营压力，

reduces the operating pressure of sellers, but also brings customers a better consumption experience.

Shopee platform does not charge usage fees, annual fees, or deposit, and the entry threshold is not very high. It is a breakthrough point suitable for small sellers to start and develop, and it is also an entry point for sellers to try the Southeast Asian market.

2.2.2   Shop Registration on Alibaba

Before registering, the materials required to register on Alibaba should be prepared first : ① business license (including company name in English, photo of business license, company registration address); ② company-to-public account information (including company-to-public account opening bank, account name, public account number); ③ business address information (including business address and business site certification); ④ certifier information (including certifier name, contact information, ID number, position, department, etc.).

【Step 1】Open the official website of Alibaba and click "Join Free" to enter the registration process (Figure 2-6).

同时也给顾客带来了更好的消费体验。

商家入驻 Shopee 平台无须缴纳平台使用费、年费或者保证金。该平台入驻门槛不是很高，是适合小卖家起步发展的突破点，同时也是卖家尝试东南亚市场的切入口。

2.2.2   阿里巴巴国际站店铺注册

在注册之前，应先准备好注册阿里巴巴国际站平台所需的材料：① 企业执照信息（包含企业中英文名称、营业执照照片、企业注册地址）；② 企业对公账户信息（包含企业对公账户开户行、开户名、对公账号）；③ 企业经营地址信息（包含企业经营地址及经营场地证明）；④ 认证人信息（包含认证人姓名、联系方式、身份证号码、职位、部门等信息）。

【步骤 1】打开阿里巴巴国际站官网，单击"免费入驻"，进入注册流程（图 2-6）。

Figure 2-6   Alibaba Registration Entry

图 2-6 阿里巴巴国际站注册入口

【Step 2】On the registration page, fill in basic information such as country/region, E-mail address, login password, mobile phone number, company name, address, etc., and click "Agree and Register" to enter the next step (Figure 2-7).

【步骤 2】在注册页面，填写国家 / 地区、电子邮箱地址、登录密码、手机号码、公司名称、地址等基本信息，单击"同意并注册"，进入下一步（图 2-7）。

Figure 2-7　Basic Registration Information

图 2-7　注册基本信息

【Step 3】Verify E-mail (Figure 2-8).

【步骤3】进行电子邮箱验证（图 2-8）。

Figure 2-8   E-mail Verification

图 2-8   电子邮箱验证

【Step 4】After the verification is completed, an Alibaba account is successfully registered. After logging into the account, complete the company's contact information (Figure 2-9).

【步骤4】验证完成后，成功注册国际站账号。登入账号后，补全企业联系信息（图 2-9）。

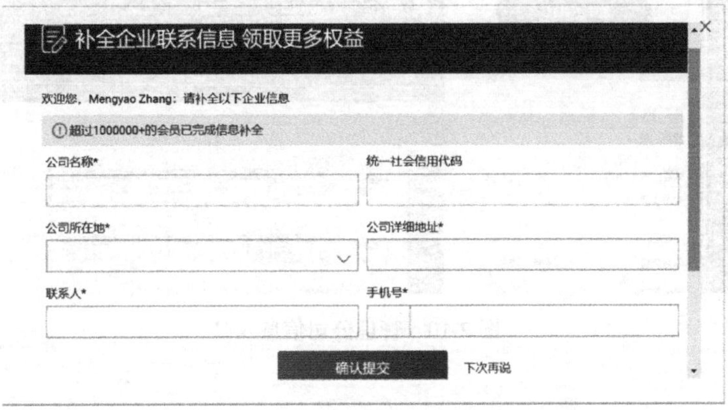

Figure 2-9   Company's Contact Information

图 2-9   企业联系信息

【Step 5】Enter the account homepage, click "Shop Management" → "Manage Company Information", select the company's "Business Mode", and click "Next" (Figure 2-10 and Figure 2-11).

【Step 6】Provide "Basic Company Details" "Manufacturing Capability" "Quality Control" "R&D Capability" "Export Capability" "Certificate Center" of the company. After filling in all the required information, click "Submit" (Figure 2-12). It takes one working day to review the company information after submission.

【步骤5】进入账号主页，单击"店铺管理"→"管理公司信息"，选择公司的"经营模式"后，单击"下一步"按钮（图 2-10 和图 2-11）。

【步骤6】提供公司的"基本信息""生产能力""质量控制""研发能力""出口能力""证书中心"。填写完成后，单击"提交"（图 2-12）。提交后需 1 个工作日对公司信息进行审核。

Figure 2-10　Manage Company Information Entry

图 2-10　管理公司信息入口

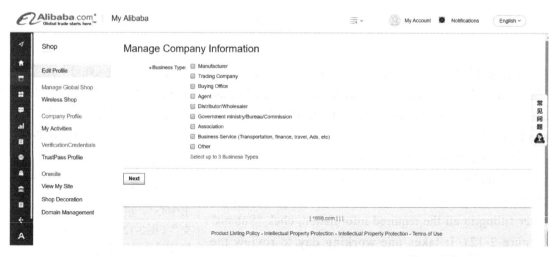

Figure 2-11　Select Company's Business Mode

图 2-11 选择公司经营模式

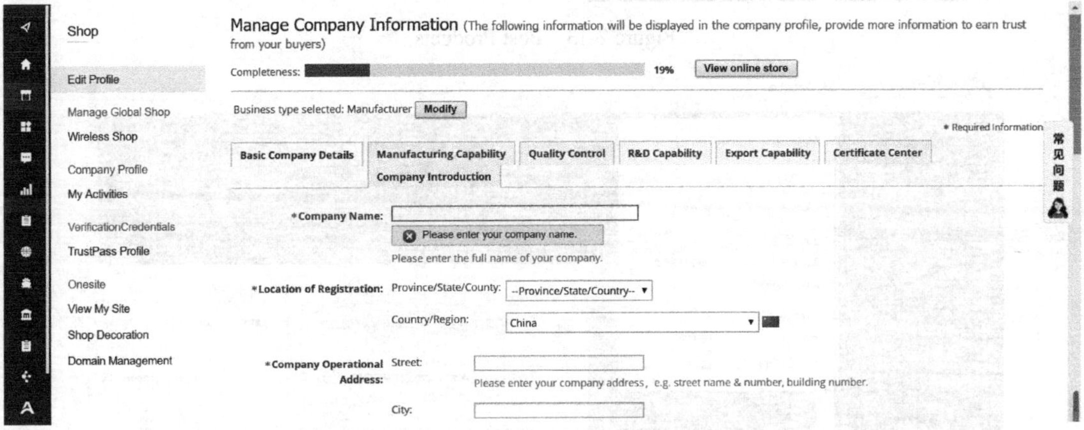

Figure 2-12 Manage Company Information

图 2-12 管理公司信息

【Step 7】After the company information gets approved, the product can be released. Click "Product Operation" → "Post Products" (Figure 2-13).

【步骤7】公司信息通过审核后，即可发布产品。单击"产品运营"→"发布产品"（图2-13）。

Figure 2-13　Post Products

图 2-13　发布产品

2.2.3　Shop Registration on AliExpress

Before registration, first prepare the materials needed for registration on AliExpress platform: ① corporate business license; ② corporate Alipay account (only corporates with business license can apply for corporate Alipay); ③ a trade mark (R/TM mark, some categories need to have pure English mark); ④ an E-mail account.

【Step 1】Open the official website of AliExpress, Click "Sell on AliExpress" → "Chinese sellers settled" to enter the registration process (Figure 2-14).

2.2.3　速卖通店铺注册

在注册之前，首先准备好注册全球速卖通平台所需的材料：① 企业营业执照；② 企业支付宝账号（有企业营业执照才可以办理企业支付宝）；③ 需要有商标（R/TM标，个别类目需要有纯英文标）；④ 国际通用的邮箱账号。

【步骤1】打开速卖通官网，单击"Sell on AliExpress"（成为速卖通卖家）→"中国卖家入驻"，进入注册流程（图2-14）。

Figure2-14   AliExpress Registration Entry

图 2-14   速卖通注册入口

【Step 2】On the registration page, "select your country" where the company is registered, and click "CONTINUE" (Figure 2-15).

【步骤 2】在注册页面，"选择"公司注册地所在的"国家"，单击"继续"按钮（图 2-15）。

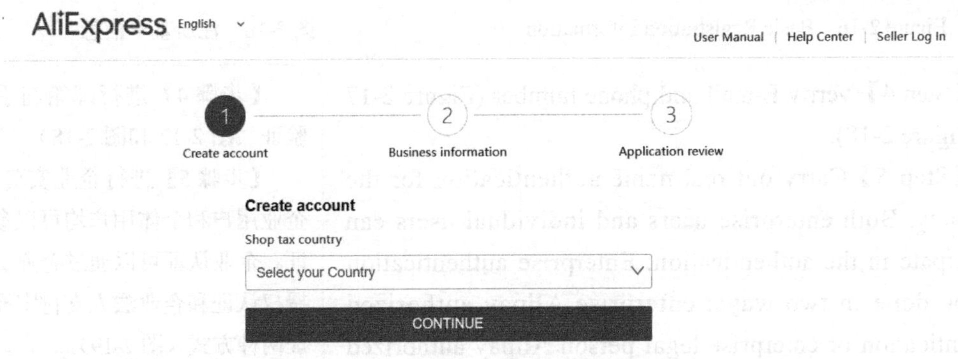

Figure 2-15   Confirm the Country Where the Company Is Registered

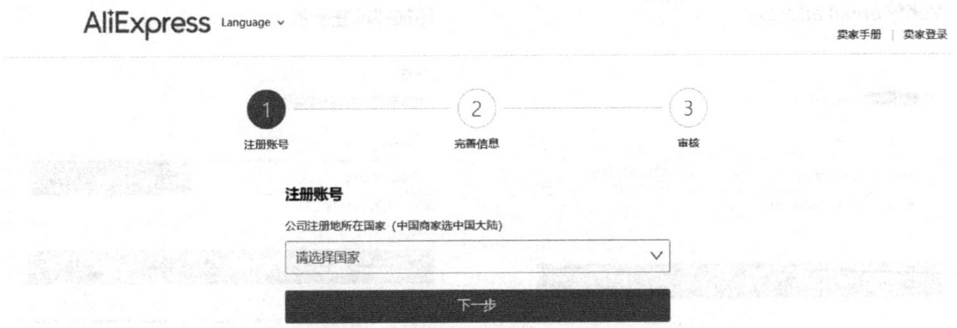

图 2-15   确认公司注册地所在国家

【Step 3】 Fill in basic information such as "E-mail" "Login Password" "Mobile Phone Number", and click "Next" (Figure 2-16).

【步骤3】填写"电子邮箱""登录密码""手机号码"等基本信息，单击"下一步"按钮（图2-16）。

Figure 2-16　Basic Registration Information

图 2-16　注册基本信息

【Step 4】 Verify E-mail and phone number (Figure 2-17 and Figure 2-18).

【Step 5】 Carry out real-name authentication for the company. Both enterprise users and individual users can participate in the authentication. Enterprise authentication can be done in two ways: enterprise Alipay authorized authentication or enterprise legal person Alipay authorized authentication (Figure 2-19).

【步骤4】进行邮箱与手机号验证（图2-17和图2-18）。

【步骤5】进行企业实名认证。企业用户和个体用户均可以参加认证。企业认证可以通过企业支付宝授权认证和企业法人支付宝授权认证两种方式（图2-19）。

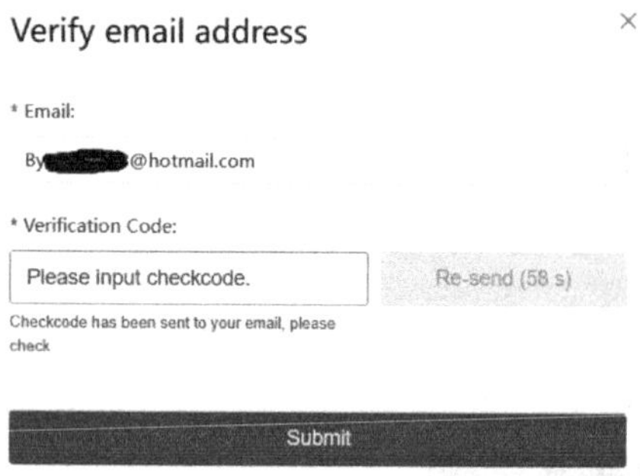

Figure 2-17　E-mail Verification

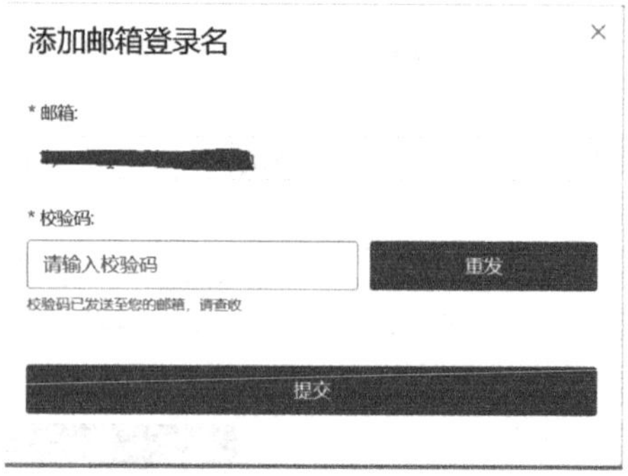

图 2-17　邮箱验证

Figure 2-18　Mobile Phone Number Verification

图 2-18　手机号验证

Figure 2-19　Enterprise Real-Name Authentication

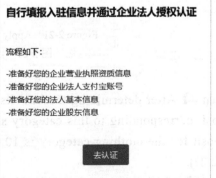

图 2-19　企业实名认证

【Step 6】After logging into the enterprise Alipay for authentication, click "Submit" (Figure 2-20).

【Step 7】Apply for business categories. According to the business direction of the enterprise, apply for the authority of business categories (Figure 2-21).

【步骤6】登录企业支付宝进行认证后，单击"提交"按钮（图 2-20）。

【步骤7】申请经营大类。根据企业经营方向，申请经营大类权限（图 2-21）。

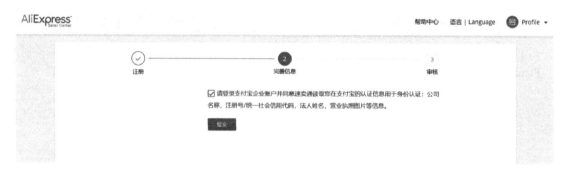

Figure 2-20　Log in to Enterprise Alipay for Authentication

图 2-20　登录企业支付宝进行认证

Figure 2-21　Apply for Business Categories

图 2-21　申请经营大类

【Step 8】After determining the business categories, the deposit corresponding to this category shall be paid. The deposit for the clothing category is 10,000.00 CNY (Figure 2-22).

【Step 9】After paying the deposit, and getting approved by AliExpress platform, you can open an operating account, release products and start operating a shop.

【步骤8】确定经营大类后，缴纳与运用该类目产品所对应的保证金。服装服饰大类的保证金是人民币 1 万元（图 2-22）。

【步骤9】缴纳保证金后，经过速卖通平台的审核，即可开通运营账号，发布商品并开始经营店铺。

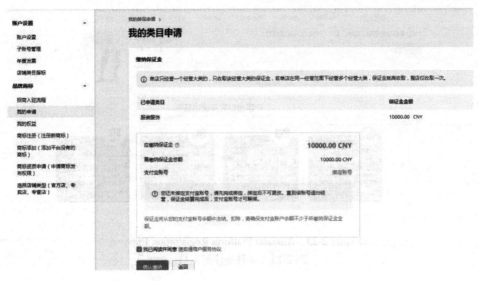

Figure 2-22   Pay the Deposit

图 2-22   支付保证金

2.2.4 Shop Registration on Amazon

Before registration, first prepare the required materials for Amazon platform registration: ① business license (including company name, address, and contact information); ② credit card (Visa, Master etc.) and billing addresses that support USD payment; ③ a valid E-mail account and mobile phone number.

【Step 1】Open the official website of Amazon, click "Register Now", and select sites in different countries to register. During the registration process, all information needs to be filled in English or Pinyin (Figure 2-23).

【Step 2】After filling in the "Your name" "E-mail address" "Password", click "Next" (Figure 2-24).

【Step 3】Verify the E-mail address (Figure 2-25).

【Step 4】After filling in "Company address" "Company type" "Company name used to register to the state or federal government", click "Agree and continue" (Figure 2-26).

2.2.4 亚马逊店铺注册

在注册之前，首先准备好注册亚马逊平台所需的材料：① 企业营业执照（公司的名称、地址、联系方式）；② 支持美元支付的信用卡（Visa、Master 等）和账单地址；③ 有效的电子邮箱账号和手机号码。

【步骤 1】打开亚马逊官网，单击"立即注册"，选择不同国家站点进行注册。在注册过程中，所有信息需使用英文或者拼音进行填写（图 2-23）。

【步骤 2】填写"您的姓名""邮箱地址""密码"后，单击"下一步"按钮（图 2-24）。

【步骤 3】验证电子邮件地址（图 2-25）。

【步骤 4】填写"公司地址""业务类型""用于向州或联邦政府登记的企业名称"后，单击"同意并继续"按钮（图 2-26）。

Figure 2-23   Amazon Platform Registration Entry
图 2-23   亚马逊注册入口

Figure 2-24   Create an Account
图 2-24   创建账户

Figure 2-25   E-mail Address Verification
图 2-25   验证电子邮件地址

Figure 2-26   Provide Company Information
图 2-26   提供公司信息

【Step 5】Fill in "Company business license registration address or Actual business address" "Legal person name" "Seller information" and fill in the phone number and keep the phone available, waiting for the phone number verification (Figure 2-27 to Figure 2-30). So far, the account registration has been completed.

【Step 5】填写"公司营业执照注册地址或实际经营地址""法定代表人""卖家信息",填写电话号码并保持电话畅通,等待接受电话验证(图 2-27 至图 2-30)。至此,账号注册完成。

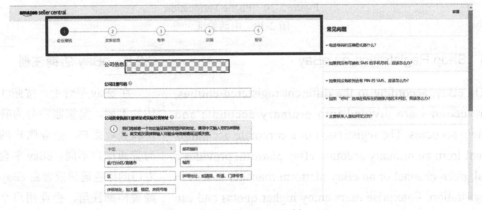

Figure 2-27　Company Address

图 2-27　公司地址

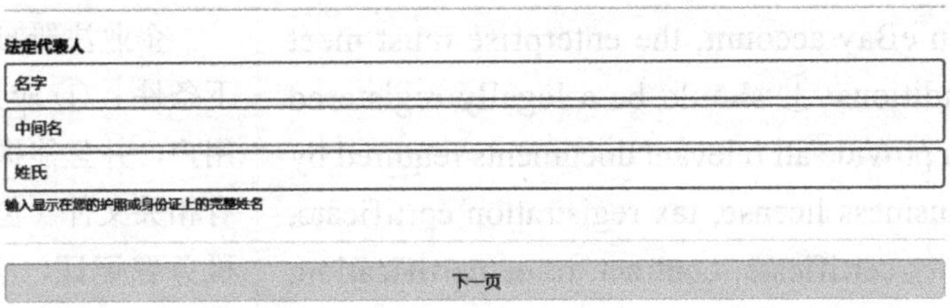

Figure 2-28　The Legal Person's Name

图 2-28　法人姓名

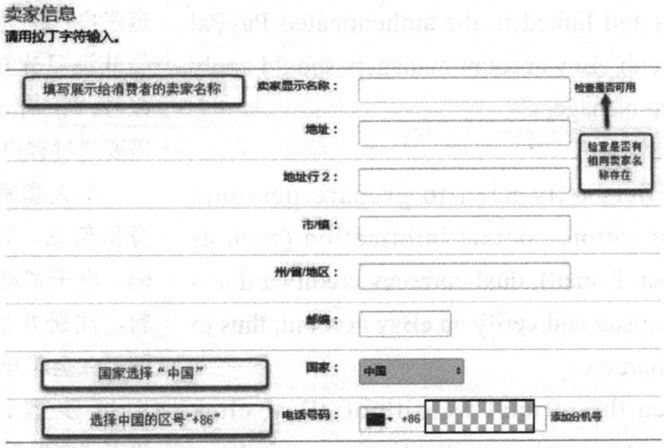

Figure 2-29　The Seller's Information

图 2-29　卖家信息

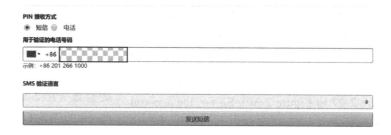

Figure 2-30　Phone Verification

图 2-30　电话验证

2.2.5　Shop Registration on eBay

On eBay, according to the different registered entities, seller accounts are divided into ordinary accounts and corporate accounts. The registration of a corporate account is different from an ordinary account. eBay platform provides a special green channel or an eBay platform manager assists in the registration. Enterprise users enjoy higher quotas and can obtain the assistance from account managers.

To register an eBay account, the enterprise must meet the following conditions: ① should be a legally registered enterprise who can provide all relevant documents required by eBay (including business license, tax registration certificate, legal person identity certificate, contract, trade certification, ISO authentication, etc.); ② be registered as a business account; ③ each seller can only apply for one enterprise entry channel account; ④ should be authenticated through the eBay seller account and linked to the authenticated PayPal account; ⑤ sellers with eBay account managers should apply through their account managers.

Individual sellers only need to prepare personal identification information, contact information (such as mobile phone number, E-mail), dual-currency credit card and other materials, to register and verify an eBay account, thus to start a global sales journey.

【Step 1】Open the official website of eBay, click "Register". After entering the registration page, set the account number and password (Figure 2-31).

2.2.5　eBay 店铺注册

在 eBay 平台上，按照注册主体的不同，卖家账户分为普通账户和企业账户。企业账户的注册与普通账户不同，eBay 平台提供专门的绿色通道或者由 eBay 平台经理协助注册。企业用户享有更高的额度并且可以获得客户经理的协助管理。

企业注册 eBay 账号需满足以下条件：① 应为合法登记的企业用户，并且能提供 eBay 要求的所有相关文件（包括企业营业执照、税务登记证、法人身份证明、合作合同、行业或产品认证、ISO 认证等）；② 注册为商业账户；③ 每个卖家只能申请一个企业入驻通道账户；④ 需要通过 eBay 卖家账号认证且连接到已认证的 PayPal 账号；⑤ 有 eBay 客户经理的卖家需要通过客户经理申请。

个人卖家只需要准备好个人身份信息、联系方式（如手机号码、电子邮箱）、双币信用卡等材料，注册并认证一个 eBay 账号，即可在全球开启销售之旅。

【步骤1】打开 eBay 官网，单击"注册"。进入 eBay 注册页面后，设置账号及密码（图2-31）。

【Step 2】Complete the verification. Click "Send me the verification code with SMS" (Figure 2-32).

【Step 3】Confirm platform terms. Click "Continue" (Figure 2-33).

【Step 4】Log in to the eBay account and click "My eBay" → "Account" → "PayPal account" → "Connect to my PayPal account" (Figure 2-34).

【步骤 2】完成验证。单击"以短讯向我提供确认码"（图 2-32）。

【步骤 3】确认平台条款。点击"继续"（图 2-33）。

【步骤 4】登录 eBay 账户，单击"我的 eBay"→"账户"→"PayPal 账户"→"连接到我的 PayPal 账户"（图 2-34）。

Figure 2-31　eBay Registration Page
图 2-31　eBay 注册页面

Figure 2-32　Complete the Verification
图 2-32　完成验证

Figure 2-33　Confirm Platform Terms
图 2-33　确认平台条款

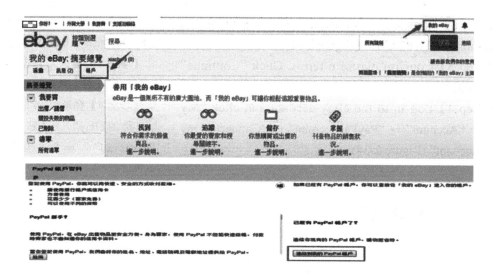

Figure 2-34　Connect to the PayPal Account

图 2-34　连接 Paypal 账户

【Step 5】Enter the PayPal account and password to complete the link between the eBay account and the PayPal account. So far, the registration of an eBay shop has been completed. (Figure 2-35).

【步骤 5】输入 Paypal 账号和密码，完成 eBay 账户与 PayPal 账户的关联。至此，一个 eBay 店铺的注册就完成了（图 2-35）。

Figure 2-35　Log into the PayPal Account

图 2-35　登录 PayPal 账户

2.2.6　Shop Registration on Shopee

Before registering, prepare the materials required for registration on the Shopee platform: ① the company's license; ② the legal person's ID card; ③ the main foreign trade shop

2.2.6　Shopee 店铺注册

在注册之前，先准备好注册 Shopee 平台所需的材料：① 公司营业执照；② 法人身份证；③ 主

link and recent sales (the number of orders needs to be displayed); ④ the company's real business address.

【Step 1】Open the offical website of Shopee，click "Register Now", to enter the registration page (Figure 2-36).

【Step 2】Click "Fill in the application form", to create a primary account (Figure 2-37 and Figure 2-38).

【Step 3】Set the basic information. After filling in "Account name" "Phone number" and "E-mail", click "Next: set the login information" (Figure 2-39).

营的外贸店铺的链接及近期销售（需显示订单数量）；④ 公司实际经营地址。

【步骤1】打开 Shopee 官网，单击"立即入驻"，进入注册界面（图 2-36）。

【步骤2】单击"填写申请表"，创建主账号（图 2-37 和图 2-38）。

【步骤3】设定基本信息。填写"账户名称""电话号码"和"电邮"后，单击"下一步：设定登入信息"按钮（图 2-39）。

Figure 2-36　Shopee Registration Entry
图 2-36　Shopee 注册入口

Figure 2-37　Fill in the Application Form
图 2-37　填写申请表

Figure 2-38   Create a Primary Account

图 2-38   创建主账号

Figure 2-39   Set up Basic Information

图 2-39   设定基本信息

【Step 4】Set the login information. After filling in the login name and password, click "Next: verify" (Figure 2-40).

【步骤4】设定登入信息。填写登入名称和密码，单击"下一步：验证"按钮（图 2-40）。

Figure 2-40   Set Login Information

图 2-40   设定登入信息

【Step 5】Verify the phone number. Enter the verification code (Figure 2-41).

【Step 6】Complete the primary account application. Click "Login now", log into the primary account, and click "Apply now" (Figure 2-42 to Figure 2-44).

【步骤 5】验证电话号码。输入验证码（图 2-41）。

【步骤 6】完成主账号申请。单击"立即登录"按钮，登入主账号，单击"立即申请入驻"按钮（图 2-42 至图 2-44）。

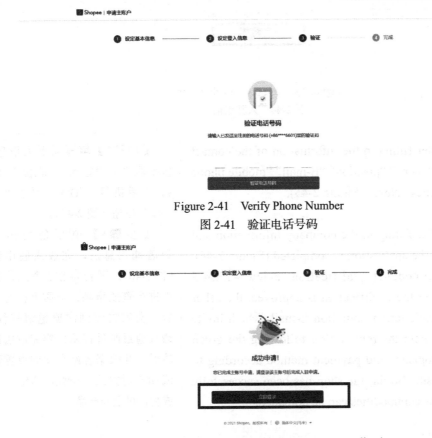

Figure 2-41　Verify Phone Number

图 2-41　验证电话号码

Figure 2-42　Complete the Primary Account Application

图 2-42　完成主账号申请

Figure 2-43　Log into the Primary Account

图 2-43　登入主账号

Figure 2-44　Apply for Admission

图 2-44　入驻申请

【Step 7】After filling in the information of the contact person, including "name" "position" "E-mail" "mobile phone number" " QQ", click "Next" (Figure 2-45).

【Step 8】After filling in the company information and shop information, the application is completed (Figure 2-46). The platform will conduct qualification review within 5 working days. After the qualification is approved, the seller will receive the registration invitation E-mail, which invite the seller to complete the registration following the given tips, and set the logistics and payment method according to the rules of each site. So far, the shop has been successfully registered, and new commodities can be uploaded.

【步骤7】填写联系人信息，包括联系人"姓名""职位""邮箱""手机号""QQ"，单击"下一步"按钮（图2-45）。

【步骤8】填写公司信息和店铺信息后，完成入驻申请（图2-46）。平台将在5个工作日内进行资质审核。资质审核通过后，卖家将收到注册邀请邮件，请其通过邮件提示内容完成店铺注册，并根据各站点规则设置物流和支付方式。至此，店铺注册成功，可上新产品。

Figure 2-45　Fill in the Contact Person Information

图 2-45　填写联系人信息

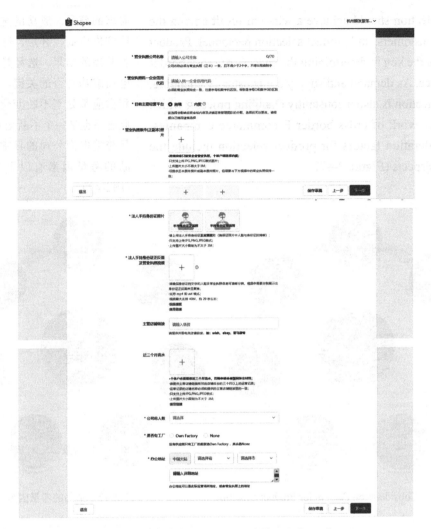

Figure 2-46   Fill in Company and Shop Information

图 2-46   填写公司和店铺信息

2.3   Cross-Border E-Commerce Product Selection

2.3.1   Basic Knowledge for Cross-Border E-Commerce Product Selection

Product selection refers to the selection of products from the supply market that suit the demand of the target market. On one hand, products should be selected according to the demand of the target market; on the other hand, products with quality, price, and appearance that best meet the demand of the target market should be selected. Successful

2.3   跨境电商选品

2.3.1   跨境电商选品认知

选品，指选品人员从供应市场中选择满足目标市场需求的商品。一方面，应以目标市场的需求为导向进行选品；另一方面，还应当从众多供应市场中选出质量、价格、外观最符合目标市场

product selection should achieve a win-win result among the suppliers, customers, and product selection personnel. Product selection is the key to determining the success of cross-border E-commerce. As demand and supply are constantly changing, product selection is also a constantly changing process, which is the daily work of cross-border E-commerce companies. The consideration factors for product selection include the following aspects (Figure 2-47).

需求的商品。成功的选品,应该达到供应商、客户、选品人员三者共赢的结果。选品是决定跨境电商成功与否的关键。由于需求和供应都处于不断变化之中,因此选品也是一个不断变化的过程,是跨境电商公司的日常工作。选品的考量因素有以下几个方面(图2-47)。

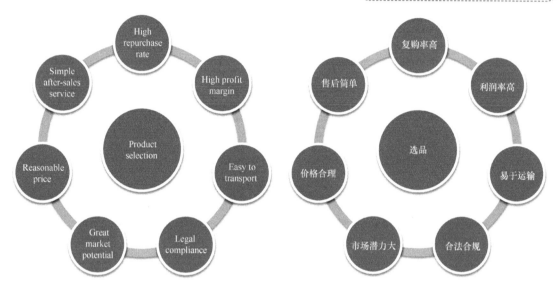

Figure 2-47　Consideration Factors for Product Selection

图 2-47　选品的考量因素

1. High profit margin

The commodity profit margin of cross-border E-commerce is about more than 50%, or even above 100%. Therefore, when selecting products, those products with higher profit margins should be considered first.

2. Easy to transport

The logistics of cross-border E-commerce has the characteristics of long transportation time and many uncertain factors, and various situations may occur during transportation, such as the damage of goods, customs detention, etc. Therefore, commodities are required to be small in size, light in weight, easy to pack and store, not easily broken, and have a long shelf life, which can greatly reduce logistics costs and the probability of cargo damage.

1. 利润率高

跨境电商的商品利润率大约在 50% 以上,甚至是 100% 以上。因此,在选品时应先要考虑那些利润空间较高的产品。

2. 易于运输

跨境电商的物流具有运输时间长、不确定因素多的特点,在运输途中可能出现各种状况,例如,货物毁损、海关扣留等。因此,要求商品体积小、质量较轻、易于包装和存储、不易破碎、保质期长,这样可以大大降低物流成本和物流环节货损的概率。

3．Simple after-sales service

It is required that the product requires simple after-sales service or doesn't need it, easy to operate, and does not require assembly or installation. Products that require after-sales service such as use and installation instructions will increase customer service cost. Once improperly handled, it will directly affect the customer's shopping experience and feedback, therefore, it is not suitable for cross-border E-commerce product selection.

4．High repurchase rate

Goods with a high repurchase rate can bring customers to the shop. The higher the repurchase rate, the higher the customer's loyalty to the shop. Generally speaking, customers will repeatedly purchase daily consumables such as snacks and facial masks; while products such as the safe basically will not be repurchased after having bought it once.

5．Reasonable price

If the price of online transactions is higher than the local market price, or higher than that of other online sellers, buyers will not be attracted to place orders.

6．Great market potential

The industry in which the product is required to have a large market potential and less competition. The selection of cross-border E-commerce products should try to avoid monopolized categories.

7．Legal compliance

Do not violate the rules of the platform or the laws and regulations of the destination country. In particular, do not sell pirated, counterfeit or contraband goods. Since the rules of each cross-border E-commerce platform are different, sellers must abide by various rules of each platform when selecting products.

2.3.2　Data Analysis for Cross-Border E-Commerce Product Selection

Cross-border E-commerce companies must conduct data analysis of the target market in advance as the basis of

3．售后简单

要求商品不需要售后服务或售后服务简单，便于操作、不需要组装或安装。需要有使用、安装说明书等售后服务的商品会加大后期的客户服务成本。一旦处理不当，会直接影响客户的购物体验及评价，因此不适合作为跨境电商的选品。

4．复购率高

复购率高的商品能够为店铺带来流量。复购率越高，表明客户对店铺的忠诚度就越高。一般来说，像零食、面膜这类的日常消耗品，客户会重复购买；但保险柜这类产品，客户购买一次后基本上不会再复购。

5．价格合理

在线交易的价格如果高于商品所在目的国的当地市场价，或者偏高与其他在线卖家，则无法吸引买家下单。

6．市场潜力大

要求商品所在的行业市场潜力较大，竞争不太激烈。跨境电商的选品应尽量避开被垄断的类目。

7．合法合规

不能违反平台的规定和目的国的法律法规。特别是，不能销售盗版、仿冒或违禁品。由于各个跨境电商平台的规则不同，卖家选品时必须了解和遵守各平台不同的规则。

2.3.2　跨境电商数据分析选品

跨境电商公司要提前对目标市场的基本情况进行数据分析，为选

product selection. Data analysis is to extract, analyze and monitor the business data, making data an effective basis for managers' decision-making and employees' execution. From the perspective of data sources, data is divided into external data and internal data. External data refers to data generated by other companies or the market, other than the company itself. Internal data refers to the data/information generated by the company itself. Companies need to conduct adequate research and analysis based on internal and external data, in order to make scientific and correct operational decisions.

1. External data analysis

External data analysis refers to the comprehensive use of various external analysis tools to fully grasp the data basis for category selection. For example, cross-border E-commerce companies can use search tools to analyze the cyclical characteristics of the category and grasp the opportunities in advance; use the tool Keyword Spy to find search popularity and keywords of the category; use the tool Alexa to find competitors' websites in this category, as a reference for the analysis and selection of products in the target market.

2. Internal data analysis

Internal data is the sales information of the products that have been released, it is the verification of the success of the product selection, and can also be used to guide the direction of future product selection. Sellers can use platform analysis tools to obtain sales information (such as customer traffic, conversion rate, bounce rate, average transaction price, etc.) of the products, so as to figure out which products are sold well and can bring traffic flow to the shop; which products are not popular in the market, and if the sales of the product have not improved for a long time, the product should be removed from the shelves.

2.3.3 Channels for Cross-Border E-Commerce Product Selection

There are two channels for choosing the source of export commodities for individual shops: one is offline sources, and

品提供依据。数据分析是通过对各个业务节点业务数据的提取、分析和监控，让数据成为管理者决策、员工执行的有效依据。从数据来源看，数据分为外部数据和内部数据。外部数据是指企业以外的其他公司、市场等产生的数据。内部数据是指企业内部经营过程中产生的数据／信息。企业需要同时对内、外部数据进行充分的调研和分析，以此做出科学、正确的运营决策。

1. 外部数据分析

外部数据分析是指综合运用各种外部分析工具，全面掌握品类选择的数据依据。例如，跨境电商公司可以借助搜索工具分析品类的周期性特点，把握商品开发先机；借助 Keyword Spy 工具发现品类搜索热度和品类关键词；借助 Alexa 工具可选择出以该品类作为主要目标市场的竞争对手的网站，作为对目标市场产品品相分析和选择的参考。

2. 内部数据分析

内部数据是已上架的商品的销售信息，是选品成功与否的验证，也可用于以后选品方向的指导。卖家可通过平台分析工具获得已上架商品的销售信息（流量、转化率、跳出率、客单价等），从而分析出哪些商品销售得好，能够为店铺带来流量；哪些商品在市场上并不受欢迎，若该产品销售情况长期没有得到改善，应下架该类产品。

2.3.3 跨境电商选品渠道

个人创业店铺的出口商品货源的选择有两种渠道：一种是线

the other is online sources.

(1) Offline source.

① Wholesale market. It is one of the most common selection channels. Purchasing in the wholesale market requires strong bargaining ability and strives to keep the price to the lowest level. At the same time, it is necessary to establish a good relationship with the wholesaler, especially to reach a consensus on the issue of exchanging goods, so as to avoid future disputes. The advantages of wholesale market sources are convenience, low transportation costs, visible physical goods, and negotiable prices.

② Factory supply. If you can cooperate with the factory, the factory supply will be the best source of goods. This way not only helps to save costs, guarantee the after-sales of the goods, but also can negotiate the style, price and quantity as well. However, factory has a high minimum order quantity, which is not suitable for small wholesale customers.

(2) Online source.

① Online platform source. Sellers can choose high-quality manufacturers through search engines or B2B platforms to purchase goods online. Online platform purchase can avoid the limitations of regional supply of goods. The advantages are convenience, low cost, and stable supply of goods, but the disadvantage is that the physical goods cannot be seen.

② Online agent source. Under this kind of sales mode, after the buyer places an order in the shop, the seller pays the superior supplier, and the superior supplier directly delivers the goods to the buyer. Therefore, this mode can reduce the seller's risk of hoarding goods, and save costs.

There are three sources of goods for the shops of brand enterprises, including self-built factories, factory contract manufacturing and brand agents.

(1) Self-built factory.

Under the mode of self-built factory, the company can independently have complete capabilities in research and development, supply chain, manufacturing, cost control, etc.

(2) Factory contract manufacturing.

下货源，另一种是线上货源。

（1）线下货源。

① 批发市场。这是最常见的选品渠道之一。在批发市场进货需要具有强大的议价能力，力争将批发价格压到最低。同时，要与批发商建立良好的关系，特别是在调换货的问题上与批发商达成共识，以免日后起纠纷。专业批发市场货源的优点是方便、运输成本低、可见实物、可议价。

② 工厂货源。如果能和工厂达成合作，工厂货源将是最好的货源渠道。这种方式不仅可以节约成本，商品售后也有保障，而且还可定款、定价、定量。然而，一般而言，厂家的起订量较高，不适合小批发客户。

（2）线上货源。

① 网络平台进货。卖家可以通过搜索引擎或者 B2B 平台选择生产厂家，选择优质厂家网上采购货源。网络平台进货可以避免地域货源的局限性，进货比较方便，成本较低，且货源稳定，但缺点是见不到实物。

② 网络代理货源。在这种销售模式下，买家在店铺下单后，店家向上级供应商支付货款，由上级供应商直接发货给买家。因此，这种模式可以降低卖家囤货的风险，而且成本很低。

品牌企业店铺的商品货源渠道有三种，包括自建工厂、工厂代工及品牌代理。

（1）自建工厂。

在自建工厂模式下，企业可以自主拥有完整的研发、供应链、制造、成本控制等综合能力。

（2）工厂代工。

Factory contract manufacturing includes OEM (Original Equipment Manufacture) and ODM (Original Design Manufacture).

OEM means that the company does not directly produce the products, but uses the core technology to design, develop the products, and control the sales channel. The specific processing tasks will be completed by other enterprises.

ODM means the company designs and produces products according to the requirements of another company. It produces goods according to the delegating contract.

Factory contract manufacturing can reduce the intermediate links in the supply chain, so that the goods and consumers are directly connected.

(3) Brand agent.

Companies can find brand suppliers to obtain brand authorization, therefore, have the agency rights to produce and sell certain brand products or services.

工厂代工包括 OEM（Original Equipment Manufacture，原始设备制造商）和 ODM（Original Design Manufacture，原始设计制造商）两种方式。

OEM 指生产者不直接生产产品，而是利用自己掌握的核心技术，负责设计和开发、控制销售渠道。由其他企业完成具体的加工任务。

ODM 指企业根据另一厂商的规格与要求设计和生产产品。企业基于授权合同生产产品。

工厂代工可以减少供应链的中间环节，让商品和消费者直接对接。

（3）品牌代理。

企业可以寻找品牌供应商，获得品牌授权许可，从而获得生产、销售某品牌产品或者服务的代理权限。

New words

1. company registration 公司注册
2. business license 营业执照
3. limited liability company 有限责任公司
4. Local Administration for Market Regulation 当地市场监督管理局
5. Alibaba 阿里巴巴国际站
6. AliExpress 速卖通
7. the Belt and Road "一带一路"
8. emerging market 新兴市场
9. Amazon 亚马逊
10. post products 发布产品
11. credit card 信用卡
12. product selection 选品
13. target market 目标市场
14. profit margin 利润率或毛利率
15. repurchase rate 复购率
16. place orders 下单
17. data analysis 数据分析
18. external data source 外部数据来源
19. internal data source 内部数据来源

Posting and Management of Cross-Border E-Commerce Products

跨境电商产品发布与管理

Lead-in case

Xiaowei has a preliminary understanding of how to register a company, open online shops on different cross-border E-commerce platforms, and use data analysis tools to select commodities. Based on data analysis and the team's resource advantages, she chooses the offline professional market or 1688 platform to buy clothes, shoes and other goods, and then sells them overseas through AliExpress, Amazon, eBay, Shopee and other platforms. In order to sell the products quickly, Xiaowei prepares to download the pictures of similar products from other online shops directly. After a little modification, the pictures will be posted on these platforms as soon as possible. Is her behaviour appropriate? Are requirements for products on different platforms the same?

Learning objectives

1. Objectives of knowledge

(1) To master the requirements of pricing, title and detail pages of products on different platforms.

(2) To master the picture requirements of main and auxiliary drawings of products on different platforms.

(3) To master the product listing rules of AliExpress and Amazon.

(4) To master the relevant complaint mechanism of AliExpress and Amazon.

2. Objectives of skills

(1) To obey the rules of each platform and select the compliant products with market potential.

(2) To complete the product image processing of cross-border E-commerce platforms as required.

(3) To write the title and detail pages of AliExpress and Amazon as required.

案例导入

小薇已经对如何注册公司、在不同跨境电商平台上开设网上店铺、利用数据分析工具选择商品有了初步了解。她依据数据分析和团队的资源优势,选择在线下的专业市场或 1688 平台购买服装、鞋类等商品以后,通过速卖通、亚马逊、eBay、Shopee 等平台,把商品卖到海外。为了快速把产品卖出去,小薇准备直接下载别的网上店铺类似产品图片。略微修改一下就把产品图片尽快上架到所有平台。这样的行为合适吗?不同平台的产品要求一样吗?

学习目标

1. 知识目标

(1)掌握不同平台的产品定价、标题和详情页的要求。

(2)掌握不同平台的产品主图和辅图的图片要求。

(3)掌握速卖通和亚马逊平台的产品上架规则。

(4)掌握速卖通和亚马逊平台的相关申诉机制。

2. 技能目标

(1)能遵守各平台规则,选择有市场潜力的合规产品。

(2)能按要求完成跨境电商平台的产品图片处理。

(3)能按要求完成速卖通与亚马逊的标题和详情页的撰写。

(4) To appeal according to the platform rules after suffering unreasonable punishment.

3．Objectives of qualities

(1) To have a diligent, patient, earnest and down-to-earth work style.

(2) To have the law-abiding awareness to obey by the rules of product listing on cross-border E-commerce platforms.

(3) To have the professional ethics of dedication, honesty, customer first, fairness and justice.

(4) To have a lasting interest in learning new knowledge and skills and the ability to change.

Not all goods can be sold on cross-border E-commerce platforms. Product posting rules on diverse platforms can vary, and even different types of goods on the same platform are slightly different. Therefore, Xiaowei and you must master the rules of commonly used E-commerce platforms such as AliExpress, Amazon and eBay, understand the similarities and differences of the rules, and prepare in advance to occupy the broad international market.

3.1 Product Posting Rules of AliExpress Platform

3.1.1 Pricing Strategy, Title and Page of Details for Products on AliExpress Platform

1．Product pricing strategy

Shops on AliExpress platform can investigate similar products online and offline, study the sales prices of homogeneous products and the sellers in the same industry, so as to provide reference to their own pricing. Specific methods are as follows:

(1) Search product categories on the home page of cross-border E-commerce platform to check the hot selling price range of the industry; search product keywords from the buyer's entrance, sort them according to different metrics, and then identify competitors according to the displayed results to analyze competitors' prices.

（4）能在遭受不合理的处罚后按平台规则申诉。

3．素质目标

（1）具有勤勉、耐心、认真和踏实的工作作风。

（2）具有遵守跨境电商平台产品上架规则的守法意识。

（3）具有爱岗敬业、诚实守信、客户至上、公平公正的职业道德。

（4）具有对新知识、新技能持久的学习兴趣和变革力。

不是所有商品都能在跨境电商平台上售卖，不同平台的产品发布规则都不相同，甚至同一平台不同类别的商品也有着细微的差别。因此，小薇与你必须掌握速卖通、亚马逊、eBay 等常用电商平台的规则，了解规则的异同，提前为攻占广阔的国际市场做准备。

3.1 速卖通平台产品发布规则

3.1.1 速卖通平台产品定价策略、标题和详情页描述

1．定价策略

速卖通店铺可以线上线下调研同类产品，研究同行业卖家、同质产品的销售价格，给自己定价作参考。具体方法为：

（1）跨境电商平台上首页搜索产品类目，查看行业热卖价格区间；从买家入口搜索产品关键词，按不同的指标排序后根据显示结果确定对手，分析对手价格。

(2) Search keywords through international social networking sites to find the prices of homogeneous products.

(3) Analyze offline shop prices and competitive advantages through various channels(Figure 3-1, Figure 3-2).

When the seller sets the price for the product, he or she needs to consider factors such as the purchase price, domestic freight, international freight, customs declaration fee, profit, platform commission, marketing activity discount, union commission withdrawal handling fee, overseas warehouse cost, etc. The calculation formula is as below.

（2）通过国际社交网站搜索关键词，查找同质产品价格。

（3）通过各种渠道分析线下实体店价格及竞争优势（图 3-1、图 3-2）。

卖家为产品定价时，需要考虑进货价、国内运费、国际运费、海关报关费、利润、平台佣金、营销活动折扣、联盟佣金提现手续费、海外仓成本等因素。计算公式如下。

Figure 3-1   Homepage of AliExpress Platform

图 3-1   速卖通平台主页

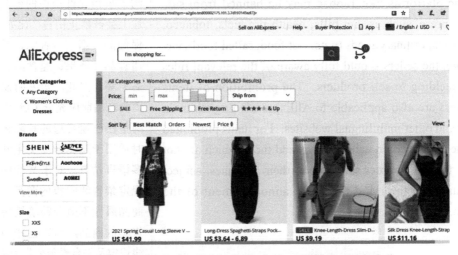

Figure 3-2   Display Page of Multiple Products on AliExpress Platform

图 3-2   速卖通平台多种产品显示页

Product price

=cost / exchange rate × (1 + cost profit margin) / (1 − various activities expense rate)

=(purchasing price + domestic freight + international freight + customs declaration fee) / exchange rate × (1 + cost profit margin) / (1−platform rate) / (1−activity discount rate)

=[purchasing price + domestic freight + (weight × international freight unit price × discount) + customs declaration fee] / foreign exchange buying rate × (1 + cost profit margin) / (1−platform rate) / (1−activity discount rate)

For example, the purchasing price of a women's coat is 30 yuan, the domestic freight is 5 yuan, the international freight unit price is 100 yuan/kg, the weight is 0.5 kg, the freight discount is 0.9, the customs declaration fee is 8 yuan, the US dollar purchase price exchange rate is 6.43, the cost profit margin is 20%, the platform rate is 5%, and the activity discount rate is 30%. How to quote the product in US dollars?

Product price = domestic cost / foreign exchange buying rate × pricing rate / (1−platform rate) / (1−activity discount rate) =(30+5+100×0.5×0.9+8)/6.43×(1+20%)/(1−5%)/(1−30%) =USD24.70

It is worth noting that not all products can be sold on the platform. Numerous items allowed posted on domestic platforms like Taobao may be banned from sale on AliExpress, such as diet pills, health products, tobacco, perfume, tea, ordinary foods (nuts, fast food, salted food), etc. Therefore, the sellers should fully aware of the relevant rules before deciding to sell products. The prohibition of items AliExpress are also applicable to AliExpress's English main website and other multilingual websites. For items prohibited or restricted by certain nation's laws and those which are not suitable for cross-border sales due to their attributes, subject to the nation's laws and the latest announcement of the platform.

产品售价

= 成本 / 汇率 ×(1+ 成本利润率)/(1− 各种活动费用率)

=(进货价 + 国内运费 + 国际运费 + 海关报关费)/ 汇率 ×(1+ 成本利润率)/(1− 平台费率)/(1− 活动折扣率)

=[进货价 + 国内运费 +(重量 × 运费单价 × 折扣)+ 海关报关费]/ 外汇买入价 ×(1+ 成本利润率)/(1− 平台费率)/(1− 活动折扣率)

例如，一件女式外套产品进货价 30 元，国内运费 5 元，国际运费单价 100 元 / 公斤，重 0.5 公斤，运费折扣 0.9，海关报关费 8 元，美元买入价汇率 6.43，成本利润率 20%，平台费率 5%，活动折扣率为 30%，产品按美元如何报价？

产品价格 = 国内成本 / 外汇买入价 × 定价率 /(1− 平台费率)/(1− 活动折扣率)=(30+5+100×0.5×0.9+8)/6.43×(1+20%)/(1−5%)/(1−30%)=24.70（美元）

值得注意的是，并非所有产品都可以在平台上卖。很多国内淘宝平台允许销售的商品，速卖通上会被禁止销售，比如减肥药、保健品、烟草、香水、茶叶、普通食品（坚果、速食品、腌制食品）等。因此，卖家朋友在决定售卖产品前应充分了解相关规则。阿里巴巴速卖通的禁限售规则同时适用于速卖通英文主站及其他多语言站点。对于某些国家法律规定禁售和限售的商品，以及因商品属性不适合跨境销售而不应售卖的商品，请以这些国家的法律规定及平台最新公告为准。

The restricted goods on AliExpress are as follows: before posting the goods, it is necessary to obtain the pre-approval, certificate operation, or authorized operation license, otherwise it is not allowed to post them. If you have obtained the relevant legal license, please provide it to the AliExpress platform first. It is strictly forbidden for users to publish and sell products involving a third-party intellectual property rights without authorization, including but not limited to trademark infringement, copyright infringement and patent infringement, which are strictly prohibited from being published on the AliExpress platform.

The prohibited goods are as follows: guns, military and police supplies, dangerous weapons; drugs, precursor chemicals, drug tools; flammable and explosive, dangerous chemicals; reactionary and other destructive information; involving personal safety, privacy; pharmaceuticals, medical devices, beauty instruments; illegal services, tickets; animals and plants, animal and plant's organs and animal killing tools; software, tools or equipment related to stealing and other illegal gains and uses; tobacco and products, e-cigarettes; virtual currency, articles related to other transportation industries, banned audio-visual products and other products.

2. Product title

Product title is an important way to attract buyers to enter and open the product details page and shop. Its main functions are as follows:

(1) Reflecting attributes of items, so that the seller can search and display your product on the platform, and then browse the image and text to see the properties, to determine whether need to click to enter.

(2) Realizing traffic flow conversion. The title text matches the preferences of potential consumers, and can have high traffic flow and ranking on the platform, which is easy for consumers to click and finally make a deal.

The characteristics of the title of AliExpress product are: accurate product keywords, product attributes that can attract buyers, service commitment and sales promotion. The number of words of the product title should be limited, and should

速卖通限售商品如下：发布商品前需取得商品销售的前置审批、凭证经营或授权经营等许可证明，否则不允许发布。若已取得相关合法的许可证明，请先提供给速卖通平台。严禁用户未经授权发布、销售涉及第三方知识产权的商品，包括但不局限于商标侵权、著作权侵权和专利侵权，都严禁在速卖通平台上发布。

禁售的商品如下：枪支、军警用品、危险武器类；毒品、易制毒化学品、毒品工具类；易燃易爆及危险化学品类；反动等破坏性信息类；涉及人身安全、隐私类；药品、医疗器械、美容仪器类；非法服务、票证类；动植物、动植物器官及动物捕杀工具类；涉及盗取等非法所得及非法用途软件、工具或设备类；烟草及制品、电子烟类；虚拟货币、其他运输行业有关的物品、禁售音像制品类等产品。

2. 产品标题

产品标题是吸引买家进入打开产品详情页和店铺的重要途径。其主要功能如下：

（1）体现产品属性，使卖家能够在平台上搜索并展示你的产品，然后再图文浏览查看属性，确定是否需要点击进入。

（2）实现流量转化。标题文字符合潜在消费者的偏好，能够在平台有较高的流量和排名，便于消费者点击并最终成交。

速卖通产品标题的特征有：准确的产品关键词、能够吸引买家的产品属性、服务承诺及促销语。产品标题的字数不应太多，应尽量准

be as accurate, complete and concise as possible, within 128 characters (if the title is copied and pasted, it is recommended to put it in notepad and fill in after removing the format). The title can be set in 17 languages (including English), and the system provides automatic translation function. Note: once other languages are set, English is not synchronized directly, and there is a reminder of earth symbol.

The compilation of titles must go through detailed investigation and research, collecting and analysis to get a vocabulary list, and then connect words in the correct order. The main ways of investigation are as follows:

(1) Data on AliExpress platform.

(2) Domestic and foreign seller and buyer forum.

(3) Foreign E-commerce websites such as eBay.

(4) Google search tool.

(5) Overseas social media.

The title is mainly composed of core words, attribute words and words to attract flows.

Shops should put the most important words for buyers in the first place, the second most important words in the second place, and the least important words in the last place. For search engines, the ranking of this title has little influence, and these words can be combined randomly according to their own products.

Core words: industry buzzwords can't really bring flow. It is usually placed at the beginning of the title to attract buyers, and the system will score when making a decision.

Attribute words: length, color and other attribute words affect sorting and click rate. Buyers can ensure that the products will stand out by category and attribute words. The system judges that the title of the product is regular, rich in information and relatively good on shelf quality.

Words to attract flows: the words that can bring flow, usually be put at the end. This kind of words is basically only used to show search engines, but if you're selling exclusive products, this kind of words could also be put at the beginning of the title.

确、完整、简洁，在 128 个字符以内（如果标题为复制与粘贴，建议放入记事本去除格式后填写）。标题可设置 17 种语言（含英文），系统提供自动翻译功能。注意：一旦设置了其他语言，则不直接同步英文，且有地球符号提醒。

标题编写必须经过详细的调查研究，收集和分析数据以得出词表，然后按正确的顺序连接词语。调研的主要途径如下：

（1）速卖通平台的数据。

（2）国内外的卖家和买家论坛。

（3）eBay 等国外电商网站。

（4）Google 搜索工具。

（5）海外社交媒体。

标题主要由核心词汇＋属性词＋引流词构成。

店铺应把对买家来说是最重要的词放在第一位，把重要的词放在第二位，把最不重要的词放在最后。对于搜索引擎来说，这个标题的排序无太大影响，可以根据自己的产品随意组合。

核心词：行业热门词并不会真的带来流量。它通常会放在标题最前面以吸引买家，系统会在进行判定时得分。

属性词：长度、颜色等属性词影响排序，影响点击率。买家通过类目和属性词去筛选，能确保产品脱颖而出。系统判断标题会认为产品标题正规、信息丰富、上架品质相对较好。

引流词：能带来流量的词，通常会把它放在最后面。这类词基本上只用于显示搜索引擎，但如果卖的是独家产品，你也可以把这类词放在第一位。

For example: 202× Spring New Fashion ××× Casual Floral Print Long Brown Coat Dress Women, 202× Autumn High Quality Fashion Women Golden Velvet Clothing Two Pieces Suit Set. The title of electronic products can add functions and supporting equipment, such as 202× ××× Mini Drone GPS L108 4K HD 5G WiFi Brush Motor FPV Dragon Flying 20 Minutes Distance RC 1km RC Quadcopter.

3. Detail page

Detail page of products is an important content for sellers to highlight their product's characteristics. After careful comparison, buyers can determine the important content of the order, including product characteristics, relevant products, shop advantages (such as factory owner, original design, their own vertical industrial chain), logistics timelines (overseas warehouses, express mail), and so on.

The first picture on the detail page should be the shop's brand or product poster; then the associated picture of the relevant product or the marketing poster.

If it belongs to garment category, put in a size list and product details, including fabrics, accessories and production process, cleaning, after-sales service and other matters of the product.Electronic products can be put in product specifications, product characteristics, system support, product packaging, etc. All indicators must be filled in correctly, and other people's products cannot be simply copied and pasted there.

As for instructional information, text-picture separation is recommended, i.e. put in pictures and text separately, instead of putting the text on pictures. Reasons are as follows.

(1) Text loads faster than pictures, so it would not be unclear at the wireless end due to equal-scale compression.

(2) By using translation plug-ins to see multilingual translations, non-English buyers can get a general idea of the product details. If the seller must write the text on the picture, he must see the actual effect on the wireless settings in order

比如：女装产品 202× Spring New Fashion ××× Casual Floral Print Long Brown Coat Dress Women，202× Autumn High Quality Fashion Women Golden Velvet Clothing Two Pieces Suit Set。电子产品标题可以加功能和配套设备，如 202× ××× Mini Drone GPS L108 4K HD 5G WiFi Brushless Motor FPV Dragon Flying 20 Minutes Distance RC 1km RC Quadcopter。

3. 详情页

产品详情页是卖家突出自己产品特征的重要内容。在仔细比较后，买家可以确定下单的重要内容，包括产品特征、关联产品、店铺优势（比如自有工厂、原创设计、自有垂直产业链）、物流时效（海外仓、特快专递）等。

在详情页的第一张图片上应是店铺的品牌或产品海报图；接着是相关产品的关联图片或营销海报。

如果是服装类，应放尺码表和产品的细节图，包括产品的面料、辅料和制作工艺、清洗、售后服务等事项。电子产品可写产品规格、产品特性、系统支持、产品包装等。所有指标必须填写正确，不能简单复制和粘贴他人产品。

对于说明类信息，建议图文分离，即图片和文字分开录入，而不是把文字写在图片上。原因如下。

（1）文字加载速度比图片快，在无线端不会因为等比例压缩的关系看不清楚。

（2）利用翻译插件看多语言的翻译，使非英语买家能大致了解商品详情。如果卖家一定要把文字写到图片上，则必须看到无

to adjust the font size on the picture and ensure that the buyer can see the text clearly when the picture is scaled down.

The relevant marketing content of AliExpress is not the buyer's biggest concern of the current commodity. If it must be displayed on one screen, you'd better put it at the end of the commodity description.

At present, the wireless user interface has an independent function of description and editing for the detail page. The content and layout of the independent detail page can be different from that of the PC end, which can help the seller better present the goods from the perspective of the wireless buyer without affecting the information acquisition of the PC buyer.

3.1.2 Photo Processing for Products on AliExpress Platform

The first main image is the key to attracting consumers to search, click to the detail page after browsing, and it is also an important entry for traffic flow. First, the picture should be simple and clear, and the main body of the product should be highlighted. The background of picture should be differentiated from your competitors' and can get more attention (Figure 3-3). Second, you should control the file size of the picture. Some nation's Internet speed is slow, and the cost it high. If the pictures are loaded slowly, the customer's inability to open

线设置的实际效果，以便调整图片上的字号，确保图片等比例缩小之后，买家能看清楚文字。

速卖通的相关营销内容不是买家在当前商品下最关注的内容，如果它必须被放在一个屏幕上，则你最好放在商品描述的最后。

目前，无线用户界面具有独立的详情页描述编辑功能。独立的详情页内容和排版都可以与PC端不一样，既可以帮助卖家更好地从无线买家的角度来展现商品，又不会影响PC买家的信息获取。

3.1.2 速卖通平台产品图片处理

第一张主图是吸引消费者搜索、浏览后点击打开详情页的关键，也是流量的重要入口。首先，图片要保证简洁和清晰，要突出产品主体。图片背景应区别于竞争对手，并能获得更多关注（图3-3）。其次，要控制好图片的文件大小。某些国家的网速较慢，上网费较贵。如果图片加载速度

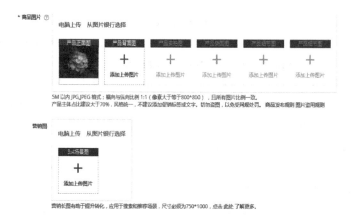

Figure 3-3　Main Image Entry Interface for AliExpress Platform Products

图3-3　速卖通平台产品主图录入界面

them will lower the experience value, which is detrimental to adding to the favorite or completing transaction. It is not recommended that different models or colors of the same product appear on one image with multiple models or puzzles of multiple products. Buyers may misinterpret one order button as containing multiple products.

Requirements of main image:

- It is recommended that the background color should be white or solid, with picture horizontal and vertical scales of 1 : 1, pixels 800×800 and above, or scales of 3 : 4, and pixels 750×1000 and above.

- The main body of the product generally accounts for more than 70%, and in a unified style. Labels or words cannot be added.
- Pictures do not require borders and watermarks, and cannot have stitching images.
- Logo is neatly placed in the upper left corner of the picture, about one-tenth the size of the main picture.
- In general, 6 pictures can be uploaded at the same time, including front, back, side, live, detail images, etc.
- Marketing images are available only in the clothing category and are called the 7th picture and do not have to be uploaded. If a marketing image has been uploaded, it will be displayed in the search or recommendation list; if not uploaded, the first main image will be displayed by default.
- It is strictly prohibited to steal images, to be suspected of banning and restricting sales or to infringe on the intellectual property rights of others.

There are slight differences in the requirements of main images for different industries, for instance, no less than 3 detail images in the main image of products should be provided in the wedding dress industry; the real models in the main image must show their heads and faces, and there should be no cuttings of their heads or mosaics on their faces; the size of products accounts for more than 80% of the pictures;

很慢，则客户无法打开图片导致拉低体验值，不利于商品收藏或成交。不建议不同型号或颜色的同一产品以多个模特或多个产品拼图的形式出现。买家可能误解为一个订单按键包含多个产品。

主图要求包括：

- 建议背景颜色为白色或纯色，图片水平和垂直比例为1：1，800 像素 ×800 像素及以上，或比例为3：4，750像素 ×1000 像素及以上。
- 产品主体占比一般为 70%以上，风格统一。不能添加标签或文字。
- 图片不需要边框和水印，不能有拼图。
- Logo 整齐地放置在图片的左上角，大约为主图的十分之一。
- 一般可以同时上传 6 张图片，包括正面、背面、侧面、实拍、细节图等。
- 营销图只在服饰类目才有，被称为第 7 张图片，非必须上传。若已上传营销图，则在搜索或者推荐表中展示营销图；若未上传则默认展示商品图片的第一张主图。
- 严禁盗图、涉嫌禁限售或侵犯他人知识产权。

不同行业的主图要求有细微差别，例如，婚纱礼服行业产品的主图中不得少于 3 张细节图；主图中的真人模特必须露出头和脸，禁止将头剪裁掉或在脸部出现马赛克；产品大小占图片比例 80%以上，多色产品的主图禁止出现

and pictures in nine square grids are prohibited in the main image of multi-color products. Two pictures stitching is allowed in the main picture of children's clothing products, but more than three pictures stitching is not allowed. It is recommended to upload six images, where the first one is a front image of the product, the second one is a side one, the third one is a back one, the fourth and the fifth are product details and the sixth is the physical picture of the product.

AliExpress platform can upload product videos and improve user conversion rate (Figure 3-4). Video requires no more than 2GB, avi, 3gp, mov and other formats, the aspect ratio is consistent with the main commercial image, and the length is less than 30 seconds. If you upload a product video, it will be displayed in the foreground main image area. Note that the basic information of the product video, whether PC or App, is displayed in the main image area on the detail page. Videos can also be added to the description of the product page, and the PC screen and the App screen can be set separately.

九宫格。童装行业产品的主图中允许有 2 张拼图，但不允许有 3 张以上的拼图。建议上传 6 张图片，第一张为正面图，第二张为侧面图，第三张为背面图，第四张与第五张为产品的细节图，第六张为实物图。

速卖通平台可以上传产品视频，可提高用户转化率（图 3-4）。视频要求不超过 2GB，具有 avi、3gp、mov 等格式，长宽比与商品主图保持一致，时长在 30 秒以内。若上传产品视频，则会展示在前台商品主图区。注意：无论是 PC 还是 App，产品视频的基本信息都显示在产品详情页的主图内。商品详情页描述中也可以添加视频，并且 PC 界面和 App 界面可以分别单独设置。

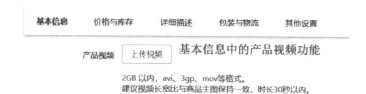

Figure 3-4　Video Entry Interface for Products of AliExpress Platform

图 3-4　速卖通平台产品视频录入界面

3.1.3　Penalties for Violations of Shops on AliExpress Platform

In order to protect the legitimate rights and the interests of consumers, business operators or AliExpress, the platform classifies violations into four sets of deduction systems according to the nature of violations: intellectual property prohibition and sale violations, transaction violations and others, violations of commodity information quality, and serious violations of intellectual property rights. The four sets of credit integrals are deducted, accumulated and punished separately.

3.1.3　速卖通平台店铺违规处罚

为保障消费者、经营者或速卖通的正当权益，平台将违规行为根据违规性质归类分为知识产权禁限售违规 、交易违规及其他、商品信息质量违规、知识产权严重违规四套积分制。对四套积分分别进行扣分、累计和处罚。

Each of the four sets' points is calculated as a cumulative points annually, which means that each deduction will be recorded for one year, such as 6 points deducted at 12:00 on March 1, 2021, which will only be cleared after 365 days. (Table 3-1).

四套积分的每个违规行为的分数按行为年累计计算，行为年是指每项扣分都会被记一年，如2021 年 3 月 1 日 12 点 被 扣 了 6分，该 6 分要到 365 天时间满后才被清零（表 3-1）。

Table 3-1   Penalties for Violations of Shops on AliExpress Platform

Violation type	Violation node	Punishment
Serious violation of intellectual property rights	First violation	Freeze (whichever violation record is shown)
	Second violation	Freeze (whichever violation record is shown)
	Third violation	Close
Intellectual property prohibition and sale violations	2 points	Warning
	6 points	Limit commodity operation for 3 days
	12 points	Freeze account for 7 days
	24 points	Freeze account for 14 days
	36 points	Freeze account for 30 days
	48 points	Close
Trading violations and others violations	12 points	Freeze account for 7 days
	24 points	Freeze account for 14 days
	36 points	Freeze account for 30 days
	48 points	Close
Violation of commodity information quality	12-point and 12-point multiples	Freeze account for 7 days

表 3-1   速卖通平台店铺违规处罚

违规类型	违规节点	处罚
知识产权严重违规	第一次违规	冻结（以违规记录展示为准）
	第二次违规	冻结（以违规记录展示为准）
	第三次违规	关闭
知识产权禁限售违规	2 分	警告
	6 分	限制商品操作 3 天
	12 分	冻结账号 7 天
	24 分	冻结账号 14 天
	36 分	冻结账号 30 天
	48 分	关闭
交易违规及其他	12 分	冻结账号 7 天
	24 分	冻结账号 14 天
	36 分	冻结账号 30 天
	48 分	关闭
商品信息质量违规	12 分及 12 分倍数	冻结账号 7 天

Common types of product release violations in shops are as follows.

(1) The product title contains unauthorized brand words.

Without brand authorization certificate, product title, description, etc. can not show brand words and logo. If complained by the brand owner, the platform will send infringement E-mail.

(2) Trademark infringement.

It is not allowed to use others' trademark and logo illegally. If it is found by the platform, it will be recorded as a serious infringement. If the infringement reaches 3 times, the shop will be closed and the penalty can't be revoked until one year later.

(3) Intellectual property right infringement.

If the product's copyright and appearance are similar, the intellectual property right owner can complain about the infringement.

3.1.4 Mechanism of Appealing for Shops on AliExpress Platform

When a shop is punished by the AliExpress platform for violation, but no violation actually occurs, the shop can appeal to the platform. The most important thing in AliExpress appeals process is evidence, which can prove that the shop has no evidence of violation. Generally, within 3 working days, the shop should send the completed protest materials to the specified mailbox, or fill in and upload the supporting materials according to the specific requirements in the complaint link. The shop must ensure the accuracy of the relevant information and evidence filled in. One complaint information corresponds to one violation punishment.

1. Appeal for stealing image

If a shop receives an E-mail complaining about the product's stolen image, and it is true that it has not stolen the image, it can appeal. The shop needs to prepare the original picture of the product, and other people's pictures are also needed to have the intellectual property rights or the authorization certificate of relevant right holders. Access to

常见的店铺产品发布违规类型如下。

（1）产品标题含有未经授权的品牌词。

未经品牌授权证明，产品标题、描述等不能出现品牌词及Logo。如果被品牌所有人投诉，平台则发送侵权邮件。

（2）商标侵权。

不得非法使用他人的商标和Logo。如果被平台查到，就会被记一次严重侵权。若侵权达到3次，则会被封店，该处罚在一年后才能被撤销。

（3）知识产权侵权。

产品著作权、外观等相似，知识产权所有人可投诉侵权店铺。

3.1.4 速卖通平台店铺申诉机制

当店铺因违规被速卖通平台处罚，而实际却未发生违规行为时，则可以向平台申诉。速卖通申诉流程最重要的就是证据，即能证明本店铺没有违规的证明材料。一般在3个工作日内，店铺将填写完整的拒付申诉资料发至指定邮箱，或按照申诉链接中具体的要求填写和上传证明材料。店铺必须保证填写的相关资料和证据的准确性。一份申诉资料对应一次违规处罚。

1. 盗图申诉

如果店铺收到产品被投诉盗图的电子邮件，并且自己确实未盗图，可以进行申诉。店铺需要准备好产品图片的原图，使用别人的图片还需要有知识产权或相关权利人的授权证明。速卖通盗图申诉人

the complaint of image theft on AliExpress is as follows: "AliExpress background" → "business performance" → "my case", click "proof" to upload relevant electronic proof materials, and wait for the platform to review. If the shop's appeal is approved, the platform will revoke the original punishment.

If the shop's original pictures are stolen by other AliExpress merchants, it can complain to the platform. First of all, the shop needs to prepare these complaint materials: the original image without editing and watermark, as well as the product link consistent with the stolen image. Shop can enter the background of AliExpress, find "violation report" → "violation of other product listings", and then fill in the product link as required, submit the original picture, etc.

2．Appeal for account closure

The account of the shop is closed because of false delivery, selling fake goods and other violations, and the shop can appeal if it doesn't correspond to the facts.

Firstly, the shop needs to prepare the brand authorization certificate, sales license, product inspection certificate, logistics documents, delivery photos and other supporting materials; secondly, the shop can contact the platform customer service to inquire about the relevant situation and procedures; and then the shop can operate according to the customer service suggestions or send E-mail to the designated mailbox.

3．Complaints of relevant shops

An enterprise can only have one account on the AliExpress platform, but it supports enterprises to open three shops under the same business category. Enterprises can make full use of the resources of these three shops and try to avoid logging in two or more shops in one IP address at the same time. If the platform misjudges the shop association, the shop can prepare its own shop opening information, product purchase invoice and other certificates to prove that it has only one shop, and then submit the complaint for review through the link in the E-mail sent by the platform. If the situations are so serious that the account

口为："速卖通后台"→"经营表现"→"我的案件"，单击"举证"上传相关电子证明材料，等待平台审核即可。若店铺的申诉通过，平台则撤销原有处罚。

若店铺自己的原创图片被其他速卖通商家盗用，则可向平台进行投诉。首先，需要准备好这些投诉材料：未经过编辑、无水印的图片原图，同时还要有与被盗图片一致的产品链接及被盗图片。店铺可以进入速卖通后台，找到"违规举报"→"其他商品发布违规"，然后按要求填写产品链接，提交原图等。

2．账户关闭申诉

店铺因为虚假发货、售假等违规导致账户被关闭，自己实际未发生违规行为，可以进行申诉。

首先，需要准备好品牌授权证明、销售许可证、产品检验证书、物流单据、发货照片等证明材料；其次，可以联系平台客服，询问有关情况和相关手续；最后，按照客服建议操作或发送电子邮件至指定邮箱。

3．店铺关联申诉

一个企业在速卖通平台上只能有一个账号，但是支持企业在同一经营大类下开通 3 家店铺。企业可以充分利用好这 3 家店铺的资源，尽可能避免在一个 IP 地址中同时登录两个及以上店铺。如果平台误判店铺关联，则该店铺可以准备好自己的开店资料、产品进货的发票等证明，来证明自己只有一个店铺，然后通过平台发送的邮件中链接提交申诉审

is closed, the probability of the appeal to be passed is low.

核。如果情节严重被封号，则申诉通过的概率较低。

3.2 Rules of Launching Products on Amazon Platform

3.2.1 Title and "Five Bulletin Points" of Products on Amazon Platform

1. Requirements of product title

An excellent title is an important factor in creating a hot product, and it is also a direct traffic flow source for buyers to search for your product. You can think of Amazon's title as the shop name of a physical shop.

Generally speaking, the title of the Amazon platform is composed of the following factors: Brand+Model+Keywords+Scope of Application+Product Features.

Here are some notes in making a title for a product on the Amazon platform:

The first letter of each word must be capitalized, except for conjunctions, articles, and prepositions (such as conjunctions: and, or, for; articles: the, a, an; prepositions of less than 5 letters: in, on, over, with), and other words cannot be all uppercase or all lowercase.

You cannot use any special characters or symbols, such as: @, #, $, &,* etc.; and you cannot enter anything in Chinese. If you want to use a number, it must be an Arabic numeral.

The title must be concise and not too long (no more than 250 characters; an English letter, space or punctuation is considered to be a character); but not too short (for example, less than 100 characters).

If it is a sale in bulk, the word "pack of" needs to be added into the title.

No promotion information could be shown in the title, such as free shipping, best sale, great promotion, new arrival, 2020 fashion, etc.

If your product has a brand, the first name of the title

3.2 亚马逊平台产品发布规则

3.2.1 亚马逊平台产品标题和"五点描述"

1. 产品标题的要求

一个优秀的标题是打造爆款的重要因素，也是买家搜索到你的产品直接流量来源。你可以把亚马逊的标题看成实体店的店名。

一般来说，亚马逊平台的标题有以下几个组成要素：品牌＋型号＋关键词＋适用范围＋产品特性。

在拟定亚马逊平台产品标题时，还需要注意以下方面：

每个单词的首字母必须大写，除了连词、冠词、介词（如连词：and、or、for；冠词：the、a、an；少于5个字母的介词：in、on、over、with），其他单词不能全部大写或小写。

你不能使用任何特殊字符或符号，例如：@、#、$、&、*等；也不能用中文输入任何内容。如果你想使用数字，则必须是阿拉伯数字。

标题必须简明扼要，不能过长（不超过250个字符，一个英文字母、空格或者标点都被认为是一个字符），但也不能太短（比如少于100个字符）。

如果是批量销售，在标题中需要添加"pack of"字样。

不能带有任何促销信息，例如，免费送货、最佳销量、最大促销、最新到货、2020时尚等。

如果你的产品有品牌，则标题

should be the brand name; if there is no one, you can write the first name as the brand name to be made in the future. However, other brands cannot appear, otherwise you may receive infringement warnings at any time. For example, "oscillating saw blade dewalt" might be thought to be a long-tail term, but in fact "dewalt" is a brand.

Do not show too many product details (It is advisable that the multi-model products should be less than 3 models).

2．Five bulletin points

The five-point description of Amazon listing is located directly below the title, and its importance is second only to the product title. Its role is to deepen the customer's impression of the product. The five-point description can be the product specifications, packaging, functions, features, uses, advantages, materials, appearance, design structure, additional functions, how to use, after-sales guarantee, etc. The first description should reflect the most attractive selling point for customers: directly distinguish the differences of other products, stimulate the desire to buy, and write the biggest features of the product. The last description is often a sentence that prompts buyers to let go of their scruples and buy directly. If the selling point is less than five descriptions, you can attach the shelf life, after-sale guarantee, gifts, etc.

Keywords that can't fit in the title can be used cleverly on bulletin points, so that the listing can facilitate the best optimization. Try to avoid repeating words in the title; avoid spelling and grammatical errors; be concise, and use the fewest words to express the meaning.

3.2.2　Image Processing of Products on Amazon Platform

The Amazon platform has stricter requirements for images than other platforms. In order to upload products smoothly, the images submitted by the seller must strictly follow the requirements of the Amazon platform.

的最前面应该是品牌名；如果没有品牌，可以将首位写成将来的品牌名。但是，不能出现其他品牌，否则，可能随时收到侵权警告。比如，"oscillating saw blade dewalt（摆动锯片 dewalt）"会让人以为是一个长尾词，其实"dewalt"是一个品牌。

不要出现过多的产品细节（多型号商品建议不超过 3 个型号）。

2．五点描述

亚马逊产品目录的五个要点描述位于标题正下方，其重要性仅次于商品标题。其作用是加深顾客对产品的印象。五个要点描述可以是产品的规格、包装、功能、特点、用途、优势、材质、外观、设计结构、附加功能、如何使用、售后保障等。其中，第一个描述应该体现最能吸引顾客的卖点：直接区分与其他产品的不同，激发购买欲，可写产品的最大特色。最后一个描述往往是促使买家放下顾忌，直接购买的句子。如果卖点较少写不满五个描述时，则可以附上保质期、售后保障、赠品等。

在标题中放不下的关键词可以巧妙地运用在要点描述上，让产品目录能有最好的优化。尽量避免和标题中的单词重复；避免拼写和语法错误；言简意赅，用最少的词汇把意思表达出来。

3.2.2　亚马逊平台产品图片要求

亚马逊平台对于图片的要求相比其他平台更严苛。为了能顺利上传产品，卖家提交的图片必须严格对照亚马逊平台的要求。

1. Requirement of main image

(1) Requirement of pixel.

The longest side must be at least 1,000 pixels. When the height or width of the picture is at least 1,000 pixels, the picture has a zoom function, and the buyer can zoom in on the part of the picture to view product details. This function has the effect of increasing sales. The shortest side (relative width or height) of the picture cannot be less than 500 pixels. Otherwise, it cannot be uploaded to the Amazon backstage. The picture is too small for the buyer to view the product. It is recommended that the seller upload the product picture with a side length of 1,001 pixels or more.

(2) Requirement of image format.

You can use JPEG, TIFF, and GIF. These are uploadable on Amazon. It is recommended to use the JPEG format. Images in this format can be uploaded faster.

(3) Requirement of background color.

The background of the image on Amazon must be pure white. The definition of a pure white background is: three-color channels of RGB, R: 255, G: 255, B: 255. Even if the product is shot on a white background paper or other materials, the background still needs to be changed to pure white through image processing. The main picture of a small part of home decorations is not mandatory to use a pure white background, such as four-piece bed sets, mosquito nets, curtains, sofas, wall paintings, and lamps.

(4) Other requirements.

The main picture is the actual picture of the product, not an illustration, let alone a hand-drawn drawing or a comic drawing.

The main image cannot carry Logo and watermark, and it is best not to have accessories, props, etc. that are not in the order (the Logo of the product itself is allowed).

The product in the main picture should occupy about 85% of the space of the picture for the best.

For products with variants, parent and subsidiary

1. 主图的要求

（1）像素的要求。

最长的边必须至少为 1 000 像素。当图片的高度或宽度至少为 1 000 像素时，该图片具有缩放功能，买家能放大图片的一部分来查看产品细节。这个功能具有增加销售量的作用。图片最短的边（相对的宽或高）不能少于 500 像素。否则无法上传到亚马逊后台。图片太小，不方便买家查看产品。建议卖家在上传产品图片时，边长为 1 001 像素或以上。

（2）图片格式的要求。

可以使用 JPEG、TIFF、GIF 格式。这几种格式适用于在亚马逊上上传。建议使用 JPEG 格式。这种格式的图片在上传时的速度比较快。

（3）背景色的要求。

亚马逊图片的背景必须是纯白的。纯白背景的定义为：RGB 三色通道，R：255，G：255，B：255。即使产品是在白色的背景纸或其他材质下拍摄的，也仍然需要通过图片处理把背景变为纯白的。小部分家居装饰用品的主图不强制一定要用纯白背景，如床上四件套、蚊帐、窗帘、沙发、墙挂画、灯。

（4）其他要求。

主图应是产品的实际图，不是插图，更不是手绘图或漫画图。

主图不能带 Logo 和水印，也最好不要有不在订单内的配件、道具等（产品本身的 Logo 是允许的）。

主图中的产品最好占据 85% 左右的图片空间。

对于有不同类型的产品，父

products must have a main image.

The product must be clearly visible in the picture, and the entire product needs to be displayed, which cannot only include a partial or multi-angle combo picture.

Some categories allow models (such as clothing, underwear and socks), and only real models can be used except humanoid models in clothing shops. The model must be standing on the front, not on the side, back, multi-angle combination drawing, sitting posture, etc. There can be no non-sale items on the model of the main picture. Models are not allowed in the main pictures of some categories (such as bag, jewelry and shoes).

No any nudity information could be presented in the main image.

2．Requirement of auxiliary image

The size of the auxiliary image is recommended to be consistent with the main image. Auxiliary pictures can show details, other sides or matching pictures, etc. The auxiliary image should show a different side of the product, the display of the product use, or supplement the product features that are not highlighted in the main image, and the seller can add up to 8 auxiliary images in the Amazon product listing.

It is best for the auxiliary image to have a pure white background like the main image, but this is not mandatory.

Logo and watermark cannot appear on the auxiliary image (the Logo of the product itself is allowed).

The product must be clearly visible in the picture. If there is a model, the model cannot be in a sitting position, preferably standing. Same as the main image, a real person model must be used.

No nude information could be presented in the auxiliary images as well.

3.2.3　Punishment for Shop Violations on Amazon Platform

The main reasons for shop violations on Amazon platform are as follows.

(1) Fake orders and evaluations. Amazon does not

产品和子产品都要有主图。

产品必须在图片中清晰可见，需要显示整个产品，不能只有部分或多角度组合图。

有些类目允许有模特（如服装、内衣、袜子），而且只能使用真人模特，不能使用服装店里的那种模型模特。模特必须是正面站立，不能是侧面、背面、多角度组合图、坐姿等。主图模特身上不能有非售物品。某些类目的主图则不允许使用模特（如包、珠宝、鞋）。

主图中不能显示任何裸体信息。

2．辅图要求

建议辅图的尺寸与主图一致，这样会比较美观。辅图可以展示细节、其他面或搭配图等。辅图应该对产品做一个不同侧面的展示、产品使用的展示，或对在主图中没凸显的产品特性做补充，在亚马逊产品目录中，卖家可以最多添加 8 张辅图。

辅图最好也和主图一样具有纯白背景，但不做强制要求。

辅图不能带 Logo 和水印（产品本身的 Logo 是允许的）。

产品必须在图片中清晰可见。如果有模特，那么模特不能采用坐姿，最好站立。与主图一样，也必须使用真人模特。

辅图中也不能显示任何裸体信息。

3.2.3　亚马逊平台店铺违规处罚

亚马逊平台店铺违规主要有以下原因。

（1）刷单、刷测评。亚马逊

allow sellers to make fake orders and evaluations. If they are found by the platform, sellers will be punished for violations.

(2) Shop association. Amazon stipulates that a business license can only have one shop on the platform. It is not recommended to log in two shops with the same IP.

(3) The product is complained by customers. If the seller's product is not relevant to the filled listing, making the buyer complain after the purchase, the platform will causing give the corresponding violation penalties.

(4) Shop infringement. Amazon has a very strict control over product infringement which may bring the closure of the shop, so that the money in the seller's account may not be withdrawn.

(5) Malicious competition. There are many competitors on the Amazon platform that maliciously place orders in your shop due to the competition, and then cancel a large number of orders, so that the platform will punish the shops for holding that they violate rules by abusing sales rankings.

The sellers' code of conduct on Amazon platform is as follows.

The policy requires sellers to act fairly and honestly on Amazon in order to ensure a safe buying and selling experience. All sellers must follow the principles below:

(1) Provide accurate information to Amazon and its customers at all time.

(2) Act fairly and not misuse Amazon's features or services.

(3) Do not attempt to damage or abuse other sellers, their items or ratings.

(4) Do not attempt to influence customers' ratings, feedback, and reviews.

(5) Do not send unsolicited or inappropriate communications.

(6) Contact buyers only by Buyer-Seller Messaging.

(7) Do not attempt to circumvent the process of Amazon

不允许卖家出现刷单、刷测评等情形。如果被平台发现，则会进行违规处罚。

（2）店铺关联。亚马逊规定一个企业营业执照只能在平台上开一个店铺。建议不在同一 IP 上登录两个店铺。

（3）产品被投诉。如果卖家的产品和填写的产品目录没有关联，导致在买家购买之后发生投诉，平台就会给予相应的违规处罚。

（4）店铺侵权。亚马逊对于产品侵权这一环节的管控非常严格，有可能做封店处理，卖家账户里的钱款也有可能无法取出。

（5）恶意竞争。亚马逊平台上不乏一些对手因竞争而在你的店铺恶意下单，然后大量取消订单，这样平台会认为店铺是滥用销售排名而违规处罚。

亚马逊平台的卖家行为准则如下。

政策要求卖家在亚马逊遵循公平、诚实的行为准则，以确保安全的购买和销售体验。所有卖家都必须遵循以下准则：

（1）始终向亚马逊和其买家提供准确的信息。

（2）公平行事，且不得滥用亚马逊的功能或服务。

（3）不得试图损害其他卖家或其商品 / 评分或者加以滥用。

（4）不得试图影响买家评分、反馈和评论。

（5）不得发送未经请求或不恰当的沟通信息。

（6）只能通过 Buyer-Seller Messaging（消息服务）联系买家。

（7）不得试图规避亚马逊销

sales.

(8) Do not operate more than one selling account on Amazon without a legitimate business need.

Violating the code of conduct or any other Amazon policies may result in actions Amazon may take corresponding actions against your account, such as cancellation of listings, suspension or forfeiture of payments, and removal of selling privileges.

3.2.4　Writing E-mail of Complaint on Amazon Platform

If an Amazon seller confirms that he has not violated the rules after reviewing his shop operations, he can appeal the violation by E-mail:

(1) Analyze the reason based on the content of the E-mail. E-mails of violation will inform Amazon sellers the reason for the violation. Sellers should check their operations, products, and listings based on the content of the E-mails to see if there is a violation of the rules and make an analysis.

(2) Measures to solve the problem. To propose solutions for this violation, that is, what actions will be taken to solve this problem?

(3) How to avoid problems in the future. In the future, what and how work will be done to avoid this problem?

Writing template for E-mail of complaint on Amazon:

(1) Explain the situation. For example, hello to Amazon team, through the notification of the platform, I know that our xx product involves brand infringement. We are very sorry for the violation of the terms of the service. In order to continue to obtain the right to sell on Amazon, we hereby assure the platform.

(2) The reason for this problem. For example, because we are not familiar with the relevant rules of the platform and not rigorous enough in operation, this violation has occurred. We are really sorry for this consequence due to our team's negligence.

售流程。

（8）在没有合法的业务需求情况下，不得在亚马逊上经营多个卖家账户。

若违反该行为准则或任何其他亚马逊政策，亚马逊可能会对你的账户采取相应措施，例如取消商品、暂停或没收付款以及撤销销售权限。

3.2.4　亚马逊平台申诉邮件的撰写

如果亚马逊的卖家在回顾自己的店铺操作后，确定自己没有违规，则可以通过邮件进行违规申诉：

（1）根据邮件内容分析原因。亚马逊的卖家违规邮件会告知违规的原因。卖家根据邮件内容对自己的操作、产品及产品目录进行检查，看看是否真的出现违规情况并进行分析。

（2）解决问题的措施。针对这次违规问题提出哪些解决措施，即通过哪些行动解决该问题。

（3）日后如何避免出现问题。日后，会从哪些方面、进行怎样的工作去避免日后再次出现该问题？

亚马逊申诉邮件的撰写模板为：

（1）说明情况。例如，尊敬的亚马逊团队，您好，通过平台的告知，知道自己的××产品涉及品牌侵权。我们很抱歉违反了平台服务条款。为了能够继续在亚马逊获得销售权，我们在此向平台做出保证。

（2）出现这一问题的原因。例如，因为对平台的相关规则不熟悉，同时在操作上也不够严谨，所以出现了本次违规情形。由于团队的疏忽导致这一后果，在此

(3) Put forward the actions to be taken. We will check every product and listing in the shop. If there is any infringing product, it will be removed from the shelves immediately.

(4) To avoid the problem from happening again. Since then, we will arrange personnel to conduct more stringent monitoring of Amazon accounts, and check each listing to see if there is any abnormal review. At the same time, we will actively learn the new policies of the Amazon platform to prevent possible violations.

(5) Positive discourse ending. We are eager to build our own brand on the Amazon platform and provide consumers with better service. For the information we need to add to the platform and answers to related questions, please let us know and we will answer truthfully, thank you very much.

Therefore, the best way for Amazon sellers to avoid penalties for violations is to be familiar with the rules of the platform and strictly control shop operations. If the seller is punished for violations, he should send an appealing E-mail to the platform in time with a sincere attitude, and this makes it easier to succeed.

3.3　Product Release Rules of Other Platforms

3.3.1　Product Release Rules of eBay Platform

Before releasing a product, you need to confirm whether it can be released on eBay platform. For details, please refer to the list of prohibited and controlled items on eBay. If the listing of product is against regulation, the product will be removed from the eBay platform, and the account will be restricted, including restrictions on buying and selling rights and the account to be frozen.

On eBay platform, the release of a product shall include three parts: product details, selling details and shipping

---

我感到很抱歉。

（3）提出采取的行动。我们会对店铺的每个产品和产品目录进行检查。若有侵权违规的产品，将马上删除下架。

（4）避免问题再次发生。自此，我们会安排人员对亚马逊账户进行更严格的监控，并对每个产品目录进行检查，看看是否有异常审查。同时，还会积极学习亚马逊平台的新政策，以防止出现可能的违规行为。

（5）积极的结束语。我们渴望在亚马逊平台建立自己的品牌，并给予消费者更优质的服务。对于平台需要我们补充的资料及相关问题解答，请告知我们，一定如实答复，非常感谢。

因此，亚马逊卖家避免违规处罚的最好方法是悉知平台的规则，对店铺操作进行严格管控。如果被违规处罚了，则要及时向平台发邮件申诉，保持诚恳的态度，这样更易成功。

3.3　其他平台产品发布规则

3.3.1　eBay 平台产品发布规则

在发布一个产品前，需要先确认产品是否可以在 eBay 平台上发布。细节可参考 eBay 违禁品和管制物品清单。若出现不符合规定的发布，该产品会被 eBay 平台移除，并且账号会受到使用限制，包括买卖权限的限制及账号被冻结。

在 eBay 平台上，产品的发布应包含三个部分：产品细节、销

details. Product details mainly include the title, attributes, pictures and detailed description of the product. Selling details include product selling format, the duration of the online selling, selling price, the quantity available and the payment method. Shipping details include the freight details of products sold to target market.

A good title not only provides information about the item, but also contains several highly relevant search keywords item. On eBay platform, there are some points we need to pay attention when writing product titles.

- Make full use of the 80 characters allowed by the system to describe your items and improve the keyword search rate.
- Don't add irrelevant label symbols, website address, E-mail and telephone number in the title.

- No profane or obscene language.
- When releasing products with brands, it must be regular and legal ones produced by brand manufacturers.
- The keywords involving infringement are not allowed to use.
- Make sure the title words are spelled correctly.

High quality images can provide a better shopping experience for buyers, making it easier for buyers to find your item, and making the seller's items easier to sell. When uploading pictures on the eBay platform, you need to pay attention to relevant policies, otherwise it may lead to the failure of product releasing or be punished by eBay.

- The image pixel is between 500-1600, and the image size cannot exceed 7 MB.
- Second hand/renovated/damaged products shall not use new product drawings.
- No shop Logo/publicity/promotion and other words in the pictures.
- No borders, shading, illustrations or icons in the pictures.
- Take pictures by yourself, do not steal images.

售细节和运输细节。产品细节主要包括产品的标题、属性、图片，以及产品详情描述。销售细节包括产品销售方式、在线销售的持续时间、销售价格、可售数量和付款方式。运输细节包括产品销往目标市场的货运细节。

好的标题不仅能提供物品信息，还包含多个高相关性的物品搜索关键词。在 eBay 平台中，产品标题的撰写需要注意。

- 尽可能充分利用系统允许的 80 个字符描述你的物品，提升关键词搜索率。
- 不要在标题中添加无关的标注符号，不得含有网站地址、电子邮件或电话号码。
- 不得含有亵渎或猥亵的语言。
- 在发布有品牌的物品时，物品必须是由品牌厂商生产的正规和合法的物品。
- 不得使用涉及侵权的关键词。
- 确保标题单词拼写正确。

高品质的图片能给买家提供更好的购物体验，更容易让买家找到你的物品，使物品更容易售出。在 eBay 平台上传图片时，需要注意相关政策，否则有可能导致产品发表失败，或受到 eBay 的惩罚。

- 图片像素为 500～1600，图片大小不能超过 7MB。
- 二手/翻新/损坏的产品不得使用新品图。
- 不能出现店铺 Logo/宣传/促销等文字。
- 不能有边框、底纹及插图或图标。
- 自行拍摄图片，请勿盗图。

3.3.2 Product Release Rules of Shopee Platform

(1) Log in to the seller's backstage, and click "New Product" in the task bar on the left side of the screen (Figure 3-5).

(2) Click "New Product" to enter the "Product Category Selection" interface (Figure 3-6).

(3) Search for the category or select the detailed category in the list, click "Next", and then the editing page of the product information appears.

(4) Fill in the product-related information. The information marked in the red box must be required.

3.3.2 Shopee 平台产品发布规则

（1）登录卖家后台，单击屏幕左侧任务栏的"新增产品"（图3-5）。

（2）单击"新增产品"进入"产品类目选择"界面（图3-6）。

（3）搜索品类或在列表中选择详细品类，单击"下一步"按钮，出现产品信息编辑页面。

（4）填写产品相关信息。红色框标注的是必填信息。

Figure 3-5　"New Product" Interface

图 3-5　"新增产品"界面

Figure 3-6　"Product Category Selection" Interface

图 3-6　"产品类目选择"界面

Fill in all the product information completely. The "sales information" includes product specification, product price, product quantity, product option, product number, etc., which should be filled in carefully. "Media management" includes product pictures, product movies and product size table, etc. Please note ① Size: the maximum is 30MB; ② Video length: 10-60 seconds; ③ Format: MP4 (VP9 video encoding format is not supported); ④ When the product video status is in processing, it can still be put on the shelves, and the product movie will be displayed on the product page after successful processing. The "freight" includes the weight of the product, the size of the package and so on. As for the size, the seller should carefully consider the size of the package, and the system will verify it. The wrong format or too large size may fail to check out for consumers.

(5) After all product information has been filled in completely, and no problem has been found out in your check, click "Save and Put on Shelf" to complete the product upload. Later, product information can also be updated according to the changes in the information and price of the product.

所有的产品信息都填写完整。其中,"销售信息"包含产品规格、产品价格、产品数量、产品选项、货号等,要仔细填写。"媒体管理"包含产品图片、产品视频和产品尺寸表等。请注意① 大小:最大 30MB;② 视频长度:10 ～ 60s;③ 格式:MP4(不支持 VP9 视频编码格式);④ 当产品视频处于处理状态时仍可上架产品,产品视频将在成功处理后显示于产品页。"运费"包含产品重量、包裹尺寸等。关于尺寸,卖家要仔细考量产品包装尺寸,系统会对其进行验证。错误或过大的尺寸可能造成消费者无法结账。

(5) 所有产品信息都填写完整且检查无误后,单击"存储并上架"就完成了产品上传。后期也可以根据产品信息、产品价格等变化进行产品信息的更新。

New words

1. listing 产品条目
2. five bullet points 五点描述
3. keyword 关键词
4. main image 主图
5. auxiliary image 辅图
6. pixel 像素
7. watermark 水印
8. zoom 缩放
9. infringement 侵权
10. shop association 店铺关联
11. brand authorized 品牌授权
12. penalty 处罚
13. violation 违反,妨碍
14. category 类目
15. detail page 详情页

Chapter 4 Online Marketing and Planning of Cross-Border E-Commerce

第4章 跨境电商网络营销与策划

Lead-in case

In early 2022, Xiaowei and her friend set up a shop on AliExpress platform. Xiaowei was responsible for the shop operation, and her friend took charge of the goods supply and delivery. After product release and shop decoration, Xiaowei found that there were few orders, and the exposure and browsing rate were also mediocre. Xiaowei was thinking, "What can I do to increase the shop impressions?" Therefore, Xiaowei looked for ways to increase shop traffic on the Internet, and the words "cross-border E-commerce marketing" deeply impressed Xiaowei. However, she knew nothing about cross-border marketing. Through the study of this chapter, you will have a better understanding of marketing and planning of cross-border E-commerce with Xiaowei.

Learning objectives

1. Objectives of knowledge

(1) To master macro and micro environment analysis methods, members and their characteristics.

(2) To master the pricing strategy of cross-border E-commerce products.

(3) To master the concept, characteristics and skills of search engine marketing, social media marketing, short video marketing and live broadcast marketing.

(4) To master promotion tools of shops and activities of AliExpress platform.

(5) To understand the concept and strategy of selection and positioning in international target market.

(6) To understand the four steps of international marketing strategy.

2. Objectives of skills

(1) To be able to use PEST method to analyze macro

案例导入

2022 年年初,小薇和她的朋友合伙在速卖通平台上开了一家店。小薇负责店铺运营,她的朋友负责供货和发货。在经历产品发布、店铺装修后,小微发现订单很少,曝光量和浏览量也是平平。小薇想:"有什么办法可以增加店铺曝光量呢?"于是,小薇就在网上查找增加店铺流量的办法,"跨境电商营销"几个字深深地映入了小薇的眼中。然而,她对跨境电商营销一无所知。通过本章学习,你将与小薇一起学习跨境电商营销与策划。

学习目标

1. 知识目标

(1) 掌握宏观、微观环境分析方法、成员及其特点。

(2) 掌握跨境电商产品的定价策略。

(3) 掌握搜索引擎营销、社交媒体营销、短视频营销、网络直播营销的概念、特点及技巧。

(4) 掌握速卖通平台店铺推广工具及平台活动。

(5) 理解国际目标市场选择与定位的概念和策略。

(6) 理解制定国际营销战略的四个步骤。

2. 技能目标

(1) 能用 PEST 分析方法对宏

environment and industry development.

(2) To be able to analyze the members in the micro environment.

(3) To be able to set the price according to the pricing strategy of cross-border E-commerce products.

(4) To be able to carry out on-site promotion of AliExpress platform shops and products.

(5) To be able to initially use social media, search engine, short video and live broadcast to attract off-site traffic.

3．Objectives of qualities

(1) To be able to use computer and other tools for daily office work and information collection and processing.

(2) To be able to reasonably use translation, video editing and other tools to assist the work.

(3) To have certain ability of innovation and learning, and to be good at finding and solving problems.

(4) To have good leadership in communication, coordination, decision-making, analysis, judgment and motivation.

(5) To obey laws and regulations of foreign trade, and to have the spirit of self-discipline.

(6) To bear hardships and pressure.

4.1   Overview of Cross-Border E-Commerce Online Marketing

Cross-border E-commerce online marketing is a new marketing method based on the Internet, which uses the interaction of digital information and online media to assist the realization of marketing objectives. In other words, cross-border E-commerce online marketing is a marketing activity that takes the Internet as the main method to achieve purposes of cross-border E-commerce marketing. This section will elaborate from four parts: international market development, selection and positioning in international target market, the steps of making international marketing strategies and pricing strategies of cross-border E-commerce products.

观环境及行业发展进行分析。

（2）能对微观环境中的各成员进行分析。

（3）能结合跨境电商产品定价策略制定价格。

（4）能开展速卖通平台店铺及产品的站内推广。

（5）能初步运用社交媒体、搜索引擎、短视频、网络直播实现站外引流。

3．素质目标

（1）能够利用计算机和其他工具进行日常办公和信息收集处理。

（2）能合理运用翻译、视频编辑等工具辅助工作。

（3）具备一定的创新能力和学习能力，善于发现和解决问题。

（4）具有良好的沟通、协调、决策、分析判断、激励等领导力。

（5）遵守外贸相关法律法规，具有自律精神。

（6）能吃苦耐劳和承受压力。

4.1   跨境电商网络营销概述

跨境电商网络营销是以国际互联网为基础，利用数字化信息和网络媒体的交互性来辅助跨境电商营销目标实现的一种新型市场营销方式。换言之，跨境电商网络营销就是以互联网为主要手段达到跨境电商营销目的的营销活动。本节将从四个部分进行阐述：国际市场开拓、国际目标市场选择与定位、制定国际市场营销战略的步骤、跨境电商产品定价策略。

4.1.1 International Market Development

Compared with domestic marketing, international marketing will face different external environments, including cultural differences, political and economic environment differences, laws and regulations differences and consumer behavior differences. Therefore, for enterprises, if they want to develop the international market, the first thing to do is to analyze the external marketing environment.

External environment includes macro environment and micro environment. The former needs to analyze four factors: politics, economy, social culture and technology; the latter refers to various factors closely related to marketing environment and those influencing marketing activities, such as, stable supply chain, competitors, partners, customers, the public, etc. Cross-border E-commerce companies need to understand their own environment and trends in order to avoid and eliminate environmental threats, seize and use environmental opportunities. Here we will focus on PEST analysis in macro environment and member analysis in micro environment.

1. PEST analysis

PEST analysis is a basic tool for analyzing the external macro environment of an enterprise. When the marketing personnel start a new project or launch products and services, they use this tool to understand the opportunities and threats in the environment. In PEST analysis, P stands for Politics, E stands for Economy, S stands for Social-culture, and T stands for Technology. Once these factors are analyzed, marketers can make better business decisions.

(1) Political factors: the political situation of the target market country, major or unexpected political events, political stability, relevant government trade policies, relevant laws and regulations, treaties, business practices, etc. All of those will have a significant impact on cross-border E-commerce companies to explore the international market.

(2) Economic factors: cross-border E-commerce

4.1.1 国际市场开拓

与国内营销相比，国际营销会面临不同的外部环境，包括文化差异、政治和经济环境差异、法律法规差异，以及消费者行为差异。因此，对于企业来说，若要开拓国际市场，首先要做的是分析外部营销环境。

外部环境包括宏观环境和微观环境。前者需具体分析政治、经济、社会文化、技术四个因素；后者是指与市场营销环境密切相关、影响市场营销活动的各种因素。例如，稳定的供应链、竞争对手、合作伙伴、客户、公众等。跨境电商企业需要了解自身所处环境及趋势，以避开和消除环境威胁，抓住和利用环境机会。这里，我们着重介绍宏观环境的PEST分析法，以及微观环境的成员分析。

1. PEST 分析法

PEST 分析法是企业外部宏观环境分析的基本工具。营销人员在开始一个新项目或推出产品和服务时，使用这个工具来了解环境中的机会和威胁。在 PEST 分析法中，P 代表政治，E 代表经济环境，S 代表社会文化，T 代表技术。一旦分析了这些因素，营销人员就可以做出更好的商业决策。

（1）政治因素：目标市场国的政治形势、重大或突发政治事件、政治稳定性、政府相关贸易政策、相关法律法规、条约、商业惯例等，这些都会对跨境电商企业开拓国际市场产生重大影响。

（2）经济因素：跨境电商企业

companies need to pay attention to the impact of home country, target market countries and international economic environment on the operation and development of enterprises, such as fluctuations of exchange rate, purchasing power of target market countries, etc.

(3) Social-cultural factors: cross-border E-commerce enterprises need to pay attention to the influence of language, social structure, religious belief, values, customs on product marketing promotion in the target market country.

(4) Technical factors: influence on enterprises brought by the overall level and changing trend of social technology, technological change and breakthrough can not only bring new products and services to cross-border E-commerce enterprises, but also develop new sales channels, such as cross-border bank payment, online bookstore, auction, etc. Technological progress can create competitive advantages, leading to the elimination of existing products, or greatly shortening the life cycle of products.

2. Member analysis of micro environment

The external micro environment members mainly include suppliers, competitors, marketing agents, customers and the public.

(1) Suppliers: suppliers are enterprises and individuals that provide resources to cross-border E-commerce enterprises. The impact of suppliers on enterprises is embodied in two aspects: one is the impact of price fluctuations; the other is the adequacy and quality of supply. Therefore, on the one hand, enterprises should maintain a long-term stable relationship with major suppliers; on the other hand, they should establish a wide range of purchasing channels to avoid the passive situation caused by over reliance on suppliers.

(2) Competitors: in terms of the close relationship with cross-border enterprises, there are four levels of competitors, that is, brand competitors, form competitors, peer competitors and desired competitors.

(3) Marketing agents: marketing agents refer to the organizations that assist the enterprise in promotion, selling and delivering products to the seller enterprise, which includes intermediaries, cross-border logistics institutions,

需要关注本国、目标市场国及国际经济环境对企业经营发展的影响，比如汇率波动、目标市场国的购买力等。

（3）社会文化因素：跨境电商企业需要关注目标市场国的语言、社会结构、宗教信仰、价值观念、风俗习惯等对产品营销推广的影响。

（4）技术因素：社会技术总水平及变化趋势、技术变迁、技术突破对企业的影响，不仅能为跨境电商企业带来新的产品与服务，也能开拓新的销售渠道，比如跨境银行支付、网上书店、拍卖等。技术进步可创造竞争优势，可导致现有产品被淘汰，或大大缩短产品的生命周期。

2. 微观环境的成员分析

外部微观环境成员主要包括供应商、竞争者、营销中介、顾客及公众。

（1）供应商：供应商是向跨境电商企业提供资源的企业和个人。供应商对企业的影响具体表现在两个方面：一是价格变动的影响；二是货源的充足性与质量。因此，企业一方面应与主要供应商保持长期稳定的关系；另一方面，应建立广泛的购货渠道，以免因过分依赖供应商造成被动局面。

（2）竞争者：从与跨境企业销售关系的密切程度看，有四个层次的竞争者，即品牌竞争者、形式竞争者、同类竞争者和愿望竞争者。

（3）营销中介：营销中介是指协助企业促销、销售，以及把产品送到企业卖方的机构。它们包括中间商、跨境物流机构、营

marketing services and financial intermediaries.

(4) Customers: customers refer to consumers and producers who use the final products or services in the field of consumption, and are also the ultimate target market of enterprise marketing activities. Customers are the main body of the market. Only when the products and services of any enterprise are recognized by customers, can they win the market. According to customers' purchase motivation, customer market can be divided into consumer market, producer market, middleman market, government market and international market.

(5) The public: the public is a group which has a real or potential impact on an organization's ability to achieve its goals. The public may help to enhance or hinder an enterprise's ability to achieve its own goals, so the enterprise should handle the relationship with the public. There are seven types of the public around enterprises: financial sector, media, government agencies, social organizations, local public, general public and internal public.

4.1.2 Selection and Positioning of International Target Market

Marketing strategies of international target market refer to three steps of implementing international marketing effectively, which are international market segmentation, selection of international market and positioning of international target market.

1. International market segmentation

International market segmentation refers to that the enterprise subdivides them into different subsidiary markets according to the obvious demand characteristics, purchase behaviors and purchase habits of different consumers in the overall market. Each subsidiary market is composed of consumers with the same needs and desires, and its internal demand characteristics are similar. Market segmentation is based on the distinct characteristics of consumers. The purpose of segmentation is to understand the heterogeneous needs of consumers, develop a matching marketing plan, and

销服务及金融中间机构。

（4）顾客：顾客是指使用进入消费领域的最终产品或劳务的消费者和生产者，也是企业营销活动的最终目标市场。顾客是市场的主体，任何企业的产品和服务，只有得到了顾客的认可，才能赢得这个市场。按照顾客的购买动机，可将顾客市场分为消费者市场、生产者市场、中间商市场、政府市场、国际市场。

（5）公众：公众是这样的一种群体，即它对一个组织完成其目标的能力有着实际或潜在的影响。公众既可能有助于增强也可能阻碍一个企业实现自己目标的能力，企业应处理好与公众的关系。围绕企业的公众有七类：金融界、媒介、政府机构、社会团体、地方公众、普通公众和内部公众。

4.1.2 国际目标市场选择与定位

国际目标市场营销战略指有效实行国际市场营销的三个步骤，依次为国际市场细分、国际目标市场选择和国际目标市场定位。

1. 国际市场细分

国际市场细分指企业根据总体市场的不同消费者的明显需求特征、购买行为和购买习惯，把它们细分为彼此有区别的不同的子市场。每个子市场由需求与欲望相同的消费者组成，其内部需求特征相似。市场细分的依据是消费者明显不同的特性。细分的目的是了解消费者的异质需求，制订匹配的营销计划，有针对性

provide targeted service to their own objects, so as to improve competitiveness, increase sales and improve market share in the segmentation market.

As its name implies, international market segmentation is the application of the concept of market segmentation in international marketing. However, due to the particularity and complexity of international marketing, international market segmentation must be divided into two steps.

The first step is macro segmentation. According to certain standards, the international market is subdivided into several subsidiary markets. Each subsidiary market is in the same marketing environment. Enterprises can choose one or several countries as their macro target markets.

The second step is micro segmentation. After entering the market of a certain country or region, according to different needs of customers in that country, enterprises further subdivide the market of that country conforming to certain standards, and then meet the needs of one or several markets according to their own conditions.

2．Selection of international target market

The selection of international target market refers to the selection of one or more segments as service objects based on market segmentation and according to their own tasks, objectives and resource conditions. International target market selection strategies include the following three types:

(1) Undifferentiated strategy of target market selection.

Undifferentiated strategy of target market selection means that enterprises regard the whole market as a big target market, and hold that there is no difference in demands of all consumers for their products in the market. Or even if there is a difference, it is so small that it can be ignored. Therefore, enterprises only launch a single standardized product to the market and sell it in a unified marketing way. With this marketing strategy, the product should not only meet the needs of different buyers in different markets, but also be easy to sell, store and transport, like towel.

地服务自己的对象，从而在细分市场中提高竞争力、增加销售量、提高市场占有率。

顾名思义，国际市场细分指市场细分概念在国际营销中的运用。但是，由于国际市场营销的特殊性和复杂性，国际市场细分必须分成两步进行。

第一步是宏观细分。根据一定的标准将国际市场细分为若干个子市场。每个子市场均在基本相同的市场营销环境中。企业可以选择一个或几个国家作为自己的宏观目标市场。

第二步是微观细分。企业进入某个国家或地区的市场以后，针对该国顾客的千差万别需求，按一定的标准对该国的市场进行细分，然后根据自己的条件满足一个或几个市场的需求。

2．国际目标市场选择

国际目标市场选择指企业在细分市场的基础上，根据自己的任务、目标和资源条件，选择一个或几个细分部分作为服务对象。国际目标市场选择策略包括以下三种：

（1）无差异性目标市场选择策略

无差异性目标市场选择策略是指企业把整体市场看作一个大的目标市场，认为市场上所有消费者对于本企业产品的需求不存在差别，或即使有差别但差别较小也可以忽略不计。因此，企业只向市场推出单一的标准化产品，并以统一的营销方式销售。采用这种市场营销策略，产品既要适应各个市场上不同购买者的需要，又要便于销售、储存和运输，比如毛巾。

(2) Differentiated strategy of target market selection.

Differentiated strategy of target market selection is to divide the whole market into several segments, and make a set of independent marketing strategies for each segment to meet the needs of different consumers and expand sales results, such as P & G's shampoo brands: Head and Shoulders, Sasson, Pantine and Rejoice.

(3) Centralized strategy of target market selection.

Centralized strategy of target market selection is not to take the overall market as the marketing goal, but to choose one or several specialized markets as the marketing goal, concentrate the overall marketing advantages of enterprises, implement specialized production and sales, and fully meet the needs of consumers to develop the market. Enterprises adopting this strategy do not seek to occupy a small share in the overall market, but to obtain a larger market share or even dominate in one or several smaller market segments. This strategy is more suitable for small and medium-sized pharmaceutical enterprises with limited resources. For example, Dong'e Ejiao focuses on the blood replenishment market, Zhengda Tianqing Pharmaceutical focuses on the liver drug market, Guizhou Yibai focuses on the cough drug market, and Modified Pharmaceutical focuses on the stomach drug market.

3. Positioning of international target market

Positioning of international target market, or product positioning, is to determine the favorable competitive position of the enterprise's products in the target market according to the market competition and the conditions of the enterprise. The core of market positioning is to seek differences between different brands. There are four kinds of positioning strategies of international target market:

(1) Counter positioning strategy: it is suitable for competing with existing competitors for the same target market when the product is sufficiently strong or equal to that of the competitors.

(2) Avoid strong positioning strategy: it avoids confrontation with competitors, positioning in the market

（2）差异性目标市场选择策略

差异性目标市场选择策略是将整体市场划分为若干个细分市场，针对每个细分市场制订一套独立的营销方案，以满足不同消费者的需求，扩大销售成果，比如宝洁的洗发水品牌：海飞丝、沙宣、潘婷和飘柔。

（3）集中性目标市场选择策略

集中性目标市场选择策略不是以整体市场作为营销目标的，而是选择一个或几个细分化的专门市场作为营销目标，集中企业的总体营销优势，实行专业化生产和销售，充分满足消费者的需要，以开拓市场。采用这种策略的企业，不是追求在整体市场上占有较小的份额，而是为了在一个或几个较小的细分市场上取得较大的市场占有率，甚至居于支配地位。这种策略比较适合资源能力有限的中小型医药企业。比如，东阿阿胶专注于补血药市场，正大天晴药业专注于肝药市场，贵州益佰专注于止咳药市场，修正药业专注于胃药市场。

3. 国际目标市场定位

国际目标市场定位也称产品定位，是指根据市场的竞争情况和本企业的条件，确定本企业产品在目标市场上的有利的竞争地位。市场定位的核心就是寻求不同品牌之间的差异。国际目标市场定位策略包括以下四种：

（1）对抗定位策略：与现有竞争者争夺同样的目标市场，适合在产品与竞争对手相比足够强劲或势均力敌的情况下采用。

（2）避强定位策略：避免与竞争对手的正面交锋，定位于市场

"blank spot".

(3) Senior club positioning strategy: it will put itself in the same league as some of the best players in the industry, in order to improve their position, applicable to the enterprise which cannot get the first position in the industry.

(4) Repositioning strategy: enterprises change the original impression of the market and adjust the strategy of the target market.

4.1.3　Steps of Making International Marketing Strategy

International marketing strategy is the way enterprises make the overall and long-term marketing goal and achieve the marketing goal based on the domestic and foreign market environment and their internal conditions. The development of international marketing strategy includes the following four steps: analyze the market environment, determine marketing objectives, develop marketing strategy and make marketing plan. (Figure 4-1).

1.　Analyze the market environment

The analysis of market environment, namely SWOT (strengths, weaknesses, opportunities, threats) analysis, is the first step of international marketing strategy. Market environment analysis includes two aspects: external environment analysis and internal environment analysis. The main purpose of external environment analysis is to find out the opportunities and threats in the external environment, which can be divided

"空白点"。

（3）高级俱乐部定位策略：将自己与行业中公认的最强的几家企业划为一个档次，借此提高自己的地位，适用于无法取得行业第一位置的企业。

（4）重新定位策略：企业改变市场对其原有印象，调整目标市场的策略。

4.1.3　制定国际市场营销战略的步骤

国际市场营销战略是指企业根据国内外市场环境及其内部条件所制定的具有全局性、长远性的营销目标和实现营销目标的途径。国际市场营销战略制定包括以下四个步骤：分析市场环境、确定市场营销目标、制定市场营销战略、编制市场营销计划（图4-1）。

1.　分析市场环境

市场环境分析，即 SWOT 分析，是国际市场营销战略制定的首要步骤。市场环境分析包括两个方面：外部环境分析和内部环境分析。外部环境分析的主要目的是找出外部环境中存在的机会与威胁，外部环境可以分为宏观和

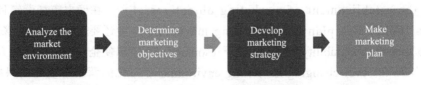

Figure 4-1　Steps of Making International Marketing Strategy

图 4-1　国际市场营销战略制定步骤

into macro and micro aspects. Among them, the macro environment analysis mainly involves the relevant national economic and industrial policies, and the micro environment analysis mainly involves the basic environment of the industry and the specific industry competitors. The main purpose of the internal environment analysis is to find out the advantages and disadvantages of the enterprise itself. The main contents include: the analysis of the basic operating conditions of the enterprise, the competitive advantages of the enterprise, the operating disadvantages of the enterprise, etc. Through SWOT analysis, we can identify the strengths and weaknesses of the enterprise, and find out factors of opportunity and threat of the international marketing environment that play a major role in the enterprise's international marketing activities.

2. Determine marketing objectives

After completing the environmental analysis of each subsidiary market, the enterprise should formulate a set of specific goals to be completed in the planning period according to different markets. Marketing objectives should be in line with the early market environment analysis and the subsidiary's own ability, while challenging and feasible. The complete marketing goals of enterprises include three parts:

(1) The product type that the enterprise should manage and the choice of the target market.

(2) Enterprises should set up challenging and feasible financial objectives.

(3) Enterprises should set the sales targets.

3. Develop marketing strategy

After the establishment of marketing objectives, enterprises should also plan corresponding marketing strategies to keep the adaptability between their resources and capabilities and the ever-changing marketing environment. Generally speaking, there are four kinds of marketing strategies that enterprises can choose: market penetration strategy, market development strategy, product development strategy and diversification strategy. Market penetration strategy refers to increasing the market share of existing products in the existing market; market development strategy

微观两个方面。其中，宏观环境分析主要涉及国家有关经济产业政策，微观环境分析主要涉及行业基本环境和具体的行业竞争对手。内部环境分析的主要目的是找出企业自身的优势与劣势。主要内容包括：企业基本经营状况分析、企业具备的竞争优势、企业存在的经营劣势等。通过 SWOT 分析，可确认企业的强项与弱项，同时找出对企业国际市场营销活动起主要影响作用的国际市场营销环境的机会因素与威胁因素。

2. 确定市场营销目标

企业在完成对各分市场的环境分析后，还要针对不同市场制定一整套在计划期内需要完成的具体目标。市场营销目标要切合前期的市场环境分析和子公司的自身能力，同时具有挑战性和可行性。完整的企业市场营销目标包括三项内容：

（1）企业应该经营的产品种类及目标市场的选择。

（2）企业应制定富有挑战性和可行性的财务目标。

（3）企业应制定销售目标。

3. 制定市场营销战略

在确立市场营销目标后，企业还要规划相应的市场营销战略，以使企业的资源和能力与不断变化的营销环境之间保持适应性。一般而言，企业有四种可选择的市场营销战略：市场渗透战略、市场开发战略、产品开发战略、多样化战略。市场渗透战略是指在现有市场上增加现有产品的市场份额；市场开发战略是指为现

refers to finding new markets for existing products; product development strategy refers to developing new products for existing markets; diversification strategy refers to developing new products for new markets.

4.　Make marketing plan

Making marketing plan is an action plan for the realization of enterprise marketing strategies. It is complex and comprehensive, involving four important factors: product, distribution, promotion and price. These four factors are called marketing combination factors. Specific contents are as follows: product factor includes product development, quality and performance indicators, varieties of designs, brands and packaging, after-sales services; price factor includes the determination of various basic prices, pricing methods, price adjustment methods; promotion factor includes the determination of promotion methods, the selection of advertising media, source sellers, and the determination of promotion costs; channel factor includes the determination of the type of sales channels, the selection of intermediaries, distribution of sales outlets, and the control and coordination of sales channels. Marketing strategies of enterprises are reflected and implemented through these combinations.

4.1.4　Pricing Strategy of Cross-Border E-Commerce Product

Product pricing is a very important link in the whole commodity sales chain. On the one hand, pricing directly affects sales and profit; on the other hand, pricing directly affects the positioning, image and competitiveness of commodities. Pricing strategies for cross-border E-commerce products mainly include: new product pricing strategy, psychological pricing strategy, discount pricing strategy, product portfolio pricing strategy, geographic pricing strategy.

(1) New product pricing strategy is a key link in the pricing strategy of an enterprise. It is of great importance to whether the products can open the market in time and occupy the market. In general, there are three strategies to be chosen.

有产品寻找新市场；产品开发战略是指为现有市场开发新产品；多样化战略是指为新市场开发新产品。

4.　编制市场营销计划

编制市场营销计划是为实现企业市场营销战略而制订的行动方案。它比较复杂又具有综合性，涉及产品、分销、促销、价格四个重要因素。这四个因素称为市场营销组合因素。具体内容为：在产品方面，包括产品研发、品质与性能指标、花色品种、品牌与包装潢、售后服务等；在价格方面，包括各种基础价格的确定、定价方法、价格调整方式等；在促销方面，包括决定促销方式、选择广告媒介、选源推销人员、确定促销费用等；在渠道方面，包括决定销售渠道的类型、选用中间商、销售网点分布、对销售渠道的控制和协调等。企业的市场营销战略正是通过这些组合来体现和实施的。

4.1.4　跨境电商产品定价策略

产品定价是整个商品销售链中非常重要的一环。一方面，定价直接关系到商品的销量和利润；另一方面，定价直接影响商品的定位、形象和竞争力。跨境电商产品的定价策略主要包括：新产品定价策略、心理定价策略、折扣定价策略、产品组合定价策略、地理定价策略。

（1）新产品定价策略是企业定价策略的关键环节。它对产品能否及时打开销路、占领市场至关重要。一般可以选择以下三种策略。

① Skimming pricing strategy, also known as high price method or liposuction prices, refers to setting the product price at a higher level at the initial stage of the product life cycle, so as to recover the investment as soon as possible and obtain considerable profits before competitors develop similar products.

② Penetration pricing strategy refers to the relatively low price of new products when they are put into the market, so as to attract a large number of customers and quickly open the market, so as to obtain a relatively high market share in the short term.

③ Satisfaction pricing strategy is a pricing strategy between skimming pricing strategy and penetration pricing strategy. Its price is lower than skimming price, but higher than penetration price. It is a middle price.

(2) Psychological pricing strategy mainly includes mantissa pricing strategy and reputation pricing strategy. The former refers to setting the mantissa of product price as 8.9, which is suitable for daily necessities or low-end products, so that consumers feel cheap psychologically and the price is calculated accurately. The latter refers to the use of consumers' admiration for famous brands and the "high price and high quality" mentality, and to set a higher price for products that enjoy prestige in consumers' minds, such as famous liquor and cigarette, perfume, jewelery, antiques and so on. When consumers buy such products, they pay special attention to the conspicuous value brought by their brands and price.

(3) Discount pricing strategy means that in order to encourage customers to pay for goods as soon as possible, to buy in large quantities, to buy in off-season and so on, enterprises can reduce the price of goods at their discretion. The main types of discount price include: cash discount, quantity discount, function discount, season discount, etc.

(4) Product portfolio pricing strategy is an economic strategy to deal with the price relationship between various products of the enterprise. The core idea of the strategy is to seek the maximum profit of the whole product portfolio.

① 撇脂定价策略又称高价法或吸脂定价，是指在产品生命周期的最初阶段，把产品价格定在较高水平，争取在竞争者研制出相似的产品之前尽快地收回投资，并且取得相当的利润。

② 渗透定价策略是指企业把新产品投入市场时的价格定得相对较低，以吸引大量顾客及迅速打开市场，在短期内获得比较高的市场占有率。

③ 满意定价策略是一种介于撇脂定价策略和渗透定价策略之间的价格策略。其所定的价格比撇脂价格低，而比渗透价格高。它是一种中间价格。

（2）心理定价策略主要包括尾数定价策略和声望定价策略。前者指将产品价格尾数定为8.9等数字，适用于日用品或低档品，以使消费者在心理上感觉便宜，同时又觉得价格是精确计算得出的。后者指利用消费者仰慕名牌和"价高质必优"的心理，对在消费者心目中享有声望的产品制定较高的价格，如名烟名酒、高级品牌的香水、珠宝、古董等。当消费者购买此类产品时，特别关注其品牌、标价所带来的炫耀价值。

（3）折扣定价策略是指企业为了鼓励顾客及早付清货款、大量购买、淡季购买等，可以酌情降低商品的价格。折扣价格的主要类型包括：现金折扣、数量折扣、功能折扣、季节折扣等。

（4）产品组合定价策略是指处理本企业各种产品之间价格关系的经济策略。该策略的核心理念即为寻求整个产品组合获得最

It includes series pricing strategy, complementary product pricing strategy (contact lens and care solution) and whole set product pricing strategy (such as toolbox and cosmetic set).

(5) Geographic pricing strategy is a kind of strategy to set different prices according to the geographical location of goods, which mainly includes unified delivery pricing, partition pricing, base point pricing, allowance freight pricing and so on. In international trade, if the enterprise pays the freight, it is beneficial to the consumers to purchase, but the profit will decrease; if the consumers pay the freight, the enterprise's profit will increase, but it is not conducive to the purchase by consumers. Therefore, the responsibilities, risks and costs between buyers and sellers can be distinguished through FOB, CIF, CFR and other price terms.

4.2　Off-Site Marketing and Promotion of Cross-Border E-Commerce

For cross-border E-commerce sellers, in addition to grasping the on-site traffic, they should also take into account the off-site one. This section will introduce the ways of off-site marketing and promotion of cross-border E-commerce, including social media marketing, search engine marketing, short video marketing and live broadcasting marketing.

4.2.1　Social Media Marketing

1．Concept of social media marketing

Social media is a very broad term. It refers to interaction with others by sharing information with others and receiving information from others. Media refers to a communication tool, such as the Internet, from which we can combine the basic definitions: social media is a Web-based communication tool that enables people to communicate with each other by sharing and using information. Social media marketing refers to the marketing method to promote and enhance product sales and brand influence by the use of social media platforms such as related

大利润。它包括系列产品定价策略、互补产品定价策略（隐形眼镜与护理液）和成套产品定价策略（如工具箱和化妆品套装）。

（5）地理定价策略是一种根据商品销售地理位置不同而规定差别价格的策略，主要包括统一交货定价 、分区定价、基点定价、津贴运费定价等方式。在国际贸易中，若企业支付运费，则有利于消费者购买，但利润会有所减少；若消费者支付运费，则企业利润有所增加，但会不利于消费者购买。因此，通过 FOB、CIF、CFR 等价格术语来区别买卖双方所承担的责任、风险和费用。

4.2　跨境电商站外营销推广

对于跨境电商卖家来说，除了要抓住站内所带来的流量，也要兼顾站外流量。本节将详细介绍跨境电商站外营销推广的方式，具体包括社交媒体营销、搜索引擎营销、短视频营销和网络直播营销。

4.2.1　社交媒体营销

1．社交媒体营销的概念

社交媒体是一个非常宽泛的术语。社交指通过与他人共享信息并从他人接收信息来与他人进行交互。媒体指一种通信工具，例如互联网，从这两个单独的术语中，我们可以将基本定义结合在一起：社交媒体是基于 Web 的交流工具，使人们可以通过共享和使用信息来相互交流。社交媒体营销是指使用社交媒体平台，

social media sites, community forums and other social media.

Social media is the main resource for enterprises to promote their brands on the Internet. As a cross-border E-commerce seller, the main task is to understand the social media sites used by target consumers. Figure 4-2 shows the number of monthly active users of each social media platform in April, 2020. Combined with previous data, we can see that the pattern of social media has remained unchanged. Facebook, YouTube and WhatsApp are still elites. The number of monthly active users of Instagram has increased to 1 billion. China's TikTok (Douyin) and WeChat have also become one of the most popular social media websites in the world.

2. Characteristics of social media marketing

(1) Precise marketing for target users.

Based on the real social circle, the platform users of social media marketing have a high degree of clustering. They

即利用相关网站、社区论坛等社交媒体进行推广，提升产品销售及品牌影响力的营销方式。

社交媒体指企业在互联网上推广自己品牌的主要资源。作为跨境电商卖家，其主要任务是了解目标受众所使用的社交网站。图 4-2 显示了 2020 年 4 月份社交媒体平台月活跃用户的数量。结合之前的数据可以看出，社交媒体的格局一直保持不变，Facebook（脸书）、YouTube 和 WhatsApp 仍然是精英。Instagram 的月活跃用户的数量有所上升，达到了 10 亿人。来自中国的 TikTok（抖音）和微信（WeChat）也已迅速成为世界上最受欢迎的社交媒体网站之一。

2. 社交媒体营销的特点

（1）实现目标用户的精准营销。

社交媒体营销的平台用户基于真实社交圈，有着高度的聚类

# ◆	Network Name ◆	Number of Users (in millions) ◆	Country of Origin ▾
1	Facebook	2,498	United States
2	YouTube	2,000	United States
3	WhatsApp	2,000	United States
4	Facebook Messenger	1,300	United States
6	Instagram	1,000	United States
11	Reddit	430	United States
13	Snapchat	398	United States
14	Twitter	386	United States
15	Pinterest	366	United States
17	LinkedIn	310	United States
19	Discord	250	United States
18	Viber	260	Israel
5	WeChat	1,165	China
7	TikTok	800	China
8	QQ	731	China
9	Qzone	517	China
10	Sina Weibo	516	China
12	Kuaishou	400	China
16	Baidu Tieba	320	China

排名	社媒平台	用户数量（单位：百万）	来源国
1	脸书	2,498	美国
2	油管	2,000	美国
3	WhatsApp	2,000	美国
4	Facebook Messenger	1,300	美国
6	Instagram	1,000	美国
11	Reddit	430	美国
13	色拉布	398	美国
14	推特	386	美国
15	Pinterest	366	美国
17	领英	310	美国
19	Discord	250	美国
18	Viber	260	以色列
5	微信	1,165	中国
7	抖音	800	中国
8	QQ	731	中国
9	QQ 空间	517	中国
10	新浪微博	516	中国
12	快手	400	中国
16	百度贴吧	320	中国

Figure 4-2　Number of Monthly Active Users of Each Social Media Platform in April 2020

Source: Tieba Baidu

图 4-2　2020 年 4 月份社交媒体平台月活跃用户的数量

资料来源：百度贴吧

show a more obvious natural division in age, preference, region, gender, economic level and other aspects, which makes it easy for enterprises to identify user groups and carry out marketing promotion.

(2) Effective reduction of the marketing cost for enterprises.

Social media marketing basically relies on soft promotion, and the cost is far lower than advertising. Even if you don't have the same advertising budget as big companies, you can at least accumulate your contacts through content marketing, improve the brand image, and gradually transform into sales performance. At the same time, because it is based on social relations, the main media of communication is users, and the main way is "word of mouth", so it can obtain natural secondary and multi-level expansion of spreading.

3．Classification of social media

Different needs of different groups promote the emergence and development of different social media platforms. The common forms of social media include social networking, social sharing, blog and forum, social news, etc.

- Social networking: social networking is one of the most famous social media. Based on social networking, people connect with friends, colleagues, classmates and other people with the same interests and background to share information and interact. Facebook, Twitter, Google + and LinkedIn are among the most famous social networkings.

- Social sharing: with social sharing, users can upload their own videos, audio or pictures, and share and interact with other netizens through the sharing website. For example, if you want to attract customers through video, YouTube is a good channel. It is the largest video sharing website overseas. In picture sharing, the photo social giant Instagram had 1 billion monthly active users, while Pinterest had 366

性。他们分别在年龄、喜好、地域、性别、经济水平等各方面呈现较为明显的自然划分，便于企业找准用户群，开展营销推广。

（2）有效降低企业的营销成本。

社交媒体营销基本上依靠软性推广，成本远远低于广告投放。即便你没有像大公司一样的广告预算，至少也可以通过内容营销积累你的人脉，提升品牌形象，并逐渐转化为销售业绩。同时，由于是基于社交关系的传播，传播的主要媒介是用户，主要方式是"众口相传"，所以可以获得自然的二次和多级扩大传播。

3．社交媒体的分类

不同人群的不同需求促进了不同社交媒体平台的产生和发展。常见的社交媒体的形式有社交网络、社交分享、博客与论坛、社交新闻等。

- 社交网络：社交网络是最知名的社交媒体之一。基于社交网络，人们与朋友、同事、同学等具有相同兴趣爱好和背景的人连接在一起，分享信息和展开互动。最知名的社交网络有Facebook、Twitter，Google+和LinkedIn。

- 社交分享：使用社交分享，用户可以上传自己的视频、音频或者图片，并通过分享网站与其他网友进行分享和互动。例如，如果你想通过视频吸引客户，YouTube是一个很好的渠道。它是海外最大的视频分享网站。在

million monthly active users in April, 2020. If you own a florist, you can share your pictures of flower arrangement for customers to buy.

- Blog and forum: blog and forum are one of the oldest forms of social media. Users promote marketing by publishing content and content-based interaction. Tumblr is one of the most popular blogging platforms with over 430 million accounts. Free blogs include blogspot.com, Wordpress.com and so on.

- Social news: through social news website, users can share or directly upload articles and news, and website users can evaluate these articles and news. Social news websites rate articles based on evaluation, and present the highest rated content to more readers. This kind of website appeared very early, and the most famous Reddit has been established for nearly 10 years. If you want to build brand awareness by spreading knowledge, Quora is a social networking site that will allow you to answer questions about the industry and help people get the information they need.

4. Steps of social media marketing

Cross-border E-commerce enterprises can gradually carry out social media marketing according to the certain steps in Figure 4-3.

4.2.2　Search Engine Marketing

1. The concept of search engine marketing

Search engine marketing (SEM) is a kind of online

图片分享上，2020 年 4 月，图片社交巨头 Instagram 拥有 10 亿名月活跃用户，而 Pinterest 也有 3.66 亿名月活跃用户。如果你拥有一家花店，则可以分享你插花的图片供客户进行选购。

- 博客与论坛：博客与论坛是历史最久的社交媒体形式之一。使用者通过发布内容和基于内容的互动进行营销推广。在博客中，Tumblr 是最受欢迎的博客平台之一，拥有超过 4.3 亿个账户。免费博客包括 blogspot.com、Wordpress.com 等。

- 社交新闻：通过社交新闻网站，用户分享或直接上传文章和新闻，网站用户可以对这些文章和新闻进行评价。社交新闻网站则基于评价对文章进行评级，并将评级最高的内容呈现给更多读者。这种网站出现得很早，最知名的 Reddit 已经创建近 10 年。如果你想通过传播知识来建立品牌知名度，Quora 就是一个社交网站，允许你回答与行业有关的问题，并帮助人们获得所需的信息。

4. 社交媒体营销的步骤

跨境电商企业开展社交媒体营销，可以按照图4-3 中的步骤逐步展开。

4.2.2　搜索引擎营销

1. 搜索引擎营销的概念

搜索引擎营销（Search Engine

Figure 4-3   Steps for Social Media Marketing

图 4-3   社交媒体营销步骤

marketing based on search engine platform. It uses people's dependence on search engine and usage habits to transfer information to target users when people retrieve information. The basic idea of search engine marketing is to let users find information, and enter the Web page by clicking to further understand the information they need. At present, the global mainstream search engines include Google, Bing, Yahoo, Baidu, Yandex, etc.

2．The general process of information transmission for search engine marketing

The basic process of search engine marketing is as follows:

(1) The enterprise publishes the information on the website and becomes the information source in the form of webpage.

(2) The search engine collects the information on websites and webpages into the side database.

(3) The user searches by using keywords and the relevant index information and its link URL are listed in the research results.

(4) According to their judgment on the results of treasure checking, users select the interested information and

Marketing，SEM），是基于搜索引擎平台的网络营销。它利用人们对搜索引擎的依赖和使用习惯，在人们检索信息时将信息传递给目标用户。搜索引擎营销的基本思想是让用户发现信息，并通过点击进入网页，进一步了解所需要的信息。目前，全球主流的搜索引擎有 Google、Bing、Yahoo、Baidu、Yandex 等。

2．搜索引擎营销信息传递的一般过程

搜索引擎营销得以实现的基本过程如下：

（1）企业将信息发布在网站上，成为以网页形式存在的信息源。

（2）搜索引擎将网站网页信息收录到旁数据库。

（3）用户利用关键词进行检索，检索结果中罗列相关的索引信息及其链接 URL。

（4）用户根据对寻宝结果的判断选择有兴趣的信息并点击

click the URL.

(5) Users enter the website where the information source is located.

In this way, the whole process is completed from enterprises publishing information to users obtaining information. This process also explains the basic principles of search engine marketing and the basic process of information transmission.

3．The characteristics of search engine marketing

(1) Search Engine Marketing (SEM) and enterprise website are inseparable.

Enterprise website promotion is one of the main purposes of search engine marketing. Therefore, the establishment of professional enterprise website is the main support for enterprises to effectively carry out search engine marketing. The professionalism of enterprise website and the friendliness of search engine will have a direct impact on the effect of search engine marketing.

(2) SEM is a kind of user-oriented online marketing.

The behavior of using search engine to retrieve information is initiated by users. What information or service to be retrieved is completely determined according to users' own needs and wishes. Moreover, users have their own preferences and judgments in choosing that information in the search results, which are not affected by other factors.

(3) SEM can achieve a higher degree of positioning.

One of the main characteristics of online marketing is that it can accurately analyze users' behaviors and achieve a high degree of positioning, especially when the keyword ads are on the search results page, which can be highly related to the keywords retrieved by them, so as to improve the degree of attention of marketing information and ultimately achieve the purpose of online marketing effect.

(4) The effect of SEM is the increase of website visits.

URL。

（5）用户进入信息源所在网页。

这样，便完成了企业从发布信息到用户获取信息的整个过程。这个过程也说明了搜索引擎营销的基本原理和信息传递基本过程。

3．搜索引擎营销的特点

（1）搜索引擎营销（SEM）与企业网站密不可分。

企业网站推广是搜索引擎营销的主要目的之一。因此，专业企业网站的建立是企业有效地开展搜索引擎营销的主要依托。企业网站的专业性和搜索引擎的友好性会对搜索引擎营销的效果产生直接影响。

（2）SEM 是一种用户主导的网络营销。

使用搜索引擎检索信息的行为是由用户主动发生的。用户检索什么信息或服务也完全是根据自己的需要和意愿决定的。而且，用户在选择搜索结果中的信息时具有自己的偏好和判断，并不受其他因素的影响。

（3）SEM 可以实现较高程度的定位。

网络营销的主要特点之一是可以对用户行为进行准确分析并实现高程度定位，尤其是在搜索结果页面的关键词广告时，完全可以实现与用户所检索的关键词高度相关，从而提高营销信息被关注的程度，最终达到网络营销效果的目的。

（4）SEM 的效果表现为网站访问量的增加。

The main task of search engine marketing for the purpose of enterprise website promotion is to increase the number of visits to the website. As for whether the increase of visits can eventually be converted into an increase in revenue, it also depends on some other factors, which cannot be determined by the search engine marketing activities.

4．Search Engine Optimization (SEO) and paid promotion

The specific methods of SEM mainly include SEO and paid promotion. As cross-border E-commerce sellers, especially sellers with independent website, they should combine the two methods to form a complementation, which can achieve the maximum effect of search engine marketing.

(1) Use the rules of search engine to improve the natural ranking of website in the relevant search engine, so as to get more traffic. Different search engines have different rules of crawling, indexing and ranking of web pages, but they also have some similarities. Therefore, cross-border E-commerce sellers can carry out search engine optimization from the following aspects: ① website and page optimization; ② keyword optimization; ③ tag optimization; ④ content optimization ; ⑤ link optimization.

(2) On the basis of SEO, cross-border E-commerce sellers also need to reasonably choose and use relevant paid promotion methods to achieve the maximum effect of search engine marketing. At present, the global mainstream search engine paid promotion methods mainly include the following: ① directory index; ② competitive ranking; ③ fixed ranking; ④ keyword advertising.

4.2.3　Short Video Marketing

1．The concept of short video marketing

Short video is a short video clip, which is mainly spread on the Internet. Compared with the traditional long video, short video is a more fashionable experience mode. The duration of short video varies from a few seconds to a few

以企业网站推广为目的的搜索引擎营销的主要任务是提高网站的访问量。访问量的增加最终是否能转化为收益的增加，还取决于其他一些因素，这是搜索引擎营销活动所无法决定的。

4．搜索引擎优化（SEO）与付费推广

SEM 的具体方法主要包括 SEO 及付费推广两大部分。作为跨境电商卖家，特别是独立网站的卖家，应让两者结合在一起，形成互补，这可以达到搜索引擎营销的最大效果。

（1）利用搜索引擎的规则提高网站在有关搜索引擎内的自然排名，从而获得更多流量。不同的搜索引擎对网页的抓取、索引、排序规则各有差异，同时也存在一定的共性。因此，跨境电商卖家开展搜索引擎优化可以从以下方面着手：① 网站及页面优化；② 关键词优化；③ 标签优化；④ 内容优化；⑤ 链接优化。

（2）在 SEO 的基础上，跨境电商卖家还需合理选择及运用相关的付费推广方式，以达到搜索引擎营销的最大效果。目前，全球主流搜索引擎付费推广方式主要包括如下几种：① 目录索引；② 竞价排名；③ 固定排名；④ 关键词广告等。

4.2.3　短视频营销

1．短视频营销的概念

短视频即时长较短的视频片段，其传播方式主要为互联网传播。短视频相对于传统意义上的长视频而言是一种更为新潮的体验方式。短

minutes. It can be spread on all kinds of new media platforms, and is more suitable for viewing in mobile state and short time. The emergence of short video is a useful supplement to the existing main content (text, pictures) of social media. At the same time, high-quality short video content can also achieve the channel advantages of social media by using "viral" transmission.

2. The characteristics of short video marketing

(1) Mobile communication.

At present, short videos are mainly spread on mobile phones. With the powerful support of mobile Internet technology, Apps have become the main front of short video applications, such as TickTok App. In 2019, the number of daily active users of Douyin exceeded 400 million.

(2) Fragmented communication.

The information age breaks the limitation of time and space, and speeds up the pace of people's life, which leads to the increase of people's fragmented time. Compared with the traditional form of video, the duration of short video is shorter, generally in a few seconds to a few minutes. This kind of video recording and viewing are more convenient, and the "short, flat and fast" content is easier to attract people's attention.

(3) Social sharing, quick results.

With the improvement of people's living standards and the continuous increase of smartphone usage, video social interaction has gradually become an important part of people's life. In the App, both video authors and users can easily use TikTok, and even realize one-click sharing, making it easier for short video to be broadcast repeatedly, so that the exposure rate of short videos will increase rapidly.

3. The mode of short video marketing

(1) Advertising placement marketing of influencers.

This kind of marketing mode is mainly promoted with the help of influencers' fans, because the traffic of non-influencers is not large, only those traffic stars and

视频的时长为几秒到几分钟不等，它可以在各类新媒体平台上传播，更适合在移动状态下及短时间内观看。短视频的出现是对社交媒体现有主要内容（文字、图片）的一种有益补充。同时，优质的短视频内容也可借助社交媒体的渠道优势实现"病毒式"传播。

2. 短视频营销的特点

（1）移动传播。

目前，短视频主要在手机上传播。在移动互联网技术的强大支持下，App已经成为短视频应用的主要阵地，比如 TickTok App。2019 年，抖音的日活跃用户数已经突破 4 亿人。

（2）碎片化传播。

信息化时代打破了时间和空间的限制，也加快了人们的生活节奏，就导致了人们碎片化时间增多。与传统的视频形式相比，短视频的时长更短，一般在几秒到几分钟之间。这种视频录制与观看都更为便捷"短平快"的内容就更容易吸引人们的视线。

（3）分享社交化，见效快。

随着人们生活水平的提高，智能手机使用率连续增高，视频社交也逐渐成为人们生活的一个重要部分。在 App 中，不管是视频作者还是用户都能轻松使用 TickTok，甚至可以做到一键分享，更加方便短视频的多次转播，让短视频的曝光率飞速增长。

3. 短视频营销的方式

（1）网红广告植入式营销。

这种营销方式主要借助网红的粉丝来进行推广，因大多数非公众人物的流量不大，只有那些

influencers have relatively large traffic and more fans. Short videos released by influencers have been widely spread by fans in a short period of time, so as to make consumption and achieve the purpose of cross-industry short video marketing. This is also mostly a short video marketing method for small and medium-sized cross-border E-commerce enterprises.

(2) Emotional resonance customized marketing.

Enterprises can make use of social hot spots for short video production and communication. This kind of communication is not simply to propagandaize, but to arouse users' emotional resonance and reflection, deliver corporate values to the public from multiple angles and in depth, and improve the public's sense of corporate identity with the help of short video content. For example, on the holiday, many enterprises use this theme to plan the content of short video marketing, breaking through the habitual marketing "selling" thinking, integrating emotion and value into it, which not only meets the emotional needs of consumers, but also realizes the marketing of enterprises.

(3) Scene immersion experiential marketing.

Many consumers are more concerned about the characteristics of products, so some advertisers prefer to create specific scenes through the characteristics of products, to increase the interesting experience of the product and stimulate the users' desire to buy. In fact, this way allows users to feel the benefits of products in advance, lets everyone realize the advantages of products, and then realizes the interest transmission of the important features of the product.

4.2.4　Live Broadcast Marketing

1. The concept of live broadcast marketing

Live broadcast marketing is a marketing means by which the marketing activity takes the live broadcasting platform as its carrier, and produces and broadcasts programs simultaneously with the occurrence and development of events in the field, so as to achieve the purpose of promoting the brand of enterprises or increasing sales. Cross-border

流量明星和网红的流量相对比较大，粉丝也比较多。通过网红发布的短视频在较短时间内引起粉丝们广为传播，从而进行消费，达到跨业做短视频营销的目的。这也大多是中小跨境电商企业的短视频营销方式。

（2）情感共鸣定制式营销。

企业可借助社会上的热点进行短视频制作传播。这种传播不是简简单单的宣传，而是借助短视频内容引发用户情感共鸣与反思，多角度、深层次地向大众传递企业价值观，提高大众对企业认同感。比如，在节日中，很多企业都借助这个题材策划短视频营销的内容，突破了惯用营销"卖货"思维，将情感和价值融入其中，这样既满足消费者的情感需求，也实现了企业的营销。

（3）场景沉浸体验式营销。

很多消费者都比较关注产品的特性，所以有的广告主就比较喜欢通过产品的特性塑造特定的场景，以增加产品的趣味体验和激发用户的购买欲。实际上，这种方式让用户可以提前感受产品所带来的好处，让每个人都认识到产品的优势，然后实现产品重要特性的趣味传递。

4.2.4　网络直播营销

1. 网络直播营销的概念

网络直播营销指营销活动以直播平台为载体，在现场随着事件的发生、发展进程同时制作和播出节目的营销方式，达到企业品牌的提升或销量的增长的目的。跨境电商卖家通过直播可以真实地展示实

E-commerce vendors can show the details of real goods through live broadcasting, providing a new shopping experience and service for overseas consumers. With the rise of 5G, big data, artificial intelligence and block chain technology, "live broadcast + cross-border E-commerce" mode will usher in a new era of traffic.

2. The characteristics of live broadcast marketing

Live broadcast marketing exhibits the following characteristics:

(1) Scene-oriented. Compared with traditional marketing methods, live broadcast marketing is more scene-oriented, which greatly improves customers' consumption experience. Scenarioization refers to the construction of specific scenarios to allow online users to have a strong sense of substitution, and awaken the needs of consumers, thus arousing consumers' desire to buy. Traditional E-commerce sellers build scenes through text, pictures, audio and video, while the E-commerce sellers of live broadcast marketing show real-time and real scenes to consumers watching live broadcast through the Internet and communication technology, which can make consumers more intuitive to understand the product, thereby increasing their trust in the product.

(2) Interactive. Live broadcast marketing contains social elements, which are mainly manifested in strong interaction with the audience. During the live broadcast, viewers can ask questions to the host and exchange ideas with him and other viewers who watch the live broadcast at the same time. Through real-time live broadcast, cross-border E-commerce sellers can realize consumers' needs and preferences, get timely feedback, and communicate with consumers in real time to provide better services, thereby increasing customers' loyalty and enhancing users' benefits.

(3) Real-time. Live broadcast marketing is instant, covering only instant users. Short videos, pictures, texts and other new media marketing methods can be used for secondary dissemination to reach more users, and dissemination of such marketing information lasts up to about 1 week. However, live broadcast marketing can only

物商品的细节，为海外消费者提供一种全新的购物体验和服务。随着5G、大数据、人工智能、区块链技术的兴起，"直播+跨境电商"模式将迎来流量的新时代。

2. 网络直播营销的特征

网络直播营销呈现以下特征：

（1）场景化。网络直播营销与传统营销方式相比，场景化更加丰富，大大提高了客户的消费体验。场景化是指通过构建特定的场景，让网络用户有强烈的代入感，唤醒消费者的需求，从而引起消费者的购买欲望。传统的电商通过文字、图片、音频和视频来构建场景，而直播营销的电商则通过互联网和通信技术给观看直播的消费者展示实时、真实的场景，能让消费者更加直观地了解产品，从而提高对产品的信任度。

（2）互动性。网络直播营销含有社交的元素，主要表现为和观众的互动性强。在网络直播时，观众可以向主播提问，与主播及其他观看网络直播的用户进行活动交流。通过实时网络直播，跨境电商卖家可以了解消费者的购买需求和喜好，得到及时的反馈，并能与消费者进行实时沟通，提供更加优质的服务，以此提高客户的忠诚度，提升用户效益。

（3）即时性。网络直播营销具有即时性，仅覆盖即时用户。短视频、图片、文字等其他新媒体营销方式可以进行二次传播，以传递给更多的用户，营销信息传播持续时间可达1周左右。但

cover instant users, and customers who have not entered the live broadcast room will miss the opportunity to intuitively understand the corresponding product information and activity information.

For cross-border E-commerce enterprises, they firstly need to make a choice between live broadcast marketing and the live broadcast platforms of major cross-border E-commerce platforms, such as Alibaba, AliExpress, Amazon, Shopee, etc. These platforms currently have their own E-commerce live broadcast platforms, and a complete E-commerce live broadcast training system.

4.3 On-Site Marketing and Promotion of Cross-Border E-Commerce

For cross-border E-commerce enterprises, in order to make the released products get more traffic, they must first optimize the products. Only the optimized products can be used for on-site marketing and promotion. Although there are differences in on-site marketing and promotion between each cross-border E-commerce platform, they are relatively similar. In this section, we will take AliExpress platform as an example to introduce its on-site marketing and promotion: keyword search, holiday activities, daily promotion activities and platform community sharing.

4.3.1 Keyword Search

In order to quickly find the product they want on the cross-border E-commerce platform, customers use their usual description to describe the product, such as brand + attribute + product name (NIKE white shoes) (Figure 4-4). These habitual descriptions include the brand, model, style, color, purpose, material, size, promotion, region, popular elements, use scene, product name, etc. All of these descriptions or their combinations can be called keywords. Keyword search is a way for buyers to buy products. High quality keywords can help sellers quickly increase their exposure. For cross-border E-commerce sellers, keywords are an important link

是，网络直播营销仅能够覆盖即时用户，没有进入网络直播间的网络用户会错失直观了解相应产品信息和活动信息的机会。

对于跨境电商企业来说，首先要选择的是做网络直播营销还是各大跨境电商平台的网络直播平台，如阿里巴巴国际站、速卖通、亚马逊、Shopee 等。这些平台目前都有自己的电商网络直播平台，而且有一套完善的电商网络直播培训系统。

4.3 跨境电商站内营销与推广

对于跨境电商企业来说，想使发布的产品有更多的流量，首先要对该产品进行优化。优化后的产品才能用于站内营销与推广。虽然每个跨境电商平台的站内营销与推广有差异，但都比较相近。本节将以速卖通平台为例，介绍其站内营销与推广：关键词搜索、节假日活动、日常促销活动，以及平台社区分享。

4.3.1 关键词搜索

客户为了在跨境电商平台上迅速找到自己想要的产品，他采用自己习惯的描述称谓来形容该产品，比如品牌＋属性＋产品名称（NIKE white shoes）（图4-4）。这些习惯性描述包括产品的品牌、型号、风格、颜色、用途、材质、尺寸、促销、地域、流行元素、使用场景、产品名称等，这些描述或者描述的组合都可以称为关键词。关键词搜索是买家购买产品的一种方

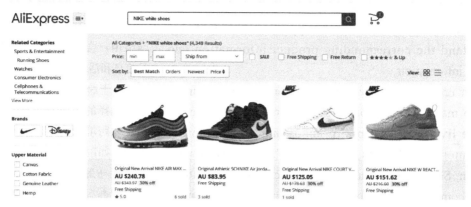

Figure 4-4　Keyword Search Page of AliExpress Platform

图 4-4　速卖通平台关键词搜索页面

for marketing customers. If the key words are not selected well, there will be no traffic, just as archery is not aimed at the target, so a lot of work is ineffective.

Keyword search methods in AliExpress are as follows.

(1) Search the keywords in the drop-down box: log into AliExpress platform, and then search the drop-down box to find the keywords, where you can find a large number of high traffic words with high accuracy.

(2) System recommendation words in P4P: if the seller in AliExpress has released P4P function, this method is also worth reference, but keyword screening should be carried out appropriately.

式。高质量的关键词可以帮助卖家快速增加曝光率。对于跨境电商卖家来说，关键词就是营销客户的重要纽带。如果关键词没有选择好，则没有流量，就像射箭没有对准靶子，很多工作都是无效的。

速卖通关键词搜索方法有如下几种。

（1）搜索下拉框的关键词：登录速卖通平台，然后通过搜索下拉框找关键词，这里可以找到大量高流量的词，而且准确度也较高。

（2）直通车中的系统推荐词：如速卖通的卖家已经发布了直通车功能，这个方法也值得参考，但要进行关键词筛选。

Knowledge Extension: AliExpress Pay for Performance (P4P)

AliExpress P4P is to set up sellers' own multi-dimensional marketing tool, display product information free of charge, welcome potential buyers by exposing a large number of products, and rapidly increase traffic by the new online promotion method of pay-per-click.

知识拓展：速卖通直通车

速卖通 P4P 是卖家建立自己的多维度营销工具，免费展示产品信息，通过曝光大量产品来吸引潜在买家，并通过点击付费的新在线推广方式快速增加流量。

(3) Hot selling products on the home page of AliExpress platform: cross-border sellers can refer to the words of hot-sale products and those in the same industry.

(4) Using search terms to analyze: it can be carried out through the data vertical and horizontal——search term analysis in the background of AliExpress, which is one of the most commonly used method. It should be noted that you must select the keywords within 30 days, so that you can obtain stable ones.

Some popular keyword query tool stations are recommended as follows:

Google Adword, Keyword Tracker, Keyword Discovery and Wordze.

4.3.2   Holiday Activities

AliExpress platform integrates relevant resources in specific holidays and uses special channels to carry out promotion activities. These activities can quickly bring a lot of traffic and exposure to shops, and the conversion rate is high. AliExpress platform carries out three promotion activities every year.

The first is the Shopping Festival on March 25th at the beginning of the year; the second is the Supernoval Sale on August 19th in the middle of the year; and the third is the "Double Eleven" at the end of the year. "Double Eleven" is the biggest promotion activity with the largest traffic flow. Every time, the platform spent a lot of resources to introduce traffic, and the effect of the activity was very significant. The massive flow of big promotion activities can lead to the rapid rise of single product ranking, so the sellers in AliExpress must catch these opportunities.

The types of platform promotion activities mainly include:

(1) Flash Sales.

(2) 50% off in the main venue.

(3) Sub venue activities.

（3）速卖通平台首页的热销产品：跨境卖家可以参考热销产品的选词，以及同行业热销产品的选词。

（4）利用搜索词进行分析：可通过速卖通后台的数据纵横——搜索词分析来进行，这是最常用的方法之一。需要注意的是，一定要选择 30 天以内的关键词，这样才可以获得稳定的关键词。

下面推荐一些比较流行的关键词查询工具站：

Google Adword、Keyword Tracker、Keyword Discovery 和 Wordze。

4.3.2   节假日活动

速卖通平台在特定的节假日，整合相关资源，利用专门设立的特定频道进行推广活动。这些活动能快速为店铺带来大量的流量和曝光，且转化率较高。速卖通平台每年开展三次大促活动：

第一次是年初的"3·25"购物节；第二次是年中的"8·19"金秋盛宴；第三次是年底的"双十一"大促。"双十一"的促销力度最大，也是流量最大的大促活动。对每次大促活动，该平台都花费大量资源引入流量，活动效果十分显著。大促活动的海量流量会使单品排名迅速上升，因此速卖通的卖家必须抓住这些机会。

平台大促活动的主要类型包括：

（1）秒杀活动。

（2）主会场五折活动。

（3）分会场活动。

(4) Theme pavilions.

(5) Quality shop promotion activities.

(6) High quality shop promotion activities.

(7) Seaview room activities.

4.3.3 Daily Promotional Activities

(1) Full shop discount: it is a discount tool that can set different discounts for the whole shop according to the commodity groups, which can help cross-border sellers quickly improve the flow and sales in a short time. According to the profit margin of different groups, different discount intensity is set, and the goods with 10% off or more are easier to generate orders.

(2) Limited time and quantity discount: it is a shop marketing tool by which the seller can choose the product and time of the activity, and set the promotion discount and inventory. It is a favorite tool for cross-border sellers to launch new products, make explosive products and clear inventory with different discounts. Use the "hot commodities" of "data vertical and horizontal" to select the active commodities, optimize the commodity information in advance, and then create the activity.

(3) ×××off on purchase over ×××: it is a kind of shop marketing tool by which the seller sets the rules for automatic price reduction and promotion of the full order system on the basis of their own average transaction value, which not only makes the buyer feel affordable, but also stimulates him to buy more in order to achieve preferential conditions, so as to improve sales and pull up the average transaction value. With the "product chain tool" to recommend related products, the effect of "×××off on purchase over ×××" can be greatly improved.

(4) Shop coupons: shop coupons are the coupons that are set by the seller and used by the buyer within the validity period after collection, which can stimulate the buyer to place orders and old buyers to buy back, and improve the purchase rate and average transaction value. At the same time, multiple shop coupon activities can be set up by sellers to meet the needs of buyers with different purchasing power, so as to

（4）主题馆。

（5）优质店铺推广活动。

（6）高品质的店铺促销活动。

（7）海景房活动。

4.3.3 日常促销活动

（1）全店折扣：是一款可以根据商品组为全店设置不同折扣的折扣工具，可以帮助跨境卖家在短时间内快速提高流量和销量。根据不同商品类别的利润率，设置不同的折扣力度，9折及以上的商品更容易产生订单。

（2）限时限量折扣：卖家可以选择活动的产品和时间，设置促销折扣和库存的店铺营销工具。这是跨境卖家推出新品、做爆款、清库存、不同折扣的首选工具。利用"数据纵横"的"热销商品"，选择活跃商品，提前优化商品信息，然后创建活动。

（3）超过多少满减：这是一种店铺营销工具，卖家根据自己的平均成交额设置订单全系统自动减价促销规则，不仅让买家觉得实惠，而且也刺激买家多买，以达到优惠条件，从而提高销量，拉高平均成交额。借助"产品链工具"推荐相关产品，可以大大提高"满×××立减×××"的效果。

（4）店铺优惠券：店铺优惠券是指由卖家设置、买家领取后在有效期内使用的优惠券，可以刺激买家下单和老买家回购，提高购买率和平均交易价值。卖家同时可以设置多个店铺优惠券活动，满足不同购买力买家的需求，

obtain more orders.

4.3.4   Platform Community Sharing

The cross-border E-commerce on-site platform community sharing refers to that the whole cross-border E-commerce platform is similar to a large online community, in which there are many users, who will recommend some product discount information and product price ratio in the community. It is recommended that the advantages of the product be written into a copy and published with humorous words to attract other users to buy. Unlike the traditional E-commerce shopping website where buyers and sellers use a single transaction method, it is a very intimate on-site marketing mode for users. At present, the cross-border E-commerce import platform, Little Red Book (Xiaohongshu), is more successful than other platforms in adopting the community sharing method.

With the operation of this mode, some high-quality users will accumulate some loyal fans, and they will often drive a certain direction, because these users have a certain degree of credibility, and a product will be more widely transmitted through high-quality users' recommendation. At present，the joining of stars makes the traffic reach a high level.

从而获得更多订单。

4.3.4   平台社区分享

跨境电商站内平台社区分享是指整个跨境电商平台类似一个大网络社区，里面有许多用户，这些用户会在社区中推荐一些产品折扣信息、产品性价比。推荐将产品优势撰写成文案以幽默的话术发布出来，以吸引其他用户去购买。不像传统的电商购物网站那样采用买卖双方单一的交易方式，这是一种对待用户非常贴心的站内营销方式。目前，采用社区分享方式且比其他平台更成功的是跨境电商进口平台小红书。

采用这种方式的运作，一些优质用户会积累成一些忠实粉丝，这些优质用户往往会带动一定的风向，因为这些用户已经有一定的信誉度，一款产品通过优质用户推荐，传播速度和范围会更广。同时，明星的加入使流量达到一个高度。

New words

1. exposure rate 曝光率
2. browsing volume 浏览量
3. traffic 流量
4. on-site and off-site marketing 站内和站外营销
5. macro environment and micro environment 宏观环境与微观环境
6. market segmentation 市场细分
7. market targeting 市场选择
8. market positioning 市场定位
9. influencer 网红
10. fragmented communication 碎片化传播

11. live broadcast marketing 网络直播营销
12. social media marketing 社交媒体营销
13. search engine marketing (SEM) 搜索引擎营销
14. search engine optimization (SEO) 搜索引擎优化
15. short video marketing 短视频营销
16. penetration pricing strategy 低价渗透策略
17. skimming pricing strategy 高价撇脂策略
18. Double Eleven 双十一
19. flash sales 秒杀
20. ××× off on purchase over ××× 满 ××× 立减 ×××
21. average transaction price 客单价

Chapter 5
第5章

Cross-Border E-Commerce Logistics and Overseas Warehouses
跨境电商物流与海外仓

Lead-in case

After learning about the connotation, platform, product selection, product management, marketing planning and related knowledge of cross-border E-commerce, Xiaowei is facing problems of solving the logistics and overseas warehouses issues. With the rapid development of cross-border logistics and the continuous evolution of related technologies, legal regulations, operating procedures, mainstream platform rules, etc., Xiaowei needs to systematically learn about the knowledge of cross-border E-commerce logistics and overseas warehouses, to master the logistics plan design, freight calculation, etc. Therefore, by learning this chapter, you and Xiaowei will master the current knowledge and skills of cross-border E-commerce logistics and overseas warehouses from both the macro and micro perspectives, and solve practical problems at the workplace, to be ready for the following procedures such as customs clearance, settlement, customer service and so on.

Learning objectives

1. Objectives of knowledge

(1) To master the logistics and transportation process of cross-border E-commerce import and export.

(2) To master the types of cross-border E-commerce logistics transportation.

(3) To grasp the concepts of cross-border container, postal parcel, and international commercial express freight.

(4) To understand the concept of overseas warehouse, process and the concept of first journey freight.

2. Objectives of skills

(1) To skillfully design the cross-border E-commerce logistics solutions.

(2) To calculate the freight of cross-border containers,

案例导入

在了解了跨境电商的内涵、平台、选品、产品管理、营销策划等知识之后，小薇面临如何处理物流及海外仓相关问题。随着跨境物流的迅速发展，与此相关的技术、法律条文、运作流程、主流平台规则等的不断演进，小薇需要对跨境电商物流与海外仓知识进行系统的学习，才能掌握相关的物流方案设计、运费计算等。因此，通过对本章的学习，你将与小薇一起从宏观及微观层面掌握当前跨境电商物流与海外仓的相关知识和技能，解决工作场所的实际问题，为随后的通关、结算、客服等工作做好准备。

学习目标

1. 知识目标

（1）掌握跨境电商进出口物流运输流程。

（2）掌握跨境电商物流运输类型。

（3）掌握跨境集装箱、邮政小包、国际商业快递运费的概念。

（4）了解海外仓的概念、流程和头程运费的概念。

2. 技能目标

（1）能熟练设计跨境电商物流方案。

（2）能根据实际问题，计算

small postal parcel, and international commercial express freight according to actual problems.

(3) To be able to analyze the operation process of overseas warehouses and to select local logistics for them.

(4) To be able to calculate the first journey freight of international sea and air transport.

3．Objectives of qualities

(1) To have a clear work motivation and a positive working attitude.

(2) To aware the laws and regulations related to cross-border E-commerce logistics.

(3) To have good teamwork and problem solving skills.

(4) To have the ability to actively learn from emerging industries.

5.1 Overview of Cross-Border E-Commerce Logistics

5.1.1 Logistics Transportation Process of Cross-Border E-Commerce Import and Export

Taking container shipping as an example, the import and export logistics transportation procedures include booking space, accepting consignment applications, issuing empty containers, Less than Container Load (LCL) cargo packing, Full Container Load (FCL) cargo handover, container handover confirmation, exchange of bills of lading, shipment, maritime transportation, unloading, FCL delivery, LCL delivery and empty container back-haul.

Booking space means that the cargo shipper fills out the shipping form and applies to the shipping company or its agent for booking space according to the terms of the trade contract or letter of credit. Accepting consignment application means that the shipping company or its agent compiles the booking list after accepting the consignment application. Issuing empty containers means that the shipper collects empty containers at the container terminal yard, and the empty containers of the LCL are collected by the container freight station. LCL cargo packing means that the consignor delivers

跨境集装箱、邮政小包、国际商业快递运费。

（3）能分析海外仓运作流程及进行海外仓本地物流选择。

（4）能计算国际海与空运头程运费。

3．素质目标

（1）具有明确的工作动机和积极向上的工作态度。

（2）了解跨境电商物流相关法律法规。

（3）具有良好的团队协作及解决问题的能力。

（4）具有对新兴产业的主动学习能力。

5.1 跨境电商物流概述

5.1.1 跨境电商进出口物流运输流程

以集装箱海运为例，进出口物流运输程序包括订舱、接受托运申请、发放空箱、拼箱货装箱、整箱货交接、集装箱交接签证、换取提单、装船、海上运输、卸船、整箱货交付、拼箱货交付、空箱回运。

订舱是指发货人或货物托运人根据贸易合同或信用证条款，填制订舱单向船公司或其代理人申请订舱。接受托运申请是指船公司或其代理人在接受托运申请后，编制订舱清单。发放空箱是指发货人到集装箱码头堆场领取空箱，拼箱的空箱由集装箱货运站负责领取。拼箱货装箱是指发货人将不足一整箱的货物交集装

less than one full container of cargoes to the container freight station, who will check the station receipt for packing. FCL cargo handover means that the consignor is responsible for packing and sealing by customs, and then transporting it to the container terminal yard. The container handover confirmation means that the signed dock receipt is returned to the shipper after the cargo and container are checked and received, and then the bill of lading is exchanged accordingly. Exchange of bill of lading means that the consignor exchanges the bill of lading with the person responsible for transportation or its agent on the basis of the dock receipt, and then goes to the bank to settle the exchange. Shipment refers to the formulation of a shipment plan by the container terminal, and it will be carried out after the ship has berthed. Maritime transportation means that the carrier is responsible for the safe transportation and custody of the container, and divides the responsibilities, obligations and rights with the cargo owner according to the bill of lading. Ship unloading refers to the formulation of an unloading plan by the container terminal in accordance with the shipping documents, and unloading the ship after it has berthed. FCL delivery means that the terminal yard delivers the container to the consignee according to the bill of lading. LCL delivery refers to the delivery of the goods to the consignee according to the bill of lading after the container freight station has unloaded the container. Empty container back-haul means that the consignee and the freight station will promptly transport the empty container back to the terminal yard after it is unloaded.

5.1.2　Types of Cross-Border E-Commerce Logistics Transportation

Methods and characteristics of cross-border E-commerce transportation are shown in Table 5-1.

The types of cross-border E-commerce logistics transportation are shown in Table 5-2.

箱货运站，由其核对场站收据装箱。整箱货交接是指发货人自行负责装箱并加海关封志，并运至集装箱码头堆场。集装箱交接签证是指在验收货物和集装箱后，将签署的场站收据交还给发货人，据此换取提单。换取提单是指发货人凭场站收据向负责运输的人或其代理换取提单，然后去银行结汇。装船是指集装箱码头制订装船计划，待船舶靠泊后装船。海上运输是指承运人负责集装箱的安全运输和保管，并依据提单条款划分与货主之间的责任、义务和权利。卸船是指集装箱码头依照货运单证制订卸船计划，待船舶靠泊后卸船。整箱货交付是指码头堆场根据提单将货箱交给收货人。拼箱货交付是指集装箱货运站在掏箱后，根据提单将货物交给收货人。空箱回运是指收货人和货运站在掏箱完毕后，及时将空箱运回码头堆场。

5.1.2　跨境电商物流运输类型

跨境电商运输方式和特征见表 5-1。

跨境电商物流运输类型见表 5-2。

Table 5-1　Methods and Characteristics of Cross-Border E-Commerce Transportation

Transportation methods	Characteristics
Ocean transport	Refers to a way of using ships to transport cargoes among ports in different countries and regions through sea lanes, and is the most important mode of transportation in international logistics, including inland water transport and maritime transport, among which the latter can be divided into coastal transport and international maritime transport
Air transport	Refers to the use of airplanes for cargo transportation, which is indispensable for the transportation of valuables, fresh cargoes and precision instruments in international trade, and has the advantage of speedy and flexible. Starting from the nature of air transportation, it is generally divided into domestic and international air transportation
Rail transport	Refers to the use of transportation methods such as vehicle transportation, container transportation or railway "land bridge", and the use of flat cars, gondola cars, tank cars, insulation and refrigerated cars and other railway vehicles in logistics. According to the different modes of operation, railway transportation can be divided into international railway through trasport and domestic railway transportation
Road transport	In medium and short distance transportation, road transportation can realize "door-to-door" direct transportation. It is not only an independent transportation system, but also an indispensable transportation method that connects water and land transportation, air transportation, and railway transportation from the beginning and the end of collection
International multi-modal transport	Refers to the transportation of cargoes in which the multi-modal transport operator transports the cargoes from a take-over location in one country to a designated delivery location in another country by adopting at least two different modes of transportation in accordance with a contract. In international trade, maritime transport occupies a dominant position in international multi-modal transport
Postal transport	The postal departments of various countries carry out the delivery of goods through the conclusion of agreements and conventions. It is a "door-to-door" mode of transportation, and has a wide range of international characteristics, suitable for light weight and small goods
Container transport	It is a modern transportation method that combines scattered goods into large containers with certain specifications and intensity that are used for multi-modal transport

表 5-1　跨境电商运输方式和特征

运输方式	特征
海洋运输	指利用船舶通过海上航道在不同国家和地区的港口之间运送货物的一种方式，是国际物流中最主要的运输方式，包括内河货物运输和海上货物运输，后者又可分为沿海货物运输和国际海上货物运输
航空运输	指利用飞机作为运输工具进行货物运输，是国际贸易中的贵重物品、鲜活货物和精密仪器运输不可或缺的，具有快速、机动的特点。从航空运输的性质出发，一般把航空运输分为国内航空运输和国际航空运输两大类
铁道运输	指采用整车运输、集装箱运输或铁路的"大陆桥"等运输方式，使用平车、散车、罐车、保温及冷藏车等铁道车辆在物流中的应用。铁路运输按经营方式的不同，可分为国际铁路货物联运和国内铁路运输
公路运输	在中、短途运输中，由于公路运输可以实现"门到门"直达运输，既是一个独立的运输体系，也是一个连接水陆运输、航空运输、铁路运输始端和末端集散物资不可或缺的运输方式
国际多式联运	指按照国际多式联运合同，以至少两种不同的运输方式，由多式联运经营人将货物从一国境内的接管地点运至另一国境内指定交付地点的货物运输。在国际贸易中，海运在国际多式联运中占据主导地位
邮政运输	各国邮政部门之间通过订立协定和公约进行货物的传递，是一种"门到门"的运输方式，并具有广泛的国际性，适用于量轻体小的货物
集装箱运输	国际多式联运是将零散的货物合并装入具有一定规格和强度的专为周转而使用的大型货箱进行集中装运的一种现代化运输方式

Table 5-2   The Types of Cross-Border E-Commerce Logistics Transportation

Types	Explanation
International parcel	The cross-border E-commerce import and export logistics transportation methods are set up by the postal system, such as the China Post network, which basically covers the world, but the transportation time is long
International express delivery	UPS, FedEx, DHL and TNT are the four major commercial express companies in the world. The logistics is fast and the customer experience is good, but the price is high
Overseas warehouses	It means that the seller stores the cargoes in the overseas warehouses, and completes the sorting, parceling and delivery of the cargoes according to the order, but is prone to over-stock and high operation and maintenance costs
Cross-border special line logistics	The cargo is transported abroad by chartering, and then the partner company completes the domestic delivery to the destination, achieving cost reduction based on the scale economy effect

表 5-2   跨境电商物流运输类型

类型	解析
国际小包	邮政系统设置的跨境电商进出口物流运输方式，如中国邮政网络基本覆盖全球，但运输时间较长
国际快递	全球四大商业快递公司 UPS、FedEx、DHL 和 TNT。物流速度快、客户体验好，但价格昂贵
海外仓	指卖家先将货物存储到海外仓库，根据订单信息完成货物的分拣、包裹及递送，存在易压货、运维成本高等问题
跨境专线物流	通过包舱方式将货物运输至国外，再通过合作公司完成目的地国内的派送，实现规模效应带来的成本降低

5.1.3   Logistics Scheme Design of Cross-Border E-Commerce

The capability requirements for the design of cross-border E-commerce logistics scheme specifically include three aspects: first, the freight can be calculated correctly according to the order; the second is to combine information such as the volume weight of the order and its destination country, and choose to design a cross-border logistics scheme with a reasonable logistics method; the third is to be able to skillfully use knowledge such as postal logistics, special line logistics and international express delivery to design logistics scheme.

Analysis of factors affecting cross-border E-commerce logistics scheme design contains the scale and strength of cross-border E-commerce companies; the nature of the cargoes (e.g. postal parcels are small, low-priced and compression-resistant, and typical goods include 3C products

5.1.3   跨境电商物流方案设计

跨境电商物流方案设计的能力要求具体包含三个方面：一是能够根据订单情况，正确计算运费；二是能结合订单产品体积重量和订单运达目的国等信息，选择设计跨境物流方案、合理选择跨境物流方式；三是能够熟练运用邮政物流、专线物流国际快递等知识进行物流方案设计。

跨境电商物流方案设计影响因素的分析包含跨境电商公司的规模和实力；货物性质（如邮政小包是小型、低价和抗压的，典型的货物有 3C 产品等）；商业快递

etc.; commercial express delivery is suitable for mobile phones, computers and high-tech products with higher value, lighter weight and items that upgrade fast; overseas warehouses are suitable for large items such as furniture, large machines, and private luxury yachts); logistics timeliness (overseas warehouses or international express delivery should be selected for items needed to be delivered in a very short time, and postal parcels are suitable for those items with lower requirement for time); logistics costs (total logistics cost = inventory costs + all costs incurred during transportation + batch costs + customer maintenance costs + order processing and information collection and processing costs + fixed and variable costs of the storage); resource support of the cross-border E-commerce platforms.

Sellers should develop logistics plans applicable to B2C platform shop, taking AliExpress as an example. Step 1: visit the website of AliExpress, enter the seller backstage of AliExpress platform, select "shipping template" from the "product management" page, and click to enter "logistics plan selection" and "list of logistics plans". Step 2: on the query page of logistics plan, figure out the corresponding logistics scheme for reference based on the receiving place, cargo type (general cargo, electrified cargo, pure electric cargo, liquid cargo, etc.), cargo value, and package information (weight, length, width and height).

Example: Take a package sent by an electronics company in Shenzhen, China to Spain as an example. The value of this batch is 28 Euros, weighs 120 grams, and the package is 12 cm long, 5 cm wide, and 7 cm high. The logistics solution will be provided by the platform by querying.

Sellers should develop logistics plans applicable to B2B platform shops, taking Alibaba as an example. The Alibaba OneTouch International Logistics Platform mainly provides logistics plans for B2B sellers such as sea, air, express and land transportation (trailers, railways).

适用于价值较高、重量较轻、更新换代较快的手机、计算机和高科技产品等物品；海外仓适用于家具类、大型机器、私人豪华游艇类的大件物品）；物流时效（对于顾客要求在极短时间内运送到的物品，可以选择海外仓或者国际快递，邮政小包适用于对时间要求不高的物品）；物流成本（物流总成本＝库存费用＋运输过程发生的所有费用＋批量的费用＋顾客维持费＋订单处理和信息收集处理费＋仓储的固定费用和变动费用）；跨境电商平台本身的资源支持。

卖家应制定适用 B2C 平台店铺的物流方案，以阿里巴巴速卖通为例。步骤1：访问速卖通网站，进入阿里巴巴速卖通平台的卖家后台，在"产品管理"页面中选择"运费模板"，单击进入"物流方案选择""物流方案例表"。步骤2：在物流方案查询页面，根据收货地、货物类型（普通货物、带电货物、纯电货物、液体货物等）、货物价值、包裹信息（重量、长宽高）等查询对应可供参考的物流方案。

举例：以中国深圳某电子公司发往西班牙的一个包裹为例。该批货物的价值为28欧元，重120g，包裹长12cm，宽5cm，高7cm。查询即能得到平台提供的物流方案。

卖家应制定 B2B 平台店铺适用的物流方案，以阿里巴巴国际站为例。阿里巴巴一达通国际物流平台主要提供海运、空运、快递、陆运（拖车、铁路）等物流方案供 B2B 卖家选择。

5.2　Calculation of Cross-Border Logistics Freight

5.2.1　Cross-Border Container Freight

The freight rate system for cross-border container cargoes is basically divided into two methods for calculating the freight charges, namely the unit of freight per ton (commonly known as the break bulk cargo price) and the unit of charge per container (commonly known as the container price).

Break bulk cargo freight contains basic rate and the surcharge. The basic rate is based on the traditional freight of break bulk cargo, and the unit is calculated in tons of freight. Most routes use class rates. The surcharge refers to additional charge related to the transportation of containerized cargo in addition to the conventional surcharges charged by traditional bulk cargo.

The container rate is based on each container as the charging unit. It is often used in the case of container delivery, namely Container Freight Station-Container Yard (CFS-CY) or Container Yard-Container Yard (CY-CY) clauses. The common container rate has the following three manifestations: the first is Freight for All Kinds (FAK), that is, the freight rate is uniformly charged for each container without subdividing the category of cargoes in the box and excluding the volume of the cargoes (within the required limit). The second is the Freight for Class (FCS), that is, the package rate is based on different cargo classes. The classification of general cargo in containers is the same as that of bulk cargo transportation, which is still 1-20. The third is the Freight for Class or Basis (FCB), that is, the container rate is formulated according to different cargo grades or categories and calculation standards.

5.2.2　Logistics Freight of Cross-Border Small Package

Cross-border small package, also called international

5.2　跨境物流运费计算

5.2.1　跨境集装箱运费

跨境集装箱货物运价体系基本上分为散货运费计算方法，即以每吨为运费计算单位（俗称散货价），和以每个集装箱收费为计费单位（俗称包箱价）两种。

散货运费包括基本费率和附加费。基本费率基于传统散货运价，以吨为运费计算单位。多数航线上采用等级费率。附加费指除传统散货所收的常规附加费外，还要加收一些与集装箱货物运输有关的附加费。

集装箱费率以每个集装箱为计费单位。它常用于集装箱交货的情况，即集装箱货运站到集装箱码头堆场交接（CFS-CY）或集装箱码头堆场到集装箱码头堆场交接（CY-CY）条款。常见的集装箱费率有以下三种表现形式：一是 FAK 集装，即对每个集装箱不细分箱内货类，不计货量（在重要限额之内）统一收取的运价。二是 FCS 集装，即按不同货物等级制定的集装箱费率。集装箱普通货物的等级划分与散货运输划分一样，仍是 1 ～ 20 级。三是 FCB 集装，即按不同货物等级或货类及计算标准制定的集装箱费率。

5.2.2　跨境小包物流运费

跨境小包，也称国际邮政小

postal parcel, mainly refers to a type of express that is limited to less than 2 kg, the total length, width and height of the outer package is less than 90 cm, and the longest one side is less than 60 cm, which is sent to various regions of the world by international post. There are two main types of cross-border small package: regular mail and registered parcels. The regular postage is low, and there is no registration fee, or tracking inquiry service. Postal registered parcels can provide inquiry and tracking services, and the price is 8 Yuan registration fee more than the regular mail, which can generally be tracked on the postal parcel official website (Table 5-3) .

包，主要指在 2kg 以下，外包装长宽高之和小于 90cm，且最长边小于 60cm，通过国际邮政邮寄到全球各个地区的一种快递。跨境小包分为两种主要类别：平邮小包和挂号小包。平邮费用低，没有挂号费，没有跟踪查询服务。邮政挂号小包可以提供查询和跟踪服务，其挂号费比平邮小包多 8 元，一般可在邮政小包官网进行跟踪（表 5-3）。

Table 5-3　Cross-Border Parcel Types and Logistics Freight

Freight calculation for regular parcels	Basic formula: regular mail freight = standard freight × actual weight × discount
	Example: a shipment to the United States weighs 200 grams, the current discount is 20% off, and the standard shipping fee is 78.5 Yuan/kg. Please calculate the regular shipping fee
	Regular postage freight: 78.5 × 200 ÷ 1000 × 0.8 = 12.56 (Yuan)
Freight calculation for registered parcels	Basic formula: registered parcel freight = standard freight × actual weight × discount + registration fee (8 Yuan)
	Example: a shipment to the United Kingdom weighs 200 grams, the current discount is 78%, and the standard shipping fee is 80.5 Yuan/kg. Please calculate the registered parcel shipping fee, with 8 Yuan registration fee
	Registered parcel freight: 80.5 × 200 ÷ 1000 × 0.78 + 8 ≈ 20.56 (Yuan)

表 5-3　跨境小包类型及物流运费

平邮小包运费计算	基本公式：平邮运费 = 标准运费 × 实际重量 × 折扣
	举例：一件运往美国的货物，重 200g，当前折扣为 8 折，标准运费为 78.5 元 /kg，请计算平邮运费
	平邮运费：78.5×200÷1000×0.8=12.56（元）
挂号小包运费计算	基本公式：挂号小包运费 = 标准运费 × 实际重量 × 折扣 + 挂号费（8 元）
	举例：一件运往英国的货物，重 200g，当前折扣为 7.8 折，标准运费为 80.5 元 /kg，请计算挂号小包运费，挂号费为 8 元
	挂号小包运费：80.5×200÷1000×0.78+8 ≈ 20.56（元）

5.2.3　International Commercial Express Freight

The four major international commercial express delivery are different in terms of timeliness, logistics services, international freight, and charging standards (Table 5-4).

5.2.3　国际商业快递运费

四大国际商业快递在时效、物流服务、国际运费、收费标准方面存在区别（表 5-4）。

Table 5-4   Freight of Four Major International Commercial Express Companies (Global Forwarding)

DHL	The charging weight is generally in units of 0.5kg
	First standard weight and additional weight: the first 0.5 kg is the first standard weight, and 0.5 kg is a continuation weight
	Chargeable weight: the weight of the freight charged during the transportation of the cargoes is calculated based on the larger one of the actual weight and volume weight
UPS	Basic charges: according to different regions, cargoes and services, etc., there are corresponding standards for each, please check the official website for details
	Fuel surcharge: it is within 19%-25% of the freight value, which is adjusted once a month
	Delivery surcharge: remote areas are settled according to the actual weight, 3.50 Yuan per kilogram, and the minimum charge is 171 Yuan
FedEx	According to the increase of 0.5 kg in weight, the charge is different; and it is charged based on the larger one of the actual weight and volume
TNT	Volume calculation: length × width × height ÷ 6 000 = volume weight, and charge according to volume weight
	Insurance fee: 3% of the declared value of the cargoes, with a minimum of 100 Yuan per shipment
	Safety surcharge, fuel surcharge: depending on the situation of the month, please check the official website for details

表 5-4   国际四大商业快递运费（国际快递）

DHL	计费重量单位一般以每 0.5kg 为一个计费重量单位
	首重与续重：以第一个 0.5kg 为首重，0.5kg 为一个续重
	计费重量：货物运输过程中收取的运费按整批货物的实际重量与体积重量两者中最高的计算
UPS	基本收费：根据运往的地区不同、运送的货物不同、相应的服务不同等，各有相应标准，具体查询官网
	燃油附加费：每月调整一次，为货运价值的 19% ～ 25%
	派送附加费：偏远地区按照实际重量结算，3.50 元 /kg，最低收取 171 元
FedEx	按照重量每增加 0.5kg 上升一档，收费不同；实际重量和体积按值大者计费
TNT	体积计算：长 × 宽 × 高 ÷ 6 000= 体积重量，并按体积重量收费
	保险费：以货物申报价值的 3% 收取，最低每票起保 100 元
	安全附加费、燃油附加费：视当月情况而定，具体查询官网

Knowledge Extension: Characteristics of DHL Logistics
Solutions from DHL are powered by trade, logistics and the drive and passion of all their employees. In every country, across all divisions at DHL, they have the potential to make a global difference. But there's more to a role at DHL than the work they do. Whether you're a global manager or a marketing assistant, driving a forklift or flying an airplane, they never forget that it's you who makes them who they are. That's why they all work as hard as possible on the team to satisfy customers and achieve maximum success.

知识拓展：DHL 物流特点
　　DHL 的解决方案由贸易、物流及所有员工的干劲和热情提供支持。在每个国家，DHL 所有部门的员工都有可能改变世界。DHL 员工从事的不仅仅是工作。无论你是全球经理还是营销助理，是开叉车还是开飞机，他们都不会忘记是你成就了他们。这就是他们在团队中都努力工作、尽可能让客户满意并取得最大成功的原因。

5.3 Logistics and Freight Calculation of Overseas Warehouse

5.3.1 Concept and Process of Overseas Warehouse

In cross-border E-commerce, overseas warehouse refers to domestic companies transporting cargoes to target market countries in the form of bulk transportation, establishing warehouses and storing cargoes locally, and then directly conducting sorting, packaging and distribution from local warehouses to meet the needs of local sales orders. The digital logistics system of overseas warehouses promotes the upgrading of the cross-border E-commerce industry chain. Using data to manage logistics and analyse time point data in the process will help sellers find problems in the distribution process and finished product delivery process, and improve efficiency in supply chain management, inventory level control, and dynamic sales management.

The specific process includes: firstly, the seller transports the cargoes to an overseas storage center, or entrusts a logistics service provider to send the cargoes to its overseas warehouse. This first journey of international freight can reach the warehouse by sea or air express. Secondly, sellers manage overseas warehousing remotely online and keep real-time updates. Furthermore, operations such as storage, sorting, packaging, and distribution of cargoes are carried out according to the seller's instructions. Finally, the system information is updated in real time so that the seller can grasp the inventory status.

5.3.2 The First Journey Freight of International Transportation by Sea or by Air

The first journey freight of international transport means the first-haul transportation costs paid by Chinese exporters to transport cargoes from China to overseas warehouses such as Amazon FBA warehouses or exporters' own overseas warehouses by sea, air or express.

5.3 海外仓物流和运费计算

5.3.1 海外仓概念及流程

在跨境电商中，海外仓是指国内企业将商品以大宗运输的形式运往目标市场国家，在当地建立仓库、储存商品，然后根据当地的销售订单，及时从当地仓库直接进行分拣、包装与配送。海外仓的数据化物流体系带动跨境电商产业链的升级。通过数据管理物流，分析流程中的时间点数据，有利于卖家在配送过程、成品发货流程等方面找出问题，在供应链管理、库存水平管控、动销管理等方面提高效率。

具体流程包含：首先，卖家将商品运至海外仓储中心，或者委托物流服务商将货发至服务商的海外仓库。这段国际货运头程可采取海运、空运快递的方式将货送达仓库。其次，卖家在线远程管理海外仓储，并保持实时更新。再次，根据卖家指令进行货物的存储、分拣、包装、配送等操作。最后，实时更新系统信息，以便卖家掌握库存状况。

5.3.2 国际海运与空运头程运费

国际海运与空运头程运费指中国出口商将货物从国内通过海运、空运或者快递等方式运到海外仓库，例如亚马逊的 FBA 仓或者出口商自有海外仓，所支付的头程运费。

1．The first journey freight of international transportation by sea

The shipping process contains packaged delivery → shipment → set sail → sea transportation → arrival at the destination port → destination customs clearance → delivery → receiving and signing → putting on shelves. International shipping is divided into Haipai and Haika, and Table 5-5 illustrates the differences between these two.

2．The first journey freight of international transportation by air

The air transportation process is making a delivery → take-off → transfer → airport → customs clearance → dispatch → sign for the cargo → put-away. The general freight rate is the most widely used rate in the IATA (International Air Transport Association) rate. Under normal circumstances, the freight rate of general cargo is divided into several important grades of demarcation point freight rates according to the weight of the cargoes. According to the order of weight points, the freight rate structure is as follows: M means the minimum freight rate; Q represents the freight rate at the cut-off point of all weight classes above 45kg, for instance, Q45 represents the freight rate of general cargo above 45 kg (including 45 kg), Q100, Q300 etc.

1．国际海运头程运费

海运流程为打包发货→装船→开船→海上运输→到达目的地港口→目的地清关→派送→签收→上架。国际海运有海派和海卡之分，具体差异见表 5-5。

2．国际空运头程运费

空运流程为发货→起飞→中转→机场→清关→派送→签收→上架。普通货物运价是国际航协（国际航空运输协会）运价中使用最为广泛的一种运价。一般情况下，普通货物运价根据货物重量再分为若干个重要等级分界点运价。按重量分界点顺序，其运价结构如下：M 表示最低运价；Q 后面加 45 或更大的数字表示 45kg 以上或者更大重量以上各种重量等级的分界点运价，例如 Q45 表示 45kg 以上（包括 45kg）的普通货物运价，Q100、Q300 等，以此类推。

Table 5-5　Comparison between Haipai and Haika

Type	Definition	Channel of maritime transport	Characteristics	Charging standard	Weight carrying capacity
Haipai	Courier delivery	Express ship	Fast delivery	Kilogram; adopt the larger one between actual weight and volume weight	21 kilograms
Haika	Truck delivery	Slow ship	Slower delivery, but lower tariff	Cubic meter; the volume weight of the cargo is not calculated	5 cubic meters

表 5-5　海派与海卡的差异

类型	定义	海上运输渠道	特征	计费标准	起重
海派	尾程采用快递派送	快船	快速送达	以 kg 为计费单位；以实际重量与体积重量中较大者为计费标准	21kg
海卡	尾程采用卡车派送	慢船	较慢送达，但关税较低	以 m³ 为计费单位；不计算货物的体积重量	5m³

Exercise: A box of fabrics sent from Shenzhen to Jingdong. The gross weight is 28.4 kg and the volume size is 82 cm × 48 cm × 32 cm. Try to calculate the air freight for the cargo.

Volume is: 82cm×48cm×32cm=125 952cm³.

Volume weight is: 125 952cm³÷6 000cm³/kg=21.0kg.

Chargeable weight is: 28.5kg (28.4kg carry).

(Because the volume weight 21.0kg is less than the actual gross weight 28.4kg, the larger value should be used.)

Applicable rate is: GCRN (General Cargo Rate Normal) = 38.67Yuan/kg.

Air freight weight charge is: 28.5×38.67=1 102 (Yuan).

5.3.3　The Local Logistics Fee of Overseas Warehouse

Overseas warehouse fee = first journey fee + handling fee + storage fee + last-mile freight + tariff / value-added tax / miscellaneous fees.

First journey fee is the expense during the handling that the seller ships the goods to the overseas warehouse in destination country through air transport, and sea transport in bulk or in containers. Handling fees include warehouse entry fees, warehouse exit fees, and order processing fees. Storage fee is the cost of storing and managing the cargoes, and generally the storage fee in the second half of the year will be higher. Last-mile freight is the local delivery freight.

The local logistics costs depend on the weight, value, volume, particularity, delivery distance and other factors of the cargoes, and have nothing to do with the order batch. We should consider how to reduce local logistics and distribution costs from a policy perspective.

Take the local logistics and transportation in the United States as an example, and make the comparison among USPS, UPS and FedEx as the following (Table5-6) .

试计算：由深圳发往京东一箱布料，毛重为 28.4kg，体积尺寸为 82cm×48cm×32cm，试计算该票货物的航空运费。

体积为：82cm×48cm×32cm=125 952cm³。

体积重量为：125952cm³÷6 000cm³/kg=21.0kg。

计费重量为：28.5kg（28.4kg 进位）。

（因体积重量 21.0kg 小于实际毛重 28.4kg，故取大值。）

适用运价为：GCRN（General Cargo Rate Normal，标准普通货物运价）=38.67 元 /kg。

航空运费为：28.5×38.67=1 102（元）。

5.3.3　海外仓的本地物流费用

海外仓费用=头程费用+处理费+仓储费+尾程运费+关税 /增值税 / 杂费。

头程费用指卖家将物品运送到海外仓的目的国，分为空运、海运散货、海运整柜等。处理费包含入库费用、出库费用、订单处理费。仓储费指仓储及管理货物产生的费用，一般下半年的仓储费会更高。尾程运费是本地派送运费。

本地物流费用取决于货物的重量、价值、体积、特殊性、配送距离等因素，与订货批量无关。应从政策上考虑如何降低本地物流配送成本。

以美国本地物流与运输为例，比较 USPS、UPS 和 FedEx（表5-6）。

Table 5-6　Comparison among USPS, UPS and FedEx

Local logistics and transportation in USA	USPS	UPS	FedEx
Domestic mailing options	Priority Express-Next day, Priority-1-3 working days, First Class-Regular mail	Express Critical-Same day, Next Day Air-Next day, 2nd Day Air-2 working days, 3 Day Select-3 working days , Ground-5 working days	Same Day, Overnight-Next day, 2 Day-2 working days, Express Saver-3 working days, Ground-7 working days

表 5-6　比较 USPS、UPS 和 FedEx

美国本地物流运输方式	USPS（美国邮政）	UPS（联合包裹服务）	FedEx（联邦快递）
境内邮寄选项	隔日、1～3 个工作日、平邮	同日、隔日、2 个工作日、3 个工作日、5 个工作日	同日、隔日、2 个工作日、3 个工作日、7 个工作日

Knowledge Extension: The Benefits of Using FBA

The benefits of using FBA include:

- Free shipping on eligible orders: With FBA, your products are eligible for Amazon Prime free Two-Day Shipping, and all Amazon.com customers can get free shipping on eligible orders.

- Customer service and returns: Amazon provides customer service on your behalf and handles returns for FBA orders.

- Opportunities to reach new customers: Programs such as FBA Subscribe & Save, FBA Small and Light, Multi-Channel Fulfillment, and FBA Export can help you maximize sales and build customer loyalty.

- Tools to help you manage your business: Choose from optional services including product preparation, labeling and repackaging, and Amazon partnered carrier options.

知识拓展：FBA 发货优点

使用 FBA 的好处如下。

- 符合条件的订单免运费：使用 FBA，您的产品有资格享受 Amazon Prime 免费两日送货服务，并且所有 Amazon.com 客户都可以获得符合条件的订单免费送货服务。

- 客户服务和退货：亚马逊将代表您提供客户服务并处理 FBA 订单的退货。

- 接触新客户的机会：FBA 订购与节约谋划、FBA 轻小商品计划、多渠道配送和亚马逊物流出口等计划可以帮助您最大限度地提高销售额并建立客户忠诚度。

- 帮助您管理业务的工具：从可选服务中进行选择，包括产品准备、标签和重新包装，以及亚马逊合作承运商选项。

New words

1. international shipping and air freight for the first journey 国际海运与空运头程运费
2. customs clearance 清关
3. chargeable weight 计费重量
4. international multi-modal transport 国际多式联运
5. oversea warehouse 海外仓
6. cross-border small package 跨境小包
7. storage fee 仓储费
8. LCL（Less than Container Load）拼箱
9. FCL（Full Container Load）整箱
10. bulk cargo 散货
11. digital logistics system 数字化物流体系
12. compression-resistant 抗压、耐压
13. regular mail 平邮
14. standard freight 标准运费
15. surcharge 附加费
16. terminal yard 集装箱码头堆场

Chapter 6

Customs Clearance Practice for Cross-Border E-Commerce

第 6 章 跨境电商通关实务

Lead-in case

After understanding the logistics methods and freight standard of various cross-border E-commerce platforms, Xiaowei chose a suitable logistics solution. Next, Xiaowei will face the procedures for exporting commodities, which are the country's management requirements for cross-border trade. Therefore, Xiaowei needs to understand the organization of cross-border E-commerce import and export management and the management system of cross-border E-commerce import and export. After studying this chapter, you will work with Xiaowei to have a preliminary understanding of the role of customs in cross-border E-commerce import and export, customs functions and cross-border customs clearance models.

Learning objectives

1. Objectives of knowledge

(1) To know the institutional framework and main duties of customs.

(2) To know the organizational reform of customs.

(3) To know related regulatory policies for cross-border E-commerce import and export customs clearance.

(4) To know tax policies related to import and export of cross-border E-commerce.

2. Objectives of skills

(1) To be able to handle the filing procedures for cross-border E-commerce import and export business.

(2) To be able to carry out import and export declarations for cross-border E-commerce products according to different regulatory methods.

(3) To be able to correctly calculate import and export taxes and fees for cross-border E-commerce.

(4) To be able to correctly fill in the cross-border

案例导入

小薇在了解了各个跨境电商平台的物流方式和运费标准之后，选择了合适的物流方案。接下来，小薇面临的是办理商品出口的手续，这是国家对于跨境贸易的管理要求。因此，小薇需要了解跨境电商进出口管理的机构，以及跨境电商进出口的管理制度。通过本章学习，你将与小薇一起初步了解海关在跨境电商进出口中的作用、海关的职能和跨境通关模式等。

学习目标

1. 知识目标

（1）了解海关组织机构及基本职能。

（2）了解海关机构改革。

（3）了解跨境电商进出口通关的相关监管政策。

（4）了解跨境电商进出口税收政策。

2. 技能目标

（1）能够办理跨境电商进出口业务的备案手续。

（2）能够针对不同监管方式进行跨境电商商品的进出口申报。

（3）能够正确计算跨境电商进出口税费。

（4）能够正确填写跨境电商

E-commerce import and export declaration list.

3．Objectives of qualities

(1) To have a patient, detailed and rigorous work style.

(2) To have the spirit of abiding by laws and regulations related to foreign trade and self-discipline.

(3) To have good leadership in communication and coordination, decision-making, analysis and judgment, motivation, etc.

(4) To have a long-lasting interest and the transformational power in new knowledge and skills.

6.1　A Brief Introduction to the Customs Declaration of Cross-Border E-Commerce

6.1.1　The Customs and Inspection and Quarantine

1．Institutional framework of the customs

The Customs of the People's Republic of China is the state's entry and exit customs supervision and management authority. In accordance with this law and other relevant laws and administrative regulations, the customs supervises the inbound and outbound means of transport, goods, luggage, postal items and other items, collects customs duties and other taxes, investigates smuggling, compiles customs statistics and handles other customs operations. The highest leading agency of the customs is the General Administration of Customs. it is an agency directly under the State Council of the People's Republic of China at the ministerial level, and manages customs across the country in a unified manner. The General Administration of Customs currently has 21 internal departments, 13 directly affiliated institutions, manages 2 social groups (the Customs Association and the China Entry and Exit Biosafety Research Association), and dispatches customs agencies in the European Union and the Chinese Hong Kong Special Administrative Region. The Central Commission for Discipline Inspection and the Ministry of Supervision dispatch the Disciplinary Inspection Team and the Supervision Bureau to the General Administration of Customs. At present, there are 47 directly-affiliated customs units (Guangdong branch, Tianjin and Shanghai special

进出口申报清单。

3．素质目标

（1）具有耐心、细致、严谨的工作作风。

（2）具有遵守外贸相关法律法规和自律精神。

（3）具有良好的沟通协调、决策、分析判断、激励等领导力。

（4）具有对新知识、新技能持久的学习兴趣和变革力。

6.1　跨境电商报关概述

6.1.1　海关与检验检疫

1．海关的组织机构

中华人民共和国海关是国家的进出境监督管理机关。海关依照本法和其他有关法律、行政法规，监管进出境的运输工具、货物、行李物品、邮递物品和其他物品，征收关税和其他税费，查缉走私，并编制海关统计和办理其他海关业务。海关的最高领导机构为海关总署。海关总署是中华人民共和国国务院下属的正部级直属机构，统一管理全国海关。海关总署现有21个内设部门、13个直属事业单位、管理2个社会团体（海关学会和中国进出境生物安全研究会），并在欧盟和中国香港特别行政区派驻海关机构。中央纪委、监察部在海关总署派驻纪检组、监察局。全国海关目前共有47个直属海关单位（广东分署，天津、上海特派办，42个直属海关，2所海关院校），超过740个隶属海关和办事处。中国海关现有关员（含海关缉私警察）

offices, 42 directly-affiliated customs offices, and 2 customs colleges), and more than 740 subordinate customs and offices in national customs. China Customs currently has about 60,000 officers (including customs anti-smuggling police). The customs implements a vertical leadership system and is not restricted by local administrative divisions.

2．Powers of the customs

According to the *Customs Law* and other laws and regulations, the powers of the customs include the power of formulating administrative regulations, the power of administrative license, the power of collecting taxes and fees, the power of administrative supervision and inspection, the power of administrative compulsion, the power of wearing and using weapons, the power of administrative penalty, the power of administrative reconsideration and other administrative processing powers.

3．Inspection and quarantine department and the customs

From April 20, 2018, the former China Entry-Exit Inspection and Quarantine Department was officially integrated into China Customs, and China Entry-Exit Inspection and Quarantine Department was unified to carry out work in the name of Customs. After the integration, the entry-exit inspection and quarantine department was merged from the original 9 links to 5 links. Entry includes: customs originally had 4 links, including declaration, on-site investigation, inspection and disposal; inspection and quarantine department originally had 5 links, including health quarantine, declaration, on-site investigation, inspection and disposal, and there are 9 links in all, with 4 combined links, and 5 links of health quarantine, declaration, on-site investigation, inspection and disposal are retained. Exit includes: customs originally had 4 links of declaration, on-site investigation, inspection, and disposal; inspection and quarantine department originally had 4 links of health and quarantine, on-site investigation, inspection and disposal, there are 8 links in all, with 3 combined links, and 5 links of health and quarantine, declaration, on-site research, inspection, and disposal are retained. At the same time, the customs and the original passenger channel of inspection and quarantine department will be merged, the supervision and

约 6 万人。海关实行垂直领导体制，不受地方行政区划限制。

2．海关的权力

根据《海关法》（注：全称为《中华人民共和国海关法》）及其他法律法规，海关的权力包括行政法规制定权、行政许可权、税费征收权、行政监督检查权、行政强制权、佩带和使用武器权、行政处罚权、行政复议权和其他行政处理权。

3．检验检疫部门与海关

自 2018 年 4 月 20 日起，原中国出入境检验检疫部门正式并入中国海关，中国出入境检验检疫部门统一以海关名义对外开展工作。合并后，出入境检验检疫部门由原来 9 个环节合并成 5 个环节。入境包括：海关原有申报、现场调研、查验、处置 4 个环节；检验检疫部门原有卫生检疫、申报、现场调研、查验、处置 5 个环节；共计 9 个环节，合并 4 个环节，保留卫生检疫、申报、现场调研、查验、处置 5 个环节。出境包括：海关原有申报、现场调研、查验、处置 4 个环节；检验检疫部门原有卫生检疫、现场调研、查验、处置 4 个环节；共计 8 个环节，合并 3 个环节，保留卫生检疫、申报、现场调研、查验、处置 5 个环节。同时，海关与检验检疫部门的原旅客通道合并，监管检查设备统一使用，行李物

inspection equipment will be used uniformly, and the luggage will only be inspected once. Institutions use customs logos uniformly to the outside world, and set up uniform policy publicity facilities.

6.1.2 Customs Declaration Platform for Cross-Border E-Commerce

1. General introduction of single window

Cross-border E-commerce is the onlineization of import and export commodity transactions. In fact, China's export trade process is also being online and digitized. This process may have a profound impact on the entire export ecology, and single window is one of the important models for online export trade.

Single window is a new attempt by Hangzhou as a pilot city for cross-border E-commerce trade. Its background is United Nations advocacy and United Nations trade facilitation. *Recommendation No. 33 of the United Nations Center for Trade Facilitation and Electronic Business* defines a single window as a single platform for all parties involved in international trade and transportation to provide standardized information and documents to meet national laws, regulations and needs.

The single window has three core elements: one-time declaration, standard data source, and submission through a unified data platform.

The single window has three basic characteristics:

First, it becomes the data exchange hub and comprehensive management service platform of the comprehensive pilot area.

Second, it provides efficient and convenient government services. The single window is a one-time declaration, and as far as possible, enterprises can make one declaration, one inspection, and one pass.

Third, it creates comprehensive service functions such as logistics, finance, and service agency, that is, to comprehensively use the accumulated data of the single window.

Advantages of single window declaration are: improved

品只接受一次查验。机构对外统一使用海关标识,设置统一的政策宣传设施。

6.1.2 跨境电商报关平台

1. 单一窗口的概况

跨境电商是将进出口商品交易线上化。实际上,中国出口贸易流程也正在实现线上化和数据化。这一流程或对整个出口生态带来深远的影响,而单一窗口则是出口贸易实现线上化的重要模式之一。

单一窗口是杭州作为跨境电商贸易试点城市的新尝试。其背景是联合国倡导、联合国贸易便利化。《联合国贸易便利化和电子商务中心第33号建议书》对单一窗口的定义是参与国际贸易及运输的各方通过单一平台提出标准化信息和单证,来满足国家的法律法规及需要。

单一窗口有三个核心元素:一次申报、标准数据源、通过统一数据平台递交。

单一窗口具有三个基本特征:

第一,成为综合试验区数据交换枢纽和综合管理服务平台。

第二,提供高效便捷的政务服务。单一窗口是一次申报,尽可能让企业做到一次申报、一次查验、一次通过等。

第三,创造物流、金融、服务代理等综合服务功能,也就是把单一窗口这些沉淀的数据综合运用。

单一窗口的申报优势为:提

enterprise efficiency, paperless throughout the process, one-time declaration, one-time release, etc. But the current single window has not fully achieved the listing goal, this is the ultimate goal of the single window.

A single window comprehensive service platform, the market is mainly connected to logistics companies, E-commerce platforms, and tripartite operating agencies. The background is connected with customs, inspection and quarantine department, and State Taxation Administration. At the same time, the single window has also achieved data docking with various local government departments in Hangzhou. At present, the single window platform has nearly 200 million pieces of data.

Taking Hangzhou as an example, more than 7,000 enterprises have registered and filed in a single window, among which E-commerce platforms or B2C E-commerce enterprises are the main ones. In addition, there are warehousing enterprises, foreign trade agency enterprises, etc., with nearly 2,500 B2B enterprises. From January to June 2020, the number of export orders through the single window in six months was 14.51 million, and the number of import orders was 15.57 million.

2. Main functions of single window

(1) Data platform.

The single window is a data-based platform, and data overlay can be better used. There are two portal websites for the single window: one is the portal website of the comprehensive pilot area; the other is the platform portal of the single window.

(2) Information sharing system.

First, export B2C business. The pilot project started in 2012, and the single window export B2C business has been very mature. At present, it has achieved three-flow integration (transaction flow, logistics flow and capital flow) and three-order preparation control. This kind of control means that after the E-commerce enterprises sends the order and logistics flow data to the single window, the single window pushes the standard index data to inspection and quarantine department and customs, and the real-time status of all exports will be

高企业效率、全程无纸化、一次申报、一次放行等。然而，目前的单一窗口还没完全实现上市目标，但这是单一窗口的终极目标。

单一窗口综合服务平台，市场端主要接入物流企业、电商平台、三方运营机构等。后台对接海关、检验检疫部门、国家税务总局。与此同时，单一窗口还和杭州市地方各个政府部门实现数据对接。目前，单一窗口平台已经有近2亿条数据。

以杭州为例，已经有7 000多家企业在单一窗口注册和备案，其中以电商平台或 B2C 电商企业为主。除此之外，还有仓储企业、外贸代理企业等，B2B 企业达到近2 500家。从 2020 年 1 月到 6 月份，在 6 个月的时间内通过单一窗口的出口单量为 1451 万单，进口单量为 1557 万单。

2．单一窗口的主要功能

（1）数据平台。

单一窗口是一个数据化平台，可以更好地使用数据叠加。单一窗口有两个门户网站：一是综合试验区门户网站；二是单一窗口的平台门户。

（2）信息共享体系。

第一，出口 B2C 业务。2012年开始试点，单一窗口出口 B2C 业务已经做得非常成熟了。目前，已经实现三流合一（交易流、物流和资金流）、三单备控。三单备控是指电商企业把订单和物流数据发送到单一窗口以后，单一窗口按照标准的指量数据推送给检验检疫部门和海关，所有出口的

returned to the single window.

Second, import B2C business. The single window platform carries out data push, one declaration and one release.

Third, cross-border B2B import and export business. In this link, there are three conditions: one is the certification of the E-commerce platform; the second is the verification of the three orders information; the third is the specific customs declaration mark. (Three orders refer to platform orders, logistics orders, and payment orders.)

Fourth, this year's single window has developed a convenient tax rebate function on the basis of last year, which is "Internet + convenient tax rebate". Many original enterprises engaged in B2B export of cross-border E-commerce finally give up the tax rebate due to its considerable details. The single window platform hopes to be able to carry out diversified matching to ensure the smooth progress of tax rebates.

Fifth, online foreign exchange collection of single window. Now it is gradually in deep docking. The advantage of Internet is full coverage. After a certain degree of coverage, this system will be very simple.

Sixth, statistical monitoring of a single window. Because the statistics of cross-border E-commerce has always been a difficult problem, the General Administration of Customs pays more attention to trade reciprocity between countries, but many cross-border E-commerce orders leave the country in the form of small parcels. Taking Hangzhou as an example, the cross-border E-commerce export value of Hangzhou in 2019 was US$6 billion, which basically reached about 13% of the total export value. The conclusion reached by the General Administration of Customs through sample survey analysis and the export data obtained through a single window are basically unanimous, and it is also recognized that Hangzhou's statistical standards, including the recognition of cross-border B2B and B2C, are relatively scientific and accurate.

实时状况会回传单一窗口。

第二，进口 B2C 业务。单一窗口平台进行数据推送，一次申报、一次放行。

第三，跨境 B2B 进出口业务。在这个环节上，有三个条件：一是电商平台认证；二是三单信息印证；三是特定报关标识。（三单指平台订单、物流订单、支付订单）

第四，今年单一窗口在去年的基础上开发了便利化退税功能，即"互联网＋便利化退税"。原来做跨境电商 B2B 出口的，因为退税涉及的细项非常多，导致很多企业最后放弃了退税。单一窗口这个平台就是希望能够进行多元化匹配，确保退税顺利进行。

第五，单一窗口在线收汇。现在逐步正在深部对接中，互联网优势就是全覆盖，覆盖到一定程度以后，这个体系会非常简单。

第六，单一窗口的统计监测。因为跨境电商的数据统计一直是一个难题，海关总署更多关注国与国之间的贸易对等，但很多跨境电商订单是通过行邮小包的形式出境的。以杭州为例，2019 年杭州全市跨境电商出口 60 亿美元，基本上达到了整个出口额 13% 左右。海关总署通过抽样调查分析达到的结论和通过单一窗口获得的出口数据基本上一致，也认定了杭州的统计标准，包括对跨境 B2B、B2C 的认定，相对而言还是比较科学和准确的。

6.2　Customs Supervision of Import and Export Commodities in Cross-Border E-Commerce

6.2.1　Supervision of Cross-Border E-Commerce B2C Import and Export Commodities

1.　The difference between customs declaration under cross-border E-commerce and traditional trade

Before the declaration of cross-border E-commerce retail imports, E-commerce enterprises or E-commerce transaction platform enterprises, payment enterprises, and logistics enterprises shall truthfully transmit transaction, payment, logistics and other electronic information to the customs through the cross-border E-commerce customs clearance service platform. Inbound and outbound express operators and postal enterprises may be entrusted by E-commerce enterprises and payment enterprises to transmit electronic information such as transactions and payments to the customs on the premise of undertaking in writing to assume corresponding legal responsibility for the authenticity of the transmitted data.

E-commerce enterprises or their agents should submit the *Declaration List of Cross-border E-commerce Retail Import and Export Commodities of the Customs of the People's Republic of China* (hereinafter referred to as the *Declaration List*). Exports are handled in the form of "release according to list, summarize declaration in total". For imports, customs declaration procedures shall be handled by means of "release according to list". The *Declaration List* has the same legal effect as the *Customs Declaration Form for Import (Export) Goods from the Customs of the People's Republic of China*.

E-commerce enterprises shall verify the identity information of individuals (orderers) who purchase cross-border E-commerce retail imports, and provide the customs with valid identity information certified by the competent national authority. If the identity information of the orderer cannot be provided or verified, the orderer and the payer shall be the same person.

Except for special circumstances, the *Declaration List*

6.2　跨境电商进出口商品的海关监管方式

6.2.1　跨境电商 B2C 进出口商品的监管

1.　跨境电商报关和传统报关方式的区别

在申报跨境电商零售进口商品前，电商企业或电商交易平台企业、支付企业、物流企业应当分别通过跨境电商通关服务平台如实向海关传输交易、支付、物流等电子信息。进出境快件运营人、邮政企业可以受电商企业、支付企业委托，在书面承诺对传输数据真实性承担相应法律责任的前提下，向海关传输交易、支付等电子信息。

电商企业或其代理人应提交《中华人民共和国海关跨境电子商务零售进出口商品申报清单》（以下简称《申报清单》）。出口采取"清单核放、汇总申报"方式办理报关手续。进口采取"清单核放"方式办理报关手续。《申报清单》与《中华人民共和国海关进（出）口货物报关单》具有同等法律效力。

电商企业应当对购买跨境电商零售进口商品的个人（订购人）身份信息进行核实，并向海关提供由国家主管部门认证的身份有效信息。若无法提供或者无法核实订购人身份信息，订购人与支付人则应为同一人。

除特殊情况外，《申报清单》

and *Customs Declaration Form for Import (Export) Goods from the Customs of the People's Republic of China* shall be declared in paperless customs clearance. The modification or cancellation of the *Declaration List* shall be handled with reference to the *Customs Declaration Form for Import (Export) Goods from the Customs of the People's Republic of China*.

Since cross-border E-commerce is characterized by a small quantity and a large number of orders, if the traditional customs clearance policy is adopted, it will bring a heavy burden to the enterprise. Most cross-border E-commerce B2C enterprises use air parcel, postal and express services. The main body of declaration is the post office and express service company. These transactions do not enter the customs statistics of import and export trade. Therefore, the customs has provided a new supervision method code "9610"to regulate those domestic individuals or companies that conduct transactions through cross-border E-commerce platforms. For those cross-border E-commerce commodities that are traded through special supervision areas (such as bonded areas), the customs has added a "1210" supervision method code.

2. Definition of "9610" and "1210"

(1) "9610".

The customs supervision method code is "9610", whose full name is "cross-border trade E-commerce", abbreviated to as"E-commerce", which is applicable to domestic individuals or E-commerce enterprises to realize transactions through E-commerce transaction platform, and adopts the "release according to list, declaration in total" method to handle E-commerce retail import and export commodities that go through customs clearance procedures (except for E-commerce retail import and export commodities that pass through special customs supervision areas or bonded supervision sites).

E-commerce enterprises, enterprises operating under supervision premises, payment enterprises, and logistics enterprises that carry out E-commerce retail import and export business under the "9610" customs supervision method code shall file with the customs in accordance

和《中华人民共和国海关进（出）口货物报关单》应当采取通关无纸化作业方式进行申报。《申报清单》的修改或者撤销，参照海关《中华人民共和国海关进（出）口货物报关单》修改或者撤销有关规定办理。

由于跨境电商的特点是数量少、订单多，因此，如果采用传统的通关政策，将给企业带来沉重的负担。跨境电商 B2C 企业大多数都采用航空包裹，邮递和快递服务，申报主体是邮局和快递服务公司。这些交易就没有进入海关的进出口贸易统计。因此，海关提供了新的监管方式代码"9610"来规范那些通过跨境电商平台进行交易的国内个人或公司。而对于那些通过特殊监管区域（例如保税区）进行交易的跨境电商商品，海关新增了"1210"的监管方式代码。

2. "9610"和"1210"的含义

（1）"9610"。

海关监管方式代码为"9610"，全称为"跨境贸易电子商务"，简称"电子商务"，适用于境内个人或电子商务企业通过电商交易平台实现交易，并采用"清单核放、汇总申报"方式办理通关手续的电商零售进出口商品（通过海关特殊监管区域或保税监管场所一线的电商零售进出口商品除外）。

以"9610"海关监管方式代码开展电商零售进出口业务的电商企业、监管场所经营企业、支付企业和物流企业应当按照规定向海关备案，并通过电商通关服

with the regulations, and submit the transaction, payment, warehousing and logistics data to the E-commerce customs clearance management platform in real time through the E-commerce customs clearance service platform.

According to "release according to list, summarize declaration in total" method for management, the customs requires enterprises to report all transactions in the form of cross-border E-commerce at the end of each month. Order transactions, payment and logistics information (excluding goods imported and exported through special supervision areas such as bonded areas) are collected electronically to the customs, which is legally equivalent to a traditional customs declaration.

(2) "1210".

The customs supervision method code is "1210", the full name is "bonded cross-border trade E-commerce", and "bonded E-commerce" for short. It is applicable to domestic individuals or E-commerce enterprises that implement cross-border transactions on E-commerce platforms approved by the customs and enter and exit E-commerce retail inbound and outbound goods through special customs supervision areas or bonded supervision places. This supervision method is not applicable to retail import and export commodities traded through E-commerce platforms among customs special supervision areas, bonded supervision places and outside the interior zone (outside the places).

The "1210" supervision method code is limited to special customs supervision areas and bonded logistics centers that have been approved to carry out cross-border trade E-commerce import pilots for import trade.

6.2.2 Supervision of Cross-Border E-Commerce B2B Import and Export Commodities

1. Customs declaration procedures for "9710" and "9810"

Definitions of "9710" and "9810" are as follows.

Export of goods in the mode of cross-border E-commerce B2B is originally supervised in the mode of general trade

务平台实时向电商通关管理平台传送交易、支付、仓储和物流数据。

针对"清单核放,汇总申报"的管理方式,海关要求企业在每个月月底以跨境电商的形式报告有关所有交易。订单交易、付款和物流信息(不包括通过保税区等特殊监管区域进出口的货物)以电子方式汇总到海关,这在法律上等同于传统的海关申报单。

(2)"1210"。

海关监管方式代码为"1210",全称为"保税跨境贸易电子商务",简称"保税电子商务"。它适用于境内个人或电商企业在经海关认可的电商平台上实现跨境交易,并通过海关特殊监管区域或保税监管场所进出的电商零售进出境商品。该监管方式不适用于海关特殊监管区域、保税监管场所与境内区外(场所外)之间通过电商平台交易的零售进出口商品。

"1210"监管方式代码用于进口时仅限经批准开展跨境贸易电商进口试点的海关特殊监管区域和保税物流中心。

6.2.2 跨境电商 B2B 进出口商品的监管

1."9710"和"9810"的报关程序

"9710"和"9810"的含义如下。

对于原跨境电商 B2B 出口,海关都按照一般贸易(代码为

(code 0110), so its customs clearance procedures are still declared in accordance with the declaration rules under traditional trade; but cross-border E-commerce enterprise, E-commerce transaction platforms, and E-commerce service enterprise need to file in advance on the single window platform, and conduct on-site interviews as required by the customs. However, with the increasing volume of cross-border E-commerce B2B exports, the customs has introduced new supervision method code, namely "9710" and "9810" (Table 6-1) .

0110）的方式进行监管，通关手续仍按照传统贸易项下的申报规则进行申报，但跨境电商企业、电商交易平台、电商服务企业需要事先在单一窗口平台进行备案，并按海关要求进行现场约谈。然而，随着跨境电商 B2B 出口量日益增长，海关又出台了新的监管方式代码"9710"和"9810"（表6-1）。

Table 6-1　Customs Clearance Requirements Under Different Customs Supervision Method Codes

Customs clearance type	Cross-border E-commerce B2B export(9710, 9810)	General trade export (0110)	Cross-border E-commerce B2C export (9610)
Attached documents	9710: order, logistics order (low value) 9810: warehouse order, logistics order (low value) (The power of attorney can be provided for the first time during customs declaration)	Power of attorney, contract, invoice, bill of lading, packing list, etc.	Orders, logistics orders, collections information
Simplified declaration	The unified export declaration is passed at the customs in the place of the comprehensive pilot area. If the list meets the conditions, you can apply for a simplified declaration based on the 6-digit HS code.		Pass the unified export declaration at the local customs of the comprehensive pilot area, and the qualified list can apply for simplified declaration according to the 4-digit HS code
Logistics	Be applied to transit or direct port export, and national customs clearance integration is applied through H2018	Be applied to direct port export or national customs clearance integration	Transit or direct port export is applicable
Examination	Be prioritized for inspection		

Resource：General Administration of Customs of China

表 6-1　不同海关监管方式代码下的通关要求

通关类型	跨境电商 B2B 出口（9710、9810）	一般贸易出口（0110）	跨境电商 B2C 出口（9610）
随附单证	9710：订单、物流单（低值） 9810：订仓单、物流单（低值） （第一次报关时提供委托书）	委托书、合同、发票、提单、装箱单等	订单、物流单、收款信息
简化申报	在综合试验区所在地海关通过出口统一版申报，符合条件的清单，可申请按 6 位 HS 编码简化申报		在综合试验区所在地海关通过出口统一版申报，符合条件的清单，可申请按 4 位 HS 编码简化申报
物流	可适用于转关或直接口岸出口，通过 H2018 申报的可适用于全国通关一体化	直接口岸出口或全国通关一体化	可适用于转关或直接口岸出口
查验	可优先安排查验		

资料来源：中国海关总署

The full name of cross-border E-commerce B2B export is "cross-border E-commerce business-to-business export", which refers to a form of trade in which domestic enterprises transport goods to overseas enterprises or overseas warehouses through cross-border logistics and complete transactions through cross-border E-commerce platforms. The enterprises transmit relevant electronic data according to customs requirements. Cross-border E-commerce B2B exports mainly include the following two modes. Enterprises can choose the corresponding mode to declare to the customs according to their business types.

The first mode is direct export in B2B.

After deals achieved on the cross-border E-commerce platforms, domestic enterprises export goods directly to overseas enterprises through cross-border logistics. In this case, supervision method code "9710" should be applied in the customs declaration.

The second mode is export to overseas warehouse.

Domestic enterprises export the goods to overseas warehouses through cross-border logistics, and then deliver the goods from overseas warehouses to overseas purchasers after orders confirmed through online platforms. In this case, supervision method code of "9810" should be applied in the customs declaration.

2．The process of the customs declaration

Enterprises should submit the customs declaration data and transmit electronic information to the customs through the "single window standard version" or "Internet + customs" cross-border E-commerce customs clearance service system and cargo declaration system. Among them, cross-border E-commerce B2B export-related electronic declaration data follow the existing B2C access channel mode of the cross-border service system, and newly support the import of B2B export declaration messages; the cargo declaration system supports B2B export declarations according to the existing pattern entry and import (Figure 6-1).

3．Important issues in the customs declaration

(1) Declaration through H2018 customs clearance management system.

跨境电商 B2B 出口的全称为 "跨境电商企业对企业出口"，是指境内企业通过跨境物流将货物运送至境外企业或海外仓，并通过跨境电商平台完成交易的贸易形式。企业根据海关要求传输相关电子数据。跨境电商 B2B 出口主要包括以下两种方式。企业可根据自身业务类型，选择相应方式向海关申报。

第一种方式是 B2B 直接出口。

境内企业通过跨境电商平台与境外企业达成交易后，通过跨境物流将货物直接出口至境外企业。在这种情况下，采用"9710"监管方式代码申报。

第二种方式是出口海外仓。

境内企业先将货物通过跨境物流出口至海外仓，通过跨境电商平台实现交易后从海外仓送达境外购买者。在这种情况下，采用"9810"监管方式代码申报。

2．申报流程

企业应通过"单一窗口标准版"或"互联网＋海关"的跨境电商通关服务系统和货物申报系统向海关提交申报数据、传输电子信息。其中，跨境电商 B2B 出口有关电子信息报文，沿用跨境服务系统现有的 B2C 接入通道方式，新增支持 B2B 出口报关单报文导入；货物申报系统支持 B2B 出口报关单按现有方式录入和导入（图 6-1）。

3．申报要点

（1）通过 H2018 通关管理系统通关。

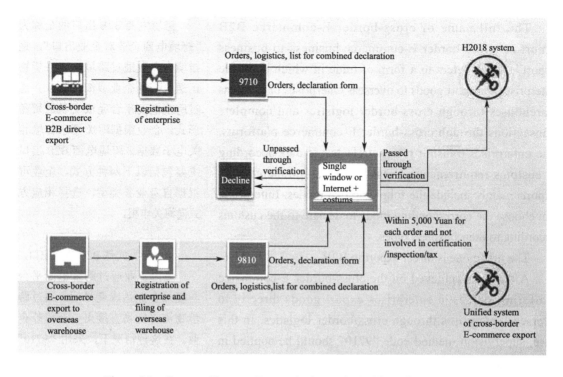

Figure 6-1　Customs Clearance Process in the Method of "9710" and "9810"

Resource：*China Customs Magazine*

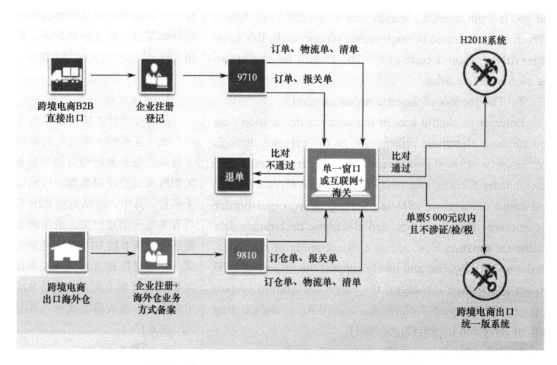

图 6-1　采用"9710"和"9810"监管方式的通关流程

资料来源：《中国海关杂志》

Firstly，electronic information transmission has to be completed. Before the declaration of cross-border E-commerce B2B direct export (9710), cross-border E-commerce enterpriese or cross-border E-commerce platform enterpriese should transmit transaction order information to the customs; before cross-border E-commerce export overseas warehouse (9810) declaration, cross-border E-commerce enterprises should transmit overseas warehouse booking information to the customs.

Next, the enterprise should submit declaration form. Cross-border E-commerce enterprises or their agents declare customs declarations to the customs. The system verifies the qualifications and declaration content of the enterprises, and declares customs declarations to H2018 if they pass.

(2) Customs clearance through the unified cross-border E-commerce export system.

Firstly, electronic information transmission has to be completed. Before cross-border E-commerce B2B direct export (9710) goods declaration, cross-border E-commerce enterpriese and logistics enterpriese should respectively transmit transaction orders and logistics information to the customs; before cross-border E-commerce export overseas warehouses (9810) goods declaration, cross-border E-commerce enterprises and logistics enterprises shall respectively transmit overseas warehouse booking information and logistics information to the customs.

Next, list declaration has to be submitted. Cross-border E-commerce enterprises or their agents declare the list to the customs. The system verifies the qualifications and declaration contents of the enterprise, and the approved declaration list is submitted to the unified export declaration. The list does not need to summarize the declaration form.

4. Customs clearance facilitation

(1) The whole process of customs declaration is digitalized.

Enterprises use "single window" or "Internet + customs" to transmit electronic information such as transaction orders and overseas warehouse orders, and all are automatically imported in standard message formats. Customs declarations

首先，完成电子信息传输。跨境电商B2B直接出口（9710）申报前，跨境电商企业或跨境电商平台企业应向海关传输交易订单信息；跨境电商出口海外仓（9810）申报前，跨境电商企业应向海关传输海外仓订仓信息。

其次，企业申报报关单。跨境电商企业或其代理人向海关申报报关单。系统对企业资质及申报内容进行校验，若通过则向H2018申报报关单。

（2）通过跨境电商出口统一版系统通关。

首先，完成电子信息传输。跨境电商B2B直接出口（9710）货物申报前，跨境电商企业、物流企业应分别向海关传输交易订单、物流信息；跨境电商出口海外仓（9810）货物申报前，跨境电商企业、物流企业应分别向海关传输海外仓订仓信息、物流信息。

其次，申报清单。跨境电商企业或其代理人向海关申报清单。系统对企业资质及申报内容进行校验，将通过的清单向出口统一版申报。清单不需要汇总申报报关单。

4. 通关便利
（1）报关全程数字化。

企业通过"单一窗口"或"互联网＋海关"网上传输交易订单、海外仓订仓单等电子信息，且全部以标准报文格式自动导入。

and declaration lists are all paperless to simplify corporate declarations formalities.

(2) New convenient declaration channel.

For goods with a single order value less than 5,000 Yuan (inclusive) and not involved in certification, inspection, or tax, customs can be cleared in the form of declaration list through the unified cross-border E-commerce export system. The items of declaration elements are less 57 than that of customs declaration, and the list does not need to summarize customs declaration forms, making it easier for small, medium and micro export enterprises to declare, further reducing customs clearance costs.

(3) Streamlined declaration for comprehensive pilot area.

With reference to the simplified declaration of cross-border E-commerce retail exports (9610) carried out by the customs in the place where the comprehensive pilot area is located, the declaration of qualified 9710 and 9810 lists at the customs in the place of the comprehensive pilot area can apply for streamlined declaration according to the 6-digit HS code.

(4) Convenient logistics and inspection.

Cross-border E-commerce B2B export goods can be transferred according to the type of "cross-border E-commerce", and customs clearance through the H2018 customs clearance management system also applies to the integration of national customs clearance. Enterprises can choose a more efficient and better combination method to transport goods according to their actual conditions, while enjoying the convenience of priority inspection.

6.3 Tax Policy of Cross-Border E-Commerce

China currently implements incentive policies for cross-border E-commerce, with relatively favorable tax conditions compared with traditional international business. Cross-border E-commerce can be divided into import and export. Import tax enjoys reduction and exemption policies, and export tax rebate enjoys convenient conditions.

报关单和申报清单均是无纸化的，以简化企业申报手续。

（2）新增便捷申报通道。

对单票金额在 5 000 元（含）以内且不涉证、不涉检、不涉税的货物，可通过跨境电商出口统一版系统以申报清单的方式进行通关。申报要素比报关单减少 57 项，清单不需要汇总报关单，让中小微出口企业申报更为便捷、通关成本进一步降低。

（3）综合试验区简化申报。

参照综合试验区所在地海关开展跨境电商零售出口（9610）简化申报的做法，在综合试验区所在地海关申报符合条件的 9710 清单、9810 清单，可申请按照 6 位 HS 编码简化申报。

（4）物流和查验便利。

跨境电商 B2B 出口货物可按照"跨境电商"类型办理转关，通过 H2018 通关管理系统通关的，同样适用全国通关一体化。企业可根据自身实际选择时效更强、组合更优的方式运送货物，同时可享受优先查验的便利。

6.3 跨境电商税收政策

中国目前对跨境电商实施鼓励政策，与传统外贸相比，税收条件相对优惠。跨境电商可分为进口与出口，对进口税收提供减免政策，对出口退税提供便利条件。

6.3.1　Comprehensive Tax on Imported Goods for Cross-Border E-Commerce

The comprehensive tax on cross-border E-commerce retail imports is applicable to the following goods imported from other countries or regions within the scope of the *List of Cross-border E-commerce Retail Import Commodities*:

All cross-border E-commerce retail imported goods that have been traded through the E-commerce transaction platform networked with the customs, can accomplish the verification among "three-order", namely transaction order, payment record, and logistics electronic information.

Cross-border E-commerce retail imported goods have not been traded through the E-commerce transaction platform networked with the customs, but express and postal enterprises can provide electronic information such as transactions, payments, and logistics in a unified manner, and promise to bear corresponding legal responsibilities for entering the country.

Cross-border E-commerce retail imports are subject to customs duties, consumption tax and value-added tax according to the goods; individuals who purchase cross-border E-commerce retail imports are taxpayers; the actual transaction price (including the retail price of goods, freight and insurance) is regarded as the duty-paid price; E-commerce enterprises, E-commerce transaction platform enterprises or logistics enterprises can act as collection and payment agents.

The single transaction limit for cross-border E-commerce retail imported goods is 5,000 Yuan, and the individual annual transaction limit is 26,000 Yuan. For cross-border E-commerce retail imported goods imported within the limit, the tariff rate is temporarily set to 0%; the import link value-added tax and consumption tax are cancelled and the tax exemption is temporarily levied at 70% of the legal tax payable. A single transaction that exceeds the single limit and the individual's annual limit after accumulation, and a single indivisible commodity with a tax value exceeding the limit of 5,000 Yuan, are all taxed in full according to the general trade method.

6.3.1　跨境电商进口商品综合税

跨境电商零售进口综合税收适用于从其他国家或地区进口的、《跨境电子商务零售进口商品清单》范围内的以下商品：

所有通过与海关联网的电商交易平台交易，能够实现交易、支付、物流电子信息"三单"比对的跨境电商零售进口商品。

未通过与海关联网的电商交易平台交易，但快递、邮政企业能够统一提供交易、支付、物流等电子信息，并承诺承担相应法律责任进境的跨境电商零售进口商品。

跨境电商零售进口商品按照货物征收关税、消费税和增值税；购买跨境电商零售进口商品的个人作为纳税义务人；实际交易价格（包括货物零售价格、运费和保险费）作为完税价格；电商企业、电商交易平台企业或物流企业可作为代收代缴义务人。

跨境电商零售进口商品的单次交易限值为 5 000 元，个人年度交易限值为 26 000 元。在限值以内进口的跨境电商零售进口商品，关税税率暂设为 0%；进口环节增值税、消费税取消免征税额，暂按法定应纳税额的 70% 征收。超过单次限值、累加后超过个人年度限值的单次交易，以及完税价格超过 5 000 元限值的单个不可分割商品，均按照一般贸易方式全额征税。

If cross-border E-commerce retail imported goods are returned within 30 days from the date of customs clearance, people can apply for a tax rebate and adjust the total amount of personal annual transactions accordingly.

In order to facilitate consumers to understand the use of personal quota, China E-Port launched an online query of annual individual quota for cross-border E-commerce retail imports on "Customs on Hand (Zhangshang Haiguan)" by using WeChat or App for every year, as shown in Figure 6-2.

Calculations of comprehensive tax on cross-border E-commerce imports are as follows.

Comprehensive tax on cross-border E-commerce imports = (tariff + consumption tax + value-added tax) × 70%.

> 跨境电商零售进口商品自海关放行之日起 30 日内退货的，可申请退税，并相应调整个人年度交易总额。
>
> 为便于消费者了解个人额度的使用情况，中国电子口岸推出微信或手机 App "掌上海关"，可在线查询年度跨境电商零售进口个人额度（图 6-2）。
>
> 跨境电商进口综合税的计算如下。
>
> 跨境电商进口综合税 =（关税 + 消费税 + 增值税）× 70%。

Cross-border personal consumption quota query

Name

***

ID No.

****

- Comsumed quota:　　　¥ 0.00
- Available quota:　　¥ 26,000.00

Query result description: cross-border personal consumption quota information from 00:00 on January 1, 2022 to 24:00 on * *, 2022

Figure 6-2　Online Query of Cross-Border Personal Consumption Quota

<　🏠　跨境个人消费额度查询　⋯　◎

跨境个人消费额度查询

姓名

***

身份证号

****

- 已消费额度：　　　¥ 0.00
- 可用额度：　　¥ 26,000.00

查询结果说明：
自2022年1月1日 00:00起，至2022年*月 ★日 24:00 的跨境个人消费额度信息。

图 6-2　在线查询跨境个人消费额度

The interim tariff rate for cross-border E-commerce imports is 0%, so the tariff is 0.

Consumption tax = [duty-paid price÷(1-consumption tax rate)] × consumption tax rate.

Value-added tax = (duty-paid price + consumption tax) × value-added tax rate.

6.3.2　Postal Tax on Imported Goods through Cross-Border E-Commerce

For personal use and a reasonable number of cross-border personal goods carried by cross-border individuals or imported by post, the postal tax is levied on the postal items in actual operation. The postal tax is aimed at non-trade inbound items, and the customs duties, import value-added tax and consumption tax are collected together, and the tax rate is generally lower than the comprehensive tax rate of similar imported goods.

The traditional overseas online shopping is that customers buy on foreign shopping websites, send them to a forwarding company, and then send them to China through the background operation of the forwarding company. Imported goods enter the country through postal channels without any transaction, payment and other information input. Therefore, the customs shall refer to the standard of *Postal Tax* when levying taxes.

With the approval of the State Council, the Customs Tariff Commission of the State Council has decided to adjust the import tax on imported articles from April 9, 2019 as follows.

(1) The tax rates of Import Tax Items 1 and 2 of imported articles will be reduced to 13% and 20% respectively.

(2) Amend the annotation of Tax Item 1 "Drugs" to read "For imported drugs that are subject to a 3% reduction in import value-added tax as stipulated by the state, the tax shall be levied at the tax rate of goods". The adjusted *Table of Import Tax Rates of Imported Articles of the People's Republic of China* is shown in Table 6-2.

跨境电商进口商品暂行关税税率为 0%，因此关税为 0。

消费税 =[完税价格 ÷(1- 消费税税率)]× 消费税税率。

增值税 =(完税价格 + 消费税税额)× 增值税税率。

6.3.2　跨境电商进口商品行邮税

个人自用、合理数量的跨境个人携带或邮递进境的海淘商品在实际操作中按照邮寄物品征收行邮税。行邮税针对的是非贸易属性的进境物品，将关税和进口环节增值税、消费税三税合并征收，税率普遍低于同类进口货物的综合税率。

传统海淘是客户先在国外购物网站购买，发往转运公司，然后通过转运公司后台操作发往国内。进口商品通过邮政渠道进入国境，没有任何交易、支付等信息录入。因此，海关在征税时参照《行邮税》的标准。

经国务院批准，国务院关税税则委员会决定自 2019 年 4 月 9 日起对进境物品进口税进行调整如下。

(1) 将进境物品进口税税目 1、2 的税率分别调降为 13%、20%。

(2) 将税目 1 " 药品 " 的注释修改为 " 对国家规定减按 3% 征收进口环节增值税的进口药品，按照货物税率征税 "。调整后的《中华人民共和国进境物品进口税税率表》见表 6-2。

Table 6-2　Table of Import Tax Rates of Imported Articles of the People's Republic of China

Tax item	Name of articles	Rate of tax
1	Books, publications, educational film and television materials; computer, video camcorders, digital cameras and other information technology products; food, beverages; gold and silver; furniture; toys, games, festivals or other entertainment products; drugs[①]	13%
2	Sporting goods (excluding golf and golf equipment), fishing supplies; textiles and their finished products; TV cameras and other electrical appliances; bicycles; other commodities not included in Tax Item 1and Tax Item 3	20%
3[②]	Tobacco, wine; precious jewelries; golf and golf equipment; luxurious watches; cosmetics	50%

Notes: ① For imported drugs that are subject to a 3% reduction in import value-added tax as stipulated by the state, tax is levied according to the tax rate of goods.

② The specific scope of commodities listed in Tax Item 3 is consistent with the scope of consumption tax collection.

Resource：General Administration of Customs of China

表 6-2　中华人民共和国进境物品进口税税率表

税目	物品名称	税率
1	书报、刊物、教育用影视资料；计算机、视频摄录一体机、数字照相机等信息技术产品；食品、饮料；金与银；家具；玩具、游戏品、节日或其他娱乐用品；药品[①]	13%
2	运动用品（不含高尔夫球及球具）、钓鱼用品；纺织品及其制成品；电视摄像机及其他电气用具；自行车；税目 1 和税目 3 中未包含的其他商品	20%
3[②]	烟、酒；贵重首饰及珠宝玉石；高尔夫球及球具；高档手表；化妆品	50%

注：① 对国家规定减按 3% 征收进口环节增值税的进口药品，按照货物税率征税。

② 税目 3 所列商品的具体范围与消费税征收范围一致。

资料来源：中国海关总署

6.3.3　Cross-Border E-Commerce Export Tax Policy

1．Scope of tax rebate

Just like traditional international business, China does not impose export duties on most exported goods, and the same goes for goods exported in cross-border E-commerce. In addition to export tax exemption, export enterprises can apply for tax rebate at the same time as the goods are declared for export and the payment is returned after receiving the value-added tax invoice.

Cross-border E-commerce enterprises that are eligible

6.3.3　跨境电商出口税收政策

1．退税范围

正如传统外贸一样，我国对于出口的绝大多数商品都是不征出口关税的，跨境电商出口的商品也一样。除出口免税外，出口企业在拿到增值税发票之后，可以在货物报关出口、回款结汇的同时申请退税。

适用出口退税、免税政策的

for export tax rebates and tax exemptions include units and individual industrial and commercial households that build their own cross-border E-commerce sales platforms or use third-party cross-border E-commerce platforms to carry out E-commerce exports. It does not include cross-border E-commerce third-party platforms that provide transaction services for E-commerce exporters.

2. Tax rebate conditions applicable to cross-border E-commerce exports

(1) For cross-border E-commerce retail export goods (customs supervision method code is "9610"), cross-border E-commerce retail export goods (except for goods that Ministry of Finance and State Administration of Taxation clearly do not allow export tax rebates or tax exemptions), and meet the following conditions at the same time, the value-added tax and consumption tax rebate policies are applicable: cross-border E-commerce retail export enterprises belong to value-added tax general taxpayers and have applied for export tax rebate qualification certification (filing) with the competent tax authority; export goods obtain customs export goods declaration form (for export tax rebate), and the electronic information of the customs export goods declaration form is consistent; export goods are closed during the tax rebate declaration period. If the cross-border E-commerce retail export enterprise is a foreign trade enterprise, the purchase of import and export goods shall obtain the corresponding special invoice for value-added tax, special payment form for consumption tax (divided bill) or special payment form for customs import value-added tax and consumption tax. And the relevant content of the above vouchers matches the relevant content of the export goods declaration form (for export tax rebates).

(2) For cross-border E-commerce enterprise-to-enterprise export goods (customs supervision method codes are "9710" and "9810"), the following basic conditions shall be met to apply for export tax rebate in accordance with the relevant policies applicable to general trade (customs supervision method code is "0110") export goods: After the goods are declared to the customs, they actually leave the country; they

跨境电商企业包括自建跨境电子商务销售平台或利用第三方跨境电商平台开展电商出口的单位和个体工商户。不包括为电商出口企业提供交易服务的跨境电商第三方平台。

2. 适用于跨境电商出口的退税条件

（1）针对跨境电商零售出口货物（海关监管方式代码为"9610"），跨境电商零售出口货物（财政部、国家税务总局明确不予出口退税或免税的货物除外），同时符合下列条件的，适用增值税、消费税退税政策：跨境电商零售出口企业属于增值税一般纳税人并已向主管税务机关办理出口退税资格认定（备案）；出口货物取得海关出口货物报关单（出口退税专用），并与海关出口货物报关单电子信息一致；出口货物在退税申报期截止之日内收汇；跨境电商零售出口企业属于外贸企业的，购进出口货物取得相应的增值税专用发票、消费税专用缴款书（分割单）或海关进口增值税、消费税专用缴款书，并且上述凭证有关内容与出口货物报关单（出口退税专用）有关内容相匹配。

（2）针对跨境电商企业对企业出口货物（海关监管方式代码为"9710"和"9810"），参照适用一般贸易（海关监管方式代码为"0110"）出口货物相关政策办理出口退税，应符合以下基本条件：货物向海关报关后实际离境；

are sold financially; the sales targets are overseas units and individuals; foreign exchange is collected on schedule.

3．Process of tax refund

Eligible cross-border E-commerce enterprises shall handle export tax refund declaration business after handling export tax refund filing.

For example: export enterprises can log in to the Zhejiang Electronic Taxation Bureau of the State Administration of Taxation to handle export tax rebates.

Cross-border E-commerce retail export business which uses the checklist may also handle tax refund. For cross-border E-commerce retail export goods (customs supervision method code is "9610"), the customs clearance method of checklist should be adopted. If export tax refund is required, a summary declaration form should be generated. Production enterprises shall declare export tax refund on the basis of the declaration form for export goods, foreign trade enterprises on the basis of the declaration form for export goods and the corresponding special invoices for VAT obtained by purchasing import and export goods. Details of the summary declaration list can be sold with special VAT invoices.

6.4　OneTouch

OneTouch was originally a comprehensive foreign trade service platform established by Shenzhen OneTouch Enterprise Services Co., Ltd. Alibaba Group acquired it as a wholly-owned subsidiary in 2004 and made OneTouch as an important part of Alibaba's foreign trade ecosystem.

At present, OneTouch provides professional and low-cost customs clearance, foreign exchange service, tax rebates and also supporting logistics and financial services for small and medium-sized enterprises by the integration of various foreign trade service resources and banking resources through the online credit data system, referred to as one-stop service (Table 6-3).

在财务上做销售处理；销售对象为境外单位和个人；按期收汇。

3．退税流程

符合条件的跨境电商企业应在办理出口退税备案后，再办理出口退税申报业务。

举例：出口企业可以登录国家税务总局浙江省电子税务局办理出口退税业务。

采用清单核放的跨境电商零售出口业务也可以办理退税。跨境电商零售出口货物（海关监管方式代码为"9610"），应采用清单核放通关方式。如果需办理出口退税，则生成汇总报关单。生产企业凭出口货物报关单，外贸企业凭出口货物报关单及购进出口货物取得相应的增值税专用发票等凭证申报出口退税。汇总报关单清单明细可随增值税专用发票销售。

6.4　一达通

一达通最初是深圳市一达通企业服务有限公司创立的外贸综合服务平台。阿里巴巴集团于2004年全资收购了一达通，并将一达通列为阿里巴巴打造外贸生态圈中的重要组成部分。

目前一达通通过线上信用数据系统，通过整合各项外贸服务资源和银行资源，为中小企业提供专业、低成本的通关、外汇、退税及配套的物流和金融服务，简称一站式服务（表6-3）。

Table 6-3　Comprehensive Service Provided by OneTouch

Procedures	Statement
Placing an order with OneTouch	As far as possible 3 working days before the goods are legally required for custom declaration; if the product requires legal (commercial) inspection, please place the order 5 working days in advance
Customs clearance	OneTouch can accomplish the custom declaration, you can check the status of the order to confirm the custom release of goods
Foreign exchange service	After the foreign exchange arrives in the account, a trade background declaration is required. After the goods are cleared, the foreign exchange must be linked to the order
VAT invoice for tax rebate	After the goods are exported, you need to issue an invoice to OneTouch for export tax refund
Upload filing documents	The tax authority requires that after the goods are exported, the filing documents must be collected for the tax authorities to verify
Advanced payment of tax	Release conditions: customs clearance is completed + original VAT invoice is received and verified + foreign exchange bills are fully collected + filed documents are reviewed + supply company has not sent a letter + supply company review status is normal + tax authority passes the next household verification +the total amount of tax refund is within the amount of tax refund available for the current month of the corresponding supplier
Settlement	Withdraw cash, after the trade background declaration is completed, you can arrange cash withdrawal and transfer Check the statement. After the goods are exported, you can check the cost of this order in the statement

表 6-3　一达通出口综合服务的流程

流程	说明
下单	尽可能在货物法定报关前 3 个工作日内报关；若产品需要法（商）检，有法（商）检备案的，则提前 5 个工作日下单
通关	一达通完成报关，可查看订单状态和报关放行情况
外汇	外汇到账后需做贸易背景申报。货物报关放行后，需将外汇关联到订单
开票	货物出口后，需开票给一达通，做出口退税
上传备案单据	税务部门要求，货物出口后需收集备案单证以备税务机关核查
垫付税款	释放条件：通关办理完毕＋收到增值税发票原件且验证通过＋外汇单已全部收齐＋备案单证审核通过＋供货企业未函调＋供货企业审核状态为正常＋税务机关通过下户核查＋退税总额在对应供货企业的当月可用垫付退税额度以内
结算	提现，在贸易背景申报后，就可以安排提现转款 查看对账单，货物出口后，可在对账单中查看此笔订单产生的费用

AliExpress cooperated with OneTouch to jointly launch the BBC (B2B2C) overseas warehouse export tax rebate service. Regardless of whether the seller has its own overseas warehouse or a cooperative third-party overseas warehouse,

速卖通联手一达通共同推出了 BBC（B2B2C）海外仓出口退税服务。无论卖家是自有海外仓还是合作的第三方海外仓，都提

it provides one-stop services such as customs clearance, logistics, tax refund, and financing; for sellers who do not use overseas warehouses, AliExpress will also provide Hong Kong Cainiao (also called rookie) warehouses. After the goods are exported to the Cainiao warehouse in Hong Kong through OneTouch, the tax refund will be handled by OneTouch. This is undoubtedly a timely rain for sellers whose profits are declining.

In addition, in the customs clearance process that is the most troublesome for sellers, there are occasions when package clearance delays affect the delivery period and cause buyers' complaints. Using this service, you can operate on the entire online platform, quickly review orders, and declare for export. In order to improve the turnover rate of sellers' funds, OneTouch will also conduct real-time foreign exchange settlement and withdrawal; as for the tax refund most concerned by sellers, the BBC can release a refund within 3 days as soon as the foreign exchange is fully collected.

供通关、物流、退税、融资等一站式服务；对于没有使用海外仓的卖家，速卖通也将提供香港菜鸟仓。货物通过一达通申报出口到香港菜鸟仓后，再由一达通操作退税。这对于利润趋减的卖家来说，无疑是一场及时雨。

此外，在卖家最为头疼的通关环节，时有包裹清关延误影响货期，造成买家投诉等情况发生。使用该项服务，可以实现完全线上平台操作，快速审单、报关出口。为提升卖家资金周转率，一达通还将实现实时结汇和提现；对于卖家最关心的退税，BBC 在外汇收齐的情况下，最快 3 天即可释放退款。

New words

1. General Administration of Customs 海关总署
2. inspection and quarantine 检验检疫
3. customs supervision 海关监管
4. customs clearance 通关
5. declaration form 报关单
6. duty/tariff 关税
7. bonded zone 保税区
8. comprehensive tax 综合税
9. value-added tax（VAT）增值税
10. consumption tax 消费税
11. quota 额度
12. levy 征收
13. *The Harmonization System Code*《商品名称及编码协调制度》
14. export tax rebate 出口退税
15. OneTouch 一达通

Chapter 7

Cross-Border E-Commerce Payments and Settlements

第7章　跨境电商支付与结算

Lead-in case

Xiaowei buys a variety of goods from China 1688 online wholesale platform or offline from Hangzhou Sijiqing, Yiwu Commodity City, Guangzhou Baiyun and other industrial clusters by using Alipay, WeChat or bank transfer payment, then sells products through cross-border E-commerce platforms, such as Alibaba, AliExpress, Amazon, eBay and Shopee or independent station to overseas. In her daily life, Xiaowei also buys imported cosmetics and clothes from Tmall Global. Domestic and foreign customers complete the transaction without direct meeting. The essence of E-commerce is the integration of information flow, logistics flow and capital flow. The difference between cross-border E-commerce and local E-commerce is that the three flows cover different regions or countries. How does Xiaowei make payment and settlement for cross-border E-commerce?

Learning objectives

1. Objectives of knowledge

(1) To master payment methods of cross-border E-commerce such as PingPong, LianLian, Alipay, WorldFirst, PayPal, and bank card.

(2) To master the revenue and payment channels of mainstream cross-border E-commerce platforms such as AliExpress and Amazon.

(3) To be familiar with China's laws and regulations on settlement of foreign exchange related to cross-border E-commerce income and payment.

(4) To master the financing methods related to different capital requirements and business scale of cross-border E-commerce enterprises.

案例导入

小薇从中国 1688 电商批发平台或线下从杭州四季青、义乌小商品城、广州白云等产业集群进货，采用支付宝、微信或银行转账支付货款；再把产品通过阿里巴巴国际站、速卖通、亚马逊、eBay、Shopee 跨境电商平台或独立站卖到国外。在日常生活中，小薇也从天猫国际购买进口化妆品和衣服。国内外客户在双方都不直接见面的情况下完成交易。电子商务本质上是对信息流、物流和资金流的整合。跨境电商和国内电商的区别是三流均涉及境内外。小薇该如何完成跨境电商支付与结算？

学习目标

1. 知识目标

(1) 掌握跨境电商乒乓（PingPong）、连连（LianLian）、支付宝（Alipay）、万里汇（WorldFirst）、贝宝（PayPal）、银行卡等支付方式。

(2) 掌握速卖通、亚马逊等跨境电商主流平台的收支渠道。

(3) 熟悉中国关于跨境电商收支外汇结算的法律法规。

(4) 掌握跨境电商企业不同资金和业务规模相关的融资方式。

2. Objectives of skills

(1) To be able to choose appropriate payment or collection channel of cross-border E-commerce platform according to the work or consumption needs.

(2) To be able to use simple and fast remittance, credit card and other payment tools from reality.

(3) To be able to handle foreign exchange settlement and purchase correctly and timely according to the requirements of national laws and regulations.

3. Objectives of qualities

(1) To have a down-to-earth, careful, rigorous and diligent work style.

(2) To have the consciousness of abiding by the relevant laws and regulations of the state on foreign exchange management.

(3) To have the professional ethics of repaying the loan on time and being honest and trustworthy.

(4) To be curious and inquisitive about new things.

7.1 Payment Methods of Cross-Border E-Commerce

7.1.1 Overview of Cross-Border E-Commerce Payment

Cross-border payment refers to the process of cross regional or national payment conducted by the parties in international economic activities. Due to online transactions, cross-border E-commerce cannot make payment by cash, and transactions are generally completed by PingPong, LianLian, AliPay, WorldFirst, PayPal, bank card and other parties approved by the buyer and seller. The funds are handed over to the third party authorized by the cross-border E-commerce platform, independent station or social networking site, which brings security to both parties: the seller delivers the goods after receiving the buyer's payment on the cross-border E-commerce platform, and the buyer's payment is first placed in the third party payment company; the goods are delivered

2. 技能目标

（1）能根据工作或消费需求，选择合适的跨境电商平台支付或收款渠道。

（2）能从实际出发，使用简单、快捷的汇款、信用卡等支付工具。

（3）能按国家法规要求，正确、及时办理外汇结汇及购汇工作。

3. 素质目标

（1）具有踏实、细心、严谨、勤奋的工作作风。

（2）具有遵守国家外汇管理相关法律法规的意识。

（3）具有按时归还借款，诚实守信的职业道德。

（4）对新生事物保持好奇心和探究力。

7.1 跨境电商支付方式

7.1.1 跨境电商支付概述

跨境支付指在国际经济活动中的当事人进行跨地区或国家的资金支付过程。跨境电商出于线上跨境交易的原因，无法采用现金交易，一般通过买卖双方认可的乒乓、连连、支付宝、万里汇、贝宝、银行卡等第三方来完成交易。资金交给跨境电商平台、独立站或社交网站授权的第三方给买卖双方带来安全保障：卖方在跨境电商平台上看到买方支付货款后发货，买方的货款先放在第三方支付公司；货物送到客户手

to the customer; the payment is transferred to the seller's account after the customer receives the goods and makes sure that there is no problem.

Although both cross-border E-commerce payment and domestic E-commerce payment are completed online, the two payments are different based on whether the transaction is offshore.

(1) Information flow is different, and the online payment platform cooperating with E-commerce platform is different.

(2) Logistics flow is different, which leads to different transportation modes, duration, inspection and quarantine, customs declaration and other processes, and prolongs the transaction time of payment-delivery-inspection-confirmation.

(3) The capital flow is different. According to *Regulations on the Administration of RMB* formulated by *Law of the People's Republic of China on the People's Bank of China*, the legal currency of China is RMB (Notes: RMB is the abbreviation of "Renminbi" pinyin; CNY stands for Chinese Yuan, which is the recognized symbol of RMB in international trade), which is used to pay all public and private debts in China. There are also import and export taxes, foreign exchange and other management regulations. Buyers and sellers of other countries also have relevant management regulations. The comparison of three flows between cross-border E-commerce and domestic E-commerce is shown in Table 7-1. The cross-border transaction involves the receipt and payment in different currencies, and the foreign currency and the local currency are settled according to the relevant national regulations. If the buyers of Chinese nationality buy goods from offline shops outside China through WeChat, Alipay, credit card or debit card, they are not cross-border E-payment.

Cross-border E-commerce payment companies can be divided into the following categories according to their background:

(1) International online payment companies established in 1990s, such as Chinese professional online payment companies like PingPong and LianLian, WeChat payment from social communication business, AliPay, and Jingdong

中，检查没有任何问题后确认收货，货款才转移至卖家账户。

跨境电商支付与国内电商支付虽然都是在线支付，但根据交易是否在境外，存在一定的区别。

（1）信息流不同，与电商平台合作的在线支付平台不同。

（2）物流不同，导致运输工具、时长、检验检疫、报关等流程不同，使卖方付款—到货—验货—确认的交易时间延长。

（3）资金流不同，根据《中华人民共和国中国人民银行法》制定的《人民币管理条例》，中国法定货币是人民币（注：RMB 是"人民币"的拼音缩写；CNY 即 Chinese Yuan，是人民币在国际贸易中被认定的符号），支付中国境内的一切公共的和私人的债务。还有进出口税收、外汇等管理规定。其他国家的买家和卖家也有其相关管理规定。跨境电商与国内电商的三流比较见表7-1。跨境交易涉及不同货币收付，按照国家有关规定对外币与本币按汇率进行结算。如果中国国籍的买方在境外的线下商店通过微信、支付宝、信用卡或借记卡支付，则不能称为跨境电商支付。

跨境电商支付公司根据其成立背景可分为以下几类：

（1）国际在线支付公司，成立于20世纪90年代，如中国的乒乓、连连专业支付公司，社交软件业务拓展的微信支付，电商

Table 7-1　The Three Flows' Comparison Between Cross-Border
E-Commerce and Domestic E-Commerce

Type	Sub-class	Source seller	Source buyer	Information flow	Logistics flow	Capital flow		Transaction and clearing duration
						payment	settlement	
Domestic E-commerce	N/A	Local	Local	Taobao, Pinduoduo, Jingdong, Suning, Dangdang and other E-commerce platforms	Local	RMB	RMB	Short, after the buyer confirms the receipt of the goods, the payment will be in the account and can be withdrawn at any time
Cross-border E-commerce	Export	Local	Over-seas	Alibaba, AliExpress, DHgate, Amazon, eBay, Shopee and other cross-border E-commerce platforms, Shopify, Shoppy, Bigcommerce and other independent stations, TikTok and other social platforms	Cross-border	FEX	RMB	Long, in order to enhance the shopping experience, overseas warehouse mode can be adopted, which is controlled by logistics, national cross-border e-commerce, foreign exchange and other laws and regulations
	Import	Overseas	Local	Cross-border E-commerce platforms, independent stations or social platforms, such as Tmall Global, NetEase Kaola, Miya, yMatou, Jingdong Global, etc.	Cross-border	RMB	FEX	Long, in order to enhance the shopping experience, bonded warehouse mode can be adopted, which is controlled by logistics, national cross-border E-commerce, foreign exchange and other laws and regulations

表 7-1　跨境电商与国内电商的三流比较

类型	子类	源头卖家	源头买家	信息流	物流	资金流		交易和清算时长
						支付	结算	
国内电商	不适用	境内	境内	淘宝、拼多多、京东、苏宁、当当等电商平台	境内	人民币	人民币	短，买方确认收货后，货款到账，可随时提现
跨境电商	出口	境内	境外	阿里巴巴国际站、速卖通、敦煌网、亚马逊、eBay、Shopee 等跨境电商平台，Shopify、Shopyy、Bigcommerce 等独立站或 TikTok 等社交平台	跨境	外币	人民币	长，为增强购物体验可采用海外仓模式，受物流、国家跨境电商、外汇等法规管制
	进口	境外	境内	天猫国际、网易考拉、蜜芽、洋码头、京东全球购等跨境电商平台，独立站或社交平台	跨境	人民币	外币	长，为增强购物体验可采用保税仓方式，受物流、国家跨境电商、外汇等法规管制

online from E-business platforms, and online payment companies such as PayPal, Payoneer, WorldFirst and Strip. These companies cooperate to provide a wide range of E-commerce financial services. Usually, different companies set the starting point of withdrawal of cash to the bank and charge for different proportions of service fee according to the withdrawal amount. You may find the latest regulations on the official website of each company.

(2) Traditional financial enterprises can be divided into commercial banks, remittance companies, international card companies, etc.

① Commercial banks, which sprouted in the 17th century, can handle electronic remittance, collection, letter of credit and other business. The currency operated by commercial banks can be in the form of paper money, coins or electronic form, which is widely used.

② Remittance companies, such as Western Union remittance company (founded in 1851) and MoneyGram company (founded in 1940), can handle small amount of US dollar collection and payment, which can arrive to the account within about 10 minutes.

③ Traditional international card issuing companies were established later than 1950s—1960s, such as China UnionPay Online, and foreign companies such as MasterCard and Visa, which can be divided into debit card and credit card. The card issuing company cooperates with the bank, so there is no handling charge for anyone to withdraw cash from the bank.

平台拓展的支付宝、京东在线等；国外的贝宝、派安盈（Payoneer）、万里汇、Strip 等。这些公司合作支付的电商业务范围较广。通常，视不同公司规定提现到银行的起点并收比例不等的手续费。可在各公司的官方网站查找最新规定。

（2）传统金融企业，可分为商业银行、汇款公司、国际卡公司等。

① 创始于 17 世纪的商业银行可以办理电子汇款、托收、信用证等业务。商业银行所经营的货币可以是纸币、铸币或使用范围很广的电子形式的货币。

② 汇款公司，如西联汇款公司（于 1851 年成立）、速汇金公司（于 1940 年成立）可以办理美元小额收付，10min 左右快速到账。

③ 传统国际发行卡公司，成立于 20 世纪 50—60 年代以后，如中国的银联在线，国外的万事达卡（MasterCard）、维萨卡（Visa）等公司，这些卡可分为借记卡与贷记卡。发行卡公司与银行合作，因此不存在提现到银行收手续费的问题。

Knowledge Extension: Debit Card and Credit Card

Debit card, by which consumers can make payment online or by POS, transfer money and withdraw cash from ATM, but cannot be overdrawn. The amount in the card is calculated and paid interest according to the current deposit. Passwords are needed before money is directly transferred out of the savings account.

知识拓展：借记卡与贷记卡

借记卡是消费者可以通过网上或 POS 机进行支付、转账和 ATM 取款的借记卡，不能透支。卡内金额按活期存款计算并支付利息。钱直接从储蓄账户转出之前需要密码。

Credit card is an electronic payment card issued by commercial banks or other financial institutions, which has all or part of the functions of consumption payment, credit loan, transfer settlement, cash deposit and withdrawal. It is not encouraged to deposit cash in advance, but to consume before repayment. Cardholders enjoy interest free repayment period, and can repay by installments (with minimum repayment amount). Consumers holding credit cards can consume in special merchants, and then the bank will settle transaction with merchants and cardholders. Cardholders can overdraft within the specified amount.

贷记卡是商业银行或其他金融机构发行的具有消费支付、信用贷款、转账、结算、现金存取。等全部或部分功能的电子支付卡。该卡不鼓励提前存入现金，而是先消费再还款。持卡人享受免息还款期，可通过分期付款方式还款（最低还款额）。持有贷记卡的消费者可先在特约商户消费，然后银行与商户和持卡人进行结算。持卡人可在规定金额内透支。

(3) Companies of payment on mobile facilities: Huawei wallets, Xiaomi wallets, Apple wallets and Samsung wallets are usually bound with mobile phones or tablets of corresponding brands. Through bank account recharge, consumers can buy products in their online cooperative mall. China's wallet payment companies can provide money transfer, cash withdrawal, financial management, small loans and other amount services. Depending on the amount of cash withdrawal, there is no or a certain proportion of service charge. At present, Apple and Samsung wallets can be recharged, but the balance cannot be withdrawn. It is difficult for ordinary companies to realize the cross-border E-commerce collection function for all wallet payment.

（3）移动设备支付公司，如华为钱包、小米钱包、苹果钱包和三星钱包等，通常与相应品牌的手机或平板电脑绑定。通过银行账户充值，消费者可在其合作商城购买产品。中国的钱包支付公司提供转账、取现、理财、小额贷款等金额服务。取现视金额不等免收或收一定比例手续费。目前，苹果和三星钱包可以充值但余额无法提现。所有钱包支付对普通公司来说很难实现跨境电商收款功能。

(4) Search engine payment companies: Baidu wallet, Google wallet, etc. can also recharge their bank accounts and buy products in their cooperative online shopping malls, provide small loan lines, and are free or charge a certain proportion of service fees depending on the amount of cash withdrawal. The cross-border E-commerce collection function is also difficult to operate.

（4）搜索引擎支付公司，如百度钱包、谷歌钱包等，也可通过银行账户充值并在其合作商城购买产品，提供小额贷款额度，取现视金额不等免收或收一定比例手续费。跨境电商收款功能较难操作。

As a buyer or seller of all kinds of cross-border online transactions, the seller should prevent the goods from being transferred back to China in RMB after export, and the buyer should also avoid the situation that the goods cannot be successfully paid for. Therefore, when choosing different

作为各种跨境线上交易的买家或卖家，卖方应防止货物出口后货款无法换成人民币调回国内，同样买方应避免发生无法顺利支付买到心仪的进口商品的情况。

companies to receive and pay for goods, we must carefully investigate the relevant provisions of the transaction countries and payment companies about cash flow and assess all the risks.

7.1.2   Payment of Cross-Border E-Commerce Platforms

1．AliPay——taking AliExpress export as an example

Xiaowei receives money by exporting goods from shops on AliExpress, so she needs to set up a RMB collection account or USD collection account. The platform receives transaction funds from different collection accounts according to buyer's choice.

When buyers pay by credit card (RMB channel), AliPay will convert US dollars into RMB to its account according to the exchange rate of buyers at the same day. Specific operations are as follows.

(1) Log in AliExpress, click the "transaction" to enter the "collection account management" interface, and select the "RMB collection account".

(2) Click "create Alipay account", or use the existing Alipay, and click "log in Alipay account" for binding.

(3) Create or log in successfully after Alipay account to complete the receipt account binding.

When buyers pay through PayPal, credit card (US dollar channel), bank wire transfer and Western Union remittance, AliPay will pay the US dollar to dollar receiving account, deducting the handling fee of US $20 each time. Specific operations are as follows.

(1) Log in to AliPay, click "transaction"→"bank account management" to enter the "collection account management" interface, and then click "create US dollar collection account".

(2) After entering the new US dollar account, you can select two account types: "company account" and "personal account".

(3) After selecting the account, fill in "Account name

因此，选择不同公司进行货款的收付时，必须认真调研交易有关的国家及支付公司资金流转的相关规定并评估风险。

7.1.2   跨境电商平台支付

1．支付宝——以阿里巴巴速卖通出口为例

小薇通过速卖通开立的店铺出口商品收款，那么她需要设置人民币收款账户和美元收款账户。平台根据买家不同的支付方式，由不同的收款账户接收交易款项。

买家通过信用卡（人民币通道）进行支付时，支付宝会按照买家支付当天的汇率将美金转换成人民币支付到支付宝中。具体操作如下。

（1）登录速卖通，单击"交易"进入"收款账户管理"界面，选择"人民币收款账户"。

（2）单击"创建支付宝账户"，也可以使用已经有的支付宝，单击"登录支付宝账户"进行绑定。

（3）创建或者登录成功支付宝账户后，即完成收款账户的绑定。

买家通过 PayPal，信用卡（美元通道）、银行电汇、西联汇款等方式进行支付时，支付宝将美元支付到美金收款账户，每次扣除手续费 20 美元。具体操作如下。

（1）登录速买通，单击"交易"→"银行账户管理"，进入"收款账户管理"界面，单击"创建美元收款账户"。

（2）单击进入新建美元账户之后，可以选择"公司账户"和"个人账户"两种账户类型。

（3）选择账户后，填写"开

(Chinese)") →"Account name (English)"→" Account bank"→"Swift code"→"Bank account number" and other required items. After filling in, buyers click the "save" button.

Operation precautions:

(1) After setting up the AliPay account, it cannot be deleted. If there is no AliPay account, the payment of the order can't be received.

(2) A single AliPay account can bind multiple sellers' shop accounts.

(3) To set a US dollar collection account, you can choose one from two account types: "company account" or "personal account". After setting successfully, you cannot delete it but modify the relevant information of the account.

➤ Company account.

• All information cannot be filled in in Chinese, otherwise you may fail to receive proceeds and pay repeated service charges.

• The company's account must have the right of import and export operation according to government regulations and be approved by the bank to open a US dollar account.

• Only by going through the customs declaration procedures in accordance with the provisions of China's import and export customs and the commodity inspection department can the company receive US dollars and convert it into RMB smoothly.

➤ Personal account.

• Don't fill in all the information in Chinese, otherwise sellers may fail to receive proceeds and pay repeated service charges.

• The personal account is a US dollar debit card, not a credit card. It must be able to receive the company's remittance to individuals in US dollars paid by Citibank in Singapore.

• There is no limit on the amount of foreign exchange

户名（中文）"→"开户名（英文）"→"开户行"→"Swift code"→"银行账号"等必填项，填写完毕后，单击"保存"按钮。

操作注意事项：

（1）设置支付宝收款账户后不能删除。因为如果没有支付宝账户，就无法收到订单货款。

（2）一个支付宝账户可以绑定多个卖家店铺账号。

（3）设置美元收款账户，可从两种账户类型中进行2选1："公司账户"或"个人账户"。设置成功后不能删除，只能修改账户相关信息。

➤ 公司账户。

• 所有信息不能使用中文填写，否则将引起收款失败，从而产生重复的收款手续费损失。

• 公司账户必须具有进出口经营权，经银行审查批准开立美元账户。

• 按中国进出口海关及商检规定办理报关手续，才能顺利收到美元并兑换成人民币。

➤ 个人账户。

• 所有信息不要使用中文填写，否则将引起放款失败，从而产生重复放款手续费损失。

• 个人账户为美元借记卡，不是贷记卡。必须能接收在新加坡的花旗银行以美元支付的公司对个人的汇款。

• 个人账户收外汇没有限制，

received by individual accounts, and the total amount of annual withdrawal can exceed 50,000 US dollars.

- Converting FEX into RMB shall comply with the regulations of the state on foreign exchange control. At present, each person has an annual settlement limit of 50,000 US dollars.

2．A variety of payment methods——by taking the export collection of Amazon platform as an example

As a famous cross-border E-commerce company in the world, Amazon's traffic accounts for half of the global traffic, and its influence goes deep into the European and American markets. According to the data disclosed by Amazon, the annual growth rate of Amazon GMV (Gross Merchandise Volume) is more than 20%, especially in 2020, which was 41.79% higher than that in 2019. In 2020, Amazon GMV (Figure 7-1) was 475 billion US dollars, among which the third-party sellers created 295 billion US dollars, and Amazon accounted for 180 billion US dollars. Amazon is a platform for international sellers to seize. Amazon sellers need to complete the corresponding settings in "Setting"→"Account Information"→"Payment Information"→"Deposit Method" of the seller platform. Collection methods mainly include International online payment company, Amazon platform payment and bank account collection.

(1) International online payment companies, such as PingPong, LianLian, WorldFirst, Payoner and other common companies, are relatively easy to apply, and can directly withdraw cash to the domestic bank card after arrival, which is almost the collection method that more than 90% of Chinese sellers choose now. Each of the four world-famous international online payment companies has its own characteristics. Comparison of four third-party payment companies in the world for Amazon is shown in Table 7-2.

(2) Amazon global collection service is a collection service launched by Amazon platform for Chinese sellers, which is calculated according to the real-time exchange rate.

年提款总额可以超过 5 万美元。

- 将美元结算成人民币需要符合国家外汇管制条例。目前，每人具有每年 5 万美元的结汇限额。

2．多种支付方式——以亚马逊平台出口收款为例

作为世界知名跨境电商公司，亚马逊的流量占据了全球流量的一半，影响力深入欧美市场。根据亚马逊披露的数据，亚马逊 GMV（商品交易总额）年增长率在 20% 以上，特别是 2020 年比 2019 年增长 41.79%。2020 年，亚马逊 GMV（图 7-1）为 4750 亿美元，第三方卖家创造 2950 亿美元，亚马逊自营 1800 亿美元。亚马逊是国际卖家纷纷抢占的平台。亚马逊卖家收款要在卖家平台的"设置"（Setting）→"账户信息"（Account Information）→"付款信息"（Payment Information）→"存款方式"（Deposit Method）中完成相应设置。收款方式主要包括国际在线支付公司、亚马逊平台支付和银行账户收款三种类型。

（1）国际在线支付公司，如乒乓、连连、万里汇、派安盈（Payoneer）等常见的公司，相对来说申请较容易，到账后可直接提现至国内银行卡，几乎是现在 9 成以上的中国卖家选择的收款方式。这四家全球知名的国际在线支付公司各有特色。亚马逊全球四家第三方支付公司的比较见表7-2。

（2）亚马逊全球收款服务是亚马逊电商平台针对中国卖家推出的收款服务，按照实时汇率计

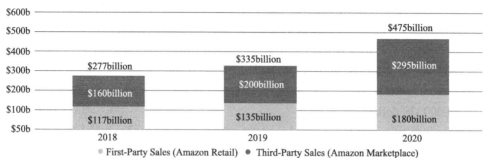

Figure 7-1   Amazon GMV

Source: Yuguo Cross-border

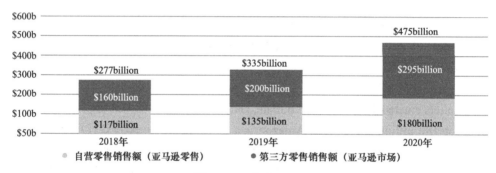

图 7-1   亚马逊 GMV

资料来源：雨果跨境。

Table 7-2   Comparison of Four Third-Party Payment Companies in the World for Amazon

Element	PingPong	LianLian	WorldFirst	Payoneer
Service site	Amazon North America, Europe, Japan, Australia, India, Singapore, UAE, Brazil and Turkey	Amazon North America, Europe, UK, Japan, Australia, India, UAE	All sites on Amazon	All sites on Amazon
Trading foreign exchange	USD, EUR, GBP, JPY, AUD etc. , CAD,SGD,IDR etc.	USD, AUD, DKK, EUR, JPY, NZD, NOK, GBP, ZAR, SEK, CHF	GBP,USD,CAD, JPY, EUR, NZD, SGD, AUD, offshore RMB etc.	There are more than 150 currencies, including USD, EUR and GBP
Converting into CNY	√	√	√	√
Service charge	1%	0.7%	0.3%	1.2%
Transfer time	T+0	T+0	T+0	T+1-3 working days
Annual fee	Free	Free	Free	Free, except physical card USD29.95
Other services	VAT payment in 7 European countries, one-stop export tax rebate, advance collection and other services	Tax rebate in 5 European countries, housekeeper, VAT payment, one click shop, claim master, cross-border logistics and other services	VAT payment covers 5 European countries, UAE and Saudi Arabia. It is a green channel for sellers to open shop all over the world	Balance direct payment on 1688 website, VAT payment, and professional consulting service

表 7-2　亚马逊全球四家第三方支付公司的比较

比较要素	PingPong	LianLian	WorldFirst	Payoneer
服务站点	亚马逊北美站、欧洲站、日本站、澳大利亚站、印度站、新加坡站、阿联酋站、巴西站、土耳其站	亚马逊北美站、欧洲站、英国站、日本站、澳大利亚站、印度站、阿联酋站	亚马逊全站点	亚马逊全站点
交易币种	美元、欧元、英镑、日元、澳大利亚元、加元、新加坡元、印度卢比等	美元、澳大利亚元、丹麦克朗、欧元、日元、新西兰元、挪威克朗、英镑、南非兰特、瑞典克朗、瑞士法郎等	英镑、美元、加元、日元、欧元、新西兰元、新加坡元、澳大利亚元、离岸人民币等	美元、欧元、英镑等150 多个币种，最全
人民币提现	√	√	√	√
手续费率	1%	0.7%	0.3%	1.2%
到账时间	当天	当天	当天	1～3 个工作日
年费	免费	免费	免费	实体卡 29.95 美元，无实体卡免费
其他服务	欧洲 7 国 VAT 缴纳、一站式出口退税、提前收款等服务	欧洲 5 国退税、管家、VAT 付款、一键开店、索赔大师、跨境物流等其他服务	VAT 缴税覆盖欧洲 5 国、阿联酋及沙特阿拉伯。开立账户证明，卖家全球开店绿色通道	1688 网采用余额直付、VAT 缴纳、专业顾问服务

Knowledge Extension: Third-party Payments

PingPong: founded in August 2014 and affiliated to Hangzhou PingPong Intelligent Technology Co., Ltd., it is a local multi regional collection brand in China. It is committed to providing low-cost overseas collection services for Chinese cross-border E-commerce sellers. Its emergence has reduced the industry's common collection rate from 3%~5% to 1%. You can use the balance of the same currency to pay VAT directly to the tax authority of seven European countries, saving your extra cost of withdrawal and remittance.

LianLian: established in 2003, it is a company dedicated to creating "simpler cross-border payment" in Hangzhou. With its strong compliance security strength and efficient and flexible global payment network, Lianlian has supported dozens of global E-commerce platforms, covering more than 100 countries and regions. Payment collected from online shops on European E-commerce platforms to LianLian can directly be used to pay VAT taxes.

乒乓：成立于 2014 年 8 月，隶属于杭州乒乓智能科技有限公司，是中国本土多区域集合品牌。该公司致力于为中国跨境电商卖家提供低成本的海外代收服务。它的出现使行业的平均收费率从 3% ～ 5% 降到 1%。可以使用同种货币的余额直接支付增值税到欧洲 7 个国家的税务部门，节省额外的提现和汇款费用。

连连：成立于 2003 年，是一家致力于在杭州打造"更简单的跨境支付"的公司。凭借其强大的合规安全实力和高效灵活的全球支付网络，连连已支持数十个全球电商平台，覆盖 100 多个国家和地区。从欧洲电商平台店铺收款到连连，可以直接用于缴纳增值税。

WorldFirst: Since its establishment in 2004, WorldFirst has handled over 70 billion pounds of capital transactions for 500,000 cross-border E-commerce customers worldwide. It joined Ant Group in 2019 and became an important component of international payment services. With the help of its business ecosystem, the company's clients can receive money within seconds when they withdraw money from Alipay or their bank cards. It also provides VAT tax services, account proof letters, and global value-added services.

万里汇：自 2004 年成立以来，已为全球 50 万名跨境电商客户处理了 700 多亿英镑的资金交易。它于 2019 年加入蚂蚁集团，成为国际支付服务的重要组成部分，并借助其商业生态系统，该公司客户在支付宝或银行卡上提款可在几秒钟内收到款项。该公司还提供增值税服务、账户证明函和全球增值服务。

Payoneer: founded in 2005 and headquartered in New York, Payoneer is a payment company specialized in transferring funds to global cross-border E-commerce customers to earn exchange losses and handling charges. The company provides simple, safe and fast transfer service for the alliance with wide distribution of payment crowd. It is also a card issuing organization authorized by MasterCard.

派安盈：成立于 2005 年，其总部位于纽约，是一家专门为全球跨境电商客户转移资金以赚取汇兑损失和手续费的支付公司。该公司为支付人群分布广泛的联盟提供简单、安全、快捷的转账服务。它也是万事达卡授权的发卡机构。

After the seller opens this service, there is no need to bind a foreign bank card or a third-party payment company's account as a collection account. It can directly use the local currency to receive global payments, and it can be deposited into the seller's domestic bank account within two working days at the soonest. At present, the service has covered Amazon's top 10 overseas sites in the United States, Canada, Germany, United Kingdom, France, Netherlands, Italy, Spain, Japan and Mexico. The seller who needs to open this service needs to click "Deposit method" in "Settings" of the seller platform, change the deposit information, select the selling country and add a domestic bank account in China. 0.4%-0.9% step-by-step service charge pricing is implemented. The rate is updated every month, and the more favorable rate ladder can be automatically upgraded every month. The disadvantage of this settlement method is that the exchange rate cannot be selected individually, and there may be losses.

算。卖家开通此项服务后，无须绑定外国银行卡或者第三方支付公司账户作为收款账户。可以直接使用本地货币接收全球付款，最快在两个工作日内就能存入卖家国内银行账户。目前，该服务已经覆盖亚马逊的美国、加拿大、德国、英国、法国、荷兰、意大利、西班牙、日本与墨西哥十大海外站点。需要开通此项服务的卖家，需要在卖家平台的"设置"中单击"存款方式"，更换存款信息，选择销售国并添加一个中国国内的银行账户即可。实行 0.4% ～ 0.9% 阶梯式手续费定价，费率每月更新，每月都可自动升级更优惠的费率阶梯。该结算方式的缺点是个人无法选择兑换汇率，且可能存在损失。

(3) Bank accounts collection, accounts in the United

（3）银行账户收款，一般接

States or Chinese Hong Kong are generally accepted. The collection violates the national regulations on foreign exchange management, the account opening is difficult, there is also exchange loss and no direct tax refund, and the transfer to the domestic RMB account is complicated and costs are incurred, so it is not recommended.

3．International online payment companies commonly used in different countries

The development level of politics, economy, finance and science and technology is different all over the world, so people's payment habits and payment methods are also different. Alipay and WeChat in the Asia Pacific region are the 2 most commonly used online payment methods in China. WebMoney and BitCash are popular online payment tools in Japan. At present, they have cooperation with three major Japanese banks and 711, Lawson, Quanjia, Ministop, NewDays and other convenience stores. Toss is the largest mobile payment application in R.O. Korea. It supports 29 banks in R.O. Korea, covering more than 98% of bank users in R.O. Korea. Users can collect the detailed information of all bank accounts on the application, fully understand their financial status, check and manage their credit scores, purchase various savings products or make small investments. Paytm is one of the largest online payment gateway and recharge portal in India, providing many online services, such as shopping, utility bill payment, travel, movie and event booking, etc. MoMo is the E-wallet of M Service company, providing users with online payment, point-to-point transfer, and public and entertainment recharge services. Currently, MoMo provides online payment services for more than 100 enterprises, and cooperates with more than 20 banks in Vietnam and payment networks of Visa, MasterCard and other card organizations.

At present, the utilization rate of credit card in Southeast Asia is relatively low, so there will be more online bank transfer or ATM payment. eNETS is a professional payment network operator in Singapore, in line with the payment habits

受美国或者中国香港银行账户。收款违反国家外汇管理规定，账户开通比较困难，存在汇兑损失且无法直接退税，转账至国内人民币账户手续烦琐且产生费用，不建议采用。

3．不同国家常用的国际在线支付公司

世界各地的政治、经济、金融和科技发展水平不同，因此国民的支付习惯和付款方式也不同。亚太地区的支付宝和微信是中国最常用的两种在线支付方式。WebMoney、BitCash 是日本流行的在线支付工具。目前，它们和日本三大银行及 711、罗森、全家、Ministop、NewDays 等便利店都有合作。Toss 是韩国最大的移动支付应用，支持韩国 29 家银行，覆盖韩国 98% 以上的银行用户。用户可在应用程序上汇总所有银行账户详细信息，全面了解其财务状况，还可以检查和管理信用评分，购买各种储蓄产品或进行小额投资等。Paytm 是印度最大的在线支付网关和充值门户之一，提供诸多在线服务，如购物、公用事业账单支付、旅行、电影和活动预订等各类支付等。MoMo 是 M Service 公司的电子钱包，为用户提供在线支付、点对点转账及公共和娱乐充值服务。MoMo 目前为 100 多家企业提供在线支付服务，并与越南 20 多家银行及 Visa、MasterCard 等卡机构的支付网络进行合作。

目前，东南亚地区的信用卡使用率较低，使用网银转账或者 ATM 机付款比较多。eNETS 是新加坡专业支付网络运营机构，符合

of local people; PayPal, AirCash and NetPay are popular used online payment tools in Malaysia, commonly used for online shopping; Dragonpay is a widely used payment method in the Philippines, and users can pay with online banking, mobile payment, ATM and offline physical stores; PayPal, TrueMoney and AirPay are the top three mobile payment tools in Thailand; OVO Wallet and DOKU Wallet are two most popular online payment companies in Indonesia, including wallet, online banking, ATM and convenience store payment.

PayPal is widely used in European countries for online payment; QIWI, Yandex Money and WebMoney are the three most commonly used E-wallets in Russia; iDEAL and PayPal are the mainstream online payment methods in Netherlands, which are widely used in cross-border transactions; DotPay, PayU, Przelewy24 and Blik are the main online payment methods in Poland; EPS is the online banking transfer method in Austria.

7.1.3 Cross-Border E-Commerce Payment Tools

When cross-border E-commerce platforms, independent stations or social networks provide two-way flow of information for buyers and sellers, cross-border E-commerce can also use payment tools of commercial banks, remittance companies, card companies and other traditional financial enterprises to complete cash flow due to factors such as transaction convenience, security and payment tools.

1. Bank Telegraphic Transfer (T/T)

Bank cross-border telegraphic transfer is one of the traditional cross-border settlement methods of import and export trade. The buyer, through its commercial bank, goes through the formalities in accordance with the relevant import regulations of the country, fills in the remittance form after approval, transfers the money to the designated bank account in the seller's country, and notifies the payee of the payment. It is often used in cross-border E-commerce B2B or B2C large amount of transaction payment, compared with

当地人支付习惯；PayPal、AirCash、NetPay 是马来西亚常用的在线支付工具，常用于在线购物；Dragonpay 是菲律宾应用较广泛的支付方式，用户可以用网银、手机支付、ATM 及线下实体店支付；PayPal、TrueMoney 和 AirPay 是泰国排名前三的移动支付工具；OVO Wallet、DOKU Wallet 是印度尼西亚两大常用在线支付公司，包括钱包、网银、ATM 和便利店支付。

欧洲国家较多使用 PayPal 完成在线支付；QIWI、Yandex Money、WebMoney 是俄罗斯最常用的三大电子钱包；iDEAL 和 PayPal 是荷兰主流在线支付方式，在跨境交易中应用非常广泛；DotPay、PayU、Przelewy24、Blik 是波兰主要在线支付方式；EPS 是奥地利在线网银转账方式。

7.1.3 跨境电商支付工具

当跨境电商平台、独立站或社交网络为买卖双方提供信息双向流动时，因为交易便利性、安全性和支付习惯等因素，跨境电商也可采用商业银行、汇款公司、信用卡公司等传统金融企业的支付工具完成资金流转。

1. 银行电汇（T/T）

银行跨境电汇是传统的进出口贸易跨境结算方式之一。买方通过其商业银行，按照该国有关进口规定办理手续审批通过后填写汇款单，将款项划转至卖方所在国指定银行账户，通知收款人货款到账。它常用于跨境电商 B2B 或 B2C 较大金额的交易付款，相比传统国际支付的信用证和托

the traditional international payment of letter of credit and collection, settlement procedures are simple and fast.

(1) Advantages: it is generally the pre T/T (payment in advance), and cross-border E-commerce sellers collect money first and then deliver goods, which can better protect the interests of sellers; bank wire transfer sets the maximum amount of remittance service charge, but there is no limit on the amount of remittance; the payment is directly to the bank account, and the seller does not need to withdraw money.

(2) Disadvantages: it involves the clearing between commercial banks in different countries, which may be higher than the handling charge of online payment companies; due to different countries and banks, the time of arrival is slower than that of online payment companies in underdeveloped financial regions; the buyer pays before receiving the goods, which bears greater risks.

2．Western Union remittance company

Western Union remittance company is the world's leading express remittance company, with an advanced electronic remittance financial network, and many express remittance agencies in nearly 200 countries and regions. The main partners of Western Union remittance company in China are China Construction Bank, China Everbright Bank, Postal Savings Bank of China, Shanghai Pudong Development Bank, etc., it is applicable to the payment of small samples, deposit or freight of US $2,000 or less for a single time, and the collection limit is US $10,000 or its equivalent in RMB.

(1) Advantages: Western Union global security ensures system provides operation password and optional password to verify the relevant information of the payment, ensuring the safety of each remittance and quickly remits to the designated payee; it operates for 365 days, and the payee can receive the remittance only a few minutes after handling the remittance procedures; there are many agency outlets, which are convenient for both parties to remit and collect money; Western Union remittance company and China UnionPay payment jointly launched online remittance method to realize online processing.

收，结算手续简单和快捷。

（1）优点：一般为前 T/T（预付货款），跨境电商卖方先收款后发货，较好地保护卖家的利益；银行电汇设置汇款手续费的最高限额，但对汇款金额不设限；货款直接付到银行账户，卖家无须提现。

（2）缺点：涉及不同国家商业银行间的清算，可能比在线支付公司的手续费高；到账时间因国家和银行不同，在金融不发达地区比在线支付公司到账慢；买方在未收货前付款，承担较大风险。

2．西联汇款公司

西联汇款公司是世界上领先的特快汇款公司，拥有先进的电子汇兑金融网络，在全球近 200 个国家和地区拥有众多特快汇款代理网点。西联汇款公司在中国的合作伙伴主要有中国建设银行、中国光大银行、中国邮政储蓄银行、上海浦发银行等多家银行，适用于支付单次 2 000 美元及以下小额样品、定金或运费，收汇限额为 1 万美元或等值人民币。

（1）优点：西联全球安全电子系统提供操作密码和自选密码以核实款项的相关信息，确保每笔汇款的安全快速汇到指定的收款人手中；365 天营业，办理汇款手续后，收款人仅在数分钟内就可收到汇款；代理网点分布众多，便于交易双方汇款和收款；西联汇款公司与中国银联电子支付共同推出在线汇款方式，实现线上办理。

(2) Disadvantages: the service charge of the remittance amount is paid according to a certain proportion, and the overall rate is on the high side; the buyer pays before goods being delivered, thus bears more risks; at present, the settlement currency is only US dollar.

3. Moneygram remittance company

Similar to Western Union remittance company, Moneygram remittance company has more than 300,000 outlets in 197 countries or regions around the world. It is a global fast remittance business between individuals, and is suitable for cross-border E-commerce retail business with annual transaction volume less than US $50,000. Relying on the special remittance route, Moneygram remittance company has business cooperation with Bank of China, Industrial and Commercial Bank of China (ICBC), China CITIC Bank, Bank of Communications and other financial institutions.

(1) Advantages: the remittance speed is fast. Under the condition that the remittance agency outlets (including the remittance outlets and the settlement outlets) can normally accept business, the remittance can reach the payee's account within ten minutes after remitting; the fee is slightly lower than that of Western Union remittance company, and the service charge is paid by the remitter, and the payee does not need to bear any service charge or surcharge; the remittance procedure is simple, and there is no need to fill in complex remittance forms. The payee is not required to open a bank account in advance.

(2) Disadvantages: Moneygram service is only available on weekdays, and can't provide remittance service for customers on non-weekdays; both remitter and payee must be individuals, which is not applicable to two parties in company identity; unlike Western Union remittance company, VIP service is not provided.

4. International credit card

Cardholders can consume by a credit card without prior deposit, and enjoy interest-free repayment period, which can be used for small payments below $1,000.

(1) Advantages: in line with the habits of buyers in

（2）缺点：按照一定的比例支付汇款金额的手续费，总体费率偏高；买方先付款后交货，承担较多风险；目前结算货币仅美元一种。

3．速汇金汇款公司

速汇金汇款公司与西联汇款公司相类似，在全球197个国家或地区拥有超过30万个网点。它是一种个人间的环球快速汇款业务，适用于年交易额在5万美元以下的跨境电商零售业务。速汇金汇款公司依托专门汇款路线，与中国银行、工商银行、中信银行、交通银行和其他金融机构有业务合作。

（1）优势：汇款速度快。在速汇金代理网点（包括汇款网点和解付网点）能够正常受理业务的情况下，速汇金汇款在汇出十分钟后可到达收款人账户；收费略低于西联汇款，手续费由汇款人支付，收款方无须承担任何的手续费或附加费；汇款手续简单，无须填写复杂的汇款路径。不要求收款人预先开立银行账户。

（2）缺点：速汇金服务仅限于工作日，非工作日无法为客户提供汇款服务；汇款人及收款人均必须为个人，不适用于公司身份的交易双方；与西联汇款不同，不提供VIP服务。

4．国际信用卡

持卡人无须事先存款，即可先行刷卡消费，并享有免息还款期，可用于1 000美元以下的小额支付。

（1）优点：符合欧美地区买家

Europe and the United States, they like to consume in advance; the payment of buyers is simple, convenient and fast, which only takes 3-5 seconds; the buyer's consumption record has real-time monitoring of bank credit data, which is conducive to reducing the risk of refusing to pay; when the transaction dispute is involved, the bank only freezes the amount of the transaction, not all transactions in the account.

(2) Disadvantages: international credit cards need to pay account opening fee and annual service fee; credit card companies generally set single transaction limit and daily transaction limit for cardholders, and payment cannot be made normally beyond the payment limit; there is a 180-day dishonor period during which cardholders can apply to the bank for dishonor, and the seller is at risk of dishonor.

7.2　Cross-Border E-Commerce Settlements

7.2.1　Overview of Cross-Border E-Commerce Settlements

People often confuse the concepts of payment and settlement. Generally, payment only involves the cross regional or national capital expenditure of the parties concerned. Cross-border E-commerce settlement focuses on checking the three flows of capital flow, logistics flow and information flow in accordance with the regulatory requirements of the authorities of foreign exchange, customs, inspection and quarantine, and taxation, so as to ensure the "real exchange value of goods". The purpose of cross-border E-commerce settlement is to ensure that all inbound and outbound transactions conform to the national policies and laws, safeguard national sovereignty and interests, and ensure people's health and property safety.

1.　Management of China's foreign exchange revenue and expenditure

The Regulations of the People's Republic of China on Foreign Exchange Administration is the basic norm in the comprehensive field of foreign exchange supervision in China, and is also the main basis of foreign exchange supervision. The import and export transactions of goods

习惯，喜欢提前消费；买家付款简单、方便、快捷，仅需 3 ~ 5s；买家消费记录具有银行信用数据实时监控，有利于降低拒付风险；当涉及交易争议时，银行仅冻结该笔交易的金额，不会冻结账户的所有交易。

（2）缺点：国际信用卡需要支付开户费和年服务费；信用卡公司一般对持卡人设置单笔限额和日交易限额，超出支付额度无法正常付款；有 180 天的拒付期，持卡人在拒付期内可以向银行申请拒付，卖方存在被拒付的风险。

7.2　跨境电商结算

7.2.1　跨境电商结算概述

人们经常混淆支付与结算的概念。支付一般仅涉及当事人跨地区或国家的资金支出。跨境电商结算重点按照外汇、海关、检验检疫、税收等监管要求，对资金流、货物流、信息流这"三流"进行检查，确保"商品的实际价值"。其目的在于保证一切进出境交易符合国家政策和法律的规范，维护国家主权和利益，保障人民健康和财产安全。

1.　中国外汇收支管理

《中华人民共和国外汇管理条例》是我国外汇监管综合领域的基础性规范，也是外汇监管的主要依据。跨境电商企业所开展的货物进出口交易属于经常项

carried out by cross-border E-commerce enterprises belong to the current account transactions involving goods. Enterprises should ensure that the transaction basis of foreign exchange collection and payment is true and legal. The legitimate foreign exchange income from the export of goods of cross-border E-commerce enterprises or individuals shall be retained in accordance with the relevant provisions of the state, or be sold to banks or third-party online payment companies authorized by the state at the foreign exchange rate, and the enterprises or individuals shall obtain the equivalent domestic currency. The act of an enterprise selling foreign exchange to financial institutions in accordance with state regulations is called settlement of foreign exchange. The foreign exchange funds needed by cross-border E-commerce enterprises or individuals to legally import goods can be paid from the foreign exchange account or to the bank or the third-party online payment company authorized by the state according to the foreign exchange rate and then paid to the seller. The purchase of foreign exchange by enterprises or individuals in accordance with national regulations is called foreign exchange purchase.

Enterprises engaged in import and export business must log in to the digital foreign exchange management platform of the State Administration of Foreign Exchange in accordance with national regulations, and handle the digital declaration of the balance of payments. The state implements the annual total amount management for the foreign exchange settlement and purchase of individuals, and the annual total amount is equivalent to USD 50,000 per person per year.

In order to prevent risks, the national financial supervision department issued the *Administrative Measures for the Online Payment Business of Non-bank Payment Institutions* to strengthen the supervision of non-bank payment institutions such as Alibaba Alipay and WeChat.The main contents are as follows.

The first is to clearly define the positioning of payment institutions. Adhere to the principle of small-value convenience and serving e-commerce, and effectively avoid cross-market risks.

目中涉及货物的交易项目，企业应确保收付汇的交易基础真实合法。跨境电商企业或个人的商品出口合法外汇收入按照国家有关规定保留或者按外汇牌价卖给银行或国家授权经营第三方在线支付公司，企业或个人拿到等值本国货币。企业将外汇按国家规定卖给金融机构的行为，称为结汇。跨境电商企业或个人合法进口商品需要使用的外汇资金，可以从外汇账户支出或向银行或国家授权经营第三方在线支付公司按外汇牌价购买后支付给卖家。企业或个人按国家规定用本国货币购买外汇的行为，称为购汇。

经营进出口业务的企业，必须按照国家规定登录国家外汇管理局数字外管平台，办理国际收支数字化申报。国家对个人结汇和境内个人购汇实行年度总额管理，年度总额分别为每人每年等值 5 万美元。

为防范风险，国家金融监管部门发布了《非银行支付机构网络支付业务管理办法》，对阿里巴巴支付宝、微信等非银行支付机构加强监管。其主要内容如下：

一是清晰界定支付机构定位。坚持小额便民、服务于电子商务的原则，有效隔离跨市场风险。

The second is to adhere to the real-name system for payment accounts. Strengthen the regulatory requirements for payment institutions to identify customer identity information through external multi-channel cross-validation, and curb illegal and criminal activities such as money laundering.

The third is to take into account payment security and efficiency. In line with the management idea that small-value payments focus on convenience and large-value payments focus on security, corresponding arrangements are made for the transaction limit of payment using the balance of the payment account, and payment institutions are guided to adopt security verification methods to ensure the safety of customer funds.

The fourth is to highlight the protection of the legitimate rights and interests of individual consumers, and improve the protection mechanism for customer rights and interests such as customer loss compensation and error dispute resolution.

The fifth is to implement classified supervision to promote innovation, and guide and promote payment institutions to carry out technological innovation, process innovation and service innovation on the premise of legal compliance.

According to the *Notice of the State Administration of Foreign Exchange on Supporting the Development of New Trade Formats*, under the conditions of meeting customer identification, transaction electronic information collection, authenticity review and other conditions, banks may, in accordance with the *Notice of the State Administration of Foreign Exchange on Printing and Distributing the Measures for the Administration of Foreign Exchange Business of Payment Institutions*, apply for providing cross-border E-commerce and foreign trade comprehensive services and other new trade market entities with electronic transaction information, payment institutions can provide cross-border E-commerce market entities with foreign exchange settlement and sales, and related fund collection and payment services based on transaction electronic information.

二是坚持支付账户实名制。强化支付机构通过外部多渠道交叉验证识别客户身份信息的监管要求，遏制洗钱等违法犯罪活动。

三是兼顾支付安全与效率。本着小额支付偏重便捷、大额支付偏重安全的管理思路，对使用支付账户余额付款的交易限额做出相应安排，引导支付机构采用安全验证手段来保障客户资金安全。

四是突出对个人消费者合法权益的保护，健全客户损失赔付、差错争议处理等客户权益保障机制。

五是实施分类监管推动创新，以引导和推动支付机构以合法合规为前提，开展技术创新、流程创新和服务创新。

根据《国家外汇管理局关于支持贸易新业态发展的通知》的规定，在满足客户身份识别、交易电子信息采集、真实性审核等条件下，银行可按照《国家外汇管理局关于印发〈支付机构外汇业务管理办法〉的通知》，申请凭交易电子信息为跨境电子商务和外贸综合服务等贸易新业态市场主体提供结售汇及相关资金收付服务，支付机构可凭交易电子信息为跨境电子商务市场主体提供结售汇及相关资金收付服务。

2. Penalty provisions for violation of foreign exchange regulations

If an enterprise or individual violates regulations by transferring domestic foreign exchange abroad, or transferring domestic capital abroad by deception, it shall be ordered to return the foreign exchange within a time limit and be fined less than 30% of the amount evaded; if the circumstances are serious, a fine of more than 30% of the evaded foreign exchange amount and less than the full amount shall be imposed; if the case constitutes a crime, it shall be investigated for criminal responsibility according to law.

If an enterprise or individual receives or pays the money that should be received or paid in RMB with foreign exchange, or fraudulently purchases foreign exchange from a financial institution engaged in foreign exchange settlement or sales with false or invalid transaction documents, the foreign exchange administration organ shall order it to redeem the illegal arbitrage funds and impose a fine of less than 30% of the illegal arbitrage amount; if the case is serious, a fine of more than 30% of the amount of illegal arbitrage and less than the full amount shall be imposed; if the case constitutes a crime, criminal responsibility shall be investigated according to law.

If a financial institution violates the regulations, it shall be ordered by the foreign exchange administration organ to make corrections within a time limit, confiscate its illegal income, and impose a fine of not less than 200,000 Yuan but not more than 1 million Yuan; if the case is serious or it fails to make corrections within the time limit, it shall be ordered by the foreign exchange administration organ to stop relevant business.

7.2.2 Cross-Border E-Commerce Export Settlement

As some cross-border E-commerce export enterprises lack the legal awareness of the state's foreign exchange management and violate the national laws and regulations, they are repatriated to foreign exchange and fined by the relevant departments of the state. If the circumstances are

2. 违反外汇法规处罚规定

若企业或个人具有违反规定将境内外汇转移境外，或者以欺骗手段将境内资本转移境外等逃汇行为，则由外汇管理机关责令限期调回外汇，处逃汇金额 30% 以下的罚款；情节严重的，处逃汇金额 30% 以上等值以下的罚款；构成犯罪的，依法追究刑事责任。

若企业或个人具有以外汇收付应当以人民币收付的款项，或者以虚假、无效的交易单证等向经营结汇、售汇业务的金融机构骗购外汇等非法套汇行为，则由外汇管理机关责令对非法套汇资金予以回兑，处非法套汇金额 30% 以下的罚款；情节严重的，处非法套汇金额 30% 以上等值以下的罚款；构成犯罪的，依法追究刑事责任。

金融机构违反规定，由外汇管理机关责令限期改正，没收违法所得，并处 20 万元以上 100 万元以下的罚款；情节严重或者逾期不改正的，由外汇管理机关责令停止经营相关业务。

7.2.2 跨境电商出口结汇

由于部分跨境电商出口企业缺乏国家外汇管理的相关法律意识，违反国家法律法规，被国家有关部门调回外汇并罚款。情节严重的构成犯罪行为。以下为近

serious, they constitute criminal acts. The following are the cases that have occurred in recent years.

Case 1: in April 2019, a cross-border E-commerce Co., Ltd. was ordered by the State Administration of Foreign Exchange to repatriate foreign exchange and imposed a fine of 810,000 RMB for its evasion of foreign exchange by transferring domestic foreign exchange abroad in violation of regulations.

Case 2: in April 2020, an enterprise mistakenly entered the "pit" of an underground bank. More than 5 million Yuan of legal income became illegal. It was suspected of illegal settlement of foreign exchange through an underground bank and was fined 5.21 million Yuan!

According to relevant national regulations, there are three basic ways of cross-border collection and settlement of foreign exchange.

1．Direct collection, collecting and settling foreign exchange by oneself or agent

Export enterprises shall, after obtaining the right to operate foreign trade in accordance with the law, go through the registration procedures of the "directory of foreign exchange income and expenditure enterprises" in the foreign exchange administration department, and then open a current account foreign exchange account in the bank (if it is necessary to obtain the approval of the State Administration of Foreign Exchange in advance through an overseas account or an offshore account) to handle the foreign exchange settlement procedures.

The state stipulates that the amount of individual export settlement of foreign exchange is 50,000 US dollars per year. Since 2014, the state has carried out foreign exchange reform pilot in Yiwu City, Zhejiang Province. Registered individual businesses in Yiwu can open foreign currency accounts to collect and settle foreign exchange. The commercial banks in Yiwu can withdraw cash and settle foreign exchange in real time through the network. There is no need to provide complicated documents, and there is no account management or handling charges. It only needs to pay about 10 Yuan for each customs declaration document.

年来发生的案例。

案例 1：2019 年 4 月，某跨境电子商务有限公司存在违反规定将境内外汇转移境外的逃汇行为被国家外汇管理局责令调回外汇，处 81 万元人民币罚款。

案例 2：2020 年 4 月，一家企业误入地下钱庄的"坑"，500 多万元合法收入变非法，涉嫌非法通过地下钱庄结汇等违规，被罚款 521 万元！

按照国家有关规定，跨境收款结汇的基本方式有如下三种。

1．直接收款、自行或代理办理收结汇

出口企业应当依法取得对外贸易经营权后在外汇管理部门办理"贸易外汇收支企业名录"的登记手续，然后到银行开立经常项目外汇账户（如需通过境外账户或者离岸账户的事先取得国家外汇管理局的批准）以办理结汇手续。

国家规定个人出口结汇每年有 5 万美元额度。自 2014 年起，国家在浙江义乌市做外汇改革试点。注册义乌个体工商户可以开外币账户收汇和结汇。义乌商业银行通过网络即可操作提现，结汇实时到账。无须提供烦琐单据，没有任何账户管理和手续费。只需支付每单约 10 元的报关单据费。

2. Channel for collection of online payment institutions

If the online payment institution cooperating with the cross-border E-commerce platform has the pilot qualification for cross-border foreign exchange payment, for example, after the payment of the overseas buyer enters the foreign exchange reserve account of the bank, the online payment institution can follow the real and legal goods trade transaction background. According to the principle of restoring transaction information under trade in goods one by one, the foreign exchange settlement and sales business will be centralized for sellers of export commodities.

7.2.3 Foreign Exchange Purchase for Import of Cross-Border E-Commerce

At present, there are four modes of cross-border E-commerce import: domestic E-commerce platform direct mail B2C, domestic E-commerce platform bonded warehouse delivery B2C, foreign individual purchasing C2C, and foreign E-commerce platform overseas online shopping B2C. Due to the legal compliance of transactions, the authenticity of goods, the timeliness of logistics and other reasons, foreign individual purchasing and overseas E-commerce platform overseas online shopping are not the mainstream cross-border E-commerce import mode. When consumers purchase goods through domestic cross-border E-commerce platform, the third-party payment institutions or commercial banks cooperating with the platform will automatically help consumers purchase foreign exchange according to the foreign exchange rate. The E-commerce platform will send the corresponding information flow, logistics flow, capital flow and other data to the customs system at the background to complete a series of procedures such as foreign exchange verification.

The differences between domestic E-commerce platform direct mail and bonded warehouse delivery are:

Direct mail means that after receiving orders, cross-border E-commerce companies send foreign goods to the entry customs through cross-border logistics, go through the customs declaration and inspection procedures, and then deliver them to consumers, which takes a long time to mail.

2. 在线支付机构通道收款

如果与跨境电商平台合作的在线支付机构具有跨境外汇支付试点资格，如境外买家的付款在进入银行的外汇备付金账户之后，该在线支付机构可按照真实合法的货物贸易交易背景，依据货物贸易项下的交易信息逐笔还原的原则，集中为出口商品的卖家办理结售汇业务。

7.2.3 跨境电商进口购汇

目前，跨境电商进口有国内电商平台直邮 B2C、国内电商平台保税仓发货 B2C、国外个人代购 C2C、国外电商平台海淘 B2C 这四种模式。国外个人代购和国外电商平台海淘出于交易的合法合规性、货物真假、物流时效等原因，现已不是主流的跨境电商进口模式。消费者通过国内跨境电商平台购买商品，与平台合作的第三方支付机构或商业银行将自动按外汇牌价帮助消费者购外汇。电商平台在后台将相应生成的信息流、物流、资金流等数据发送到海关系统后，完成外汇核销等一系列手续。

国内电商平台直邮与保税仓发货的区别：

直邮是指跨境电商公司接到订单后，将国外货物通过跨境物流发至入境海关，办理报关报检手续后，再送达消费者手里，邮寄时间较长。

The bonded warehouse delivery refers to that the cross-border E-commerce company transports the whole batch of foreign goods to the domestic bonded warehouse in advance, and uses the cross-border E-commerce mode for customs declaration and inspection; after the consumers place an order on the E-commerce platform and finish the payment, the platform sends the correspondingly generated order, payment form, logistics form and other data to the customs system for declaration, and after the customs release, the bonded warehouse packages the goods according to the order and sends them to the domestic express delivery to the recipient. When a cross-border E-commerce company sells a commodity, it will clear the customs. Unsold goods cannot be out of the bonded center, but there is no need to declare, so unsold goods can be directly returned abroad.

NetEase Kaola has built cross-border bonded warehouses in Hangzhou, Ningbo, Zhengzhou and other places. Through cooperation with cross-border free trade zones, Tmall Global has established its own cross-border commodity logistics warehouses in bonded logistics centers all over the country, which shortens the time from placing an order to arrival, and greatly meets consumers' demand for timeliness of goods.

Since January 1, 2019, China has increased the single transaction limit of consumers' cross-border E-commerce retail imports from RMB 2,000 to RMB 5,000, and the annual transaction limit from RMB 20,000 to RMB 26,000. Consumers can only purchase imported goods through cross-border E-commerce platforms such as domestic Tmall Global, NetEase Kaola, Jingdong Global, yMatou, and Shunfeng Haitao. For goods purchased within the quota, they can enjoy the preferential treatment of no tariff, with a 70% discount on value-added tax and consumption tax. After placing an order, consumers can query their cross-border E-commerce consumption details through the "customs cross-border E-commerce annual personal quota query" website. It should be pointed out that: the goods purchased by consumers are only for personal use, and the imported goods purchased by cross-border E-commerce retailers are not allowed to enter the domestic market for resale; the imported goods purchased

保税仓发货是指跨境电商公司预先将整批国外货物运至国内保税仓库，采用跨境电商模式报关报检；消费者在电商平台上下单付款后，电商平台将相应生成的订单、支付单、物流单等数据发送到海关系统进行申报，海关放行后，保税仓根据订单将商品打包并由国内快递送达收件人。跨境电商公司卖一件商品，就清关一件。没卖掉的商品就不能出保税中心，但也无须报关。卖不掉商品的可直接退回国外。

网易考拉海购在杭州、宁波、郑州等地建有跨境保税仓。天猫国际通过与跨境自贸区的合作，在全国各地的保税物流中心建立自己的跨境商品物流仓库，缩短了从下单到到货的时间，极大地满足了消费者对商品及时性的需求。

自 2019 年 1 月 1 日开始，我国将消费者跨境电商零售进口商品的单次交易限值由人民币 2 000 元提高至 5 000 元，年度交易限值由人民币 20 000 元提高至 26 000 元。消费者只能通过国内天猫国际、网易考拉、京东全球购、洋码头、顺丰海淘等跨境电商平台购买进口商品，在额度内购买的商品，可以享受免征收关税的待遇，而增值税及消费税享受 7 折优惠。下单之后，消费者可通过"海关跨境电商年度个人额度查询"网站查询本人跨境电商消费明细。需要指出的是：消费者所购商品仅限于个人自用，对于已购买的跨境电商零售进口商品，不得进入国内市场再次销售；

beyond the quota will not be released by the customs.

Open the mini program on WeChat "Customs on Hand" or download the App. After registering and logging in as prompted, you can query the personal consumption information of the cross-border E-commerce (Figure 7-2).

超额度购买的进口商品，海关将不予放行。

在微信上打开"掌上海关"小程序或下载手机 App。根据提示注册并登录后，可查询跨境电商个人消费信息（图 7-2）。

Figure 7-2   Open the "Customs on Hand" Mini Program to Find Your Personal Consumption Information of Cross-Border E-Commerce

图 7-2   打开"掌上海关"小程序以查询跨境电商个人消费信息

7.2.4   Import and Export Financing of Cross-Border E-Commerce

Cross-border E-commerce providers are new industries that are supported by national policies. Consumers who purchase imported goods can obtain small loans in advance through credit card, AliPay Huabei and Jiebei. This section will focus on the import and export financing of enterprises. The fundamental purpose of cross-border E-commerce platform, E-commerce sellers or service providers and other ecosystem enterprises' financing is to obtain operating funds, maintain abundant cash flow and keep sustainable development. Financing can be borrowing in the name of the whole enterprise, or businesses engaged in cross-border

7.2.4   跨境电商进出口融资

跨境电商是国家政策扶持的新兴行业。购买进口商品的消费者可以通过信用卡、支付宝花呗和借呗获得小额借款提前消费。本节将着重探讨企业进出口融资。跨境电商平台、电商卖家或服务商等生态圈企业融资的根本目的是获取经营用资金，保持现金流充沛，保持可持续发展。融资可以是以整体企业名义借款，或者从事跨境业务的商家专门为某项

business obtain financial support from financial service providers for a certain export or import business.

1. Capital financing

The financing of large cross-border E-commerce enterprises has been favored by the capital market since the rise of the industry in 2015. In 2020, China's economy recovered rapidly after the test of epidemic situation, and cross-border E-commerce flourishes. According to the *2020 China Cross-Border E-commerce Financing Data List* released by the research center of E-commerce of ECOSOC, the "electronic data treasure" E-commerce database of ECOSOC showed that, in 2020, 33 platforms in China's cross-border E-commerce field obtained financing, with a total financing amount of more than 7.09 billion Yuan. There were nine import cross-border E-commerce financing case, exceeding 3.08 billion Yuan, including Xingyun Group, KK Group, Pea Princess, Hello World, yMatou, etc. Nine export cross-border E-commerce financing cases exceeded 1.85 billion Yuan, including fashion cross-border E-commerce website SheIn, VanTop Group, Starlink, Full Speed Online, OrderPlus Network, etc. Ten cross-border E-commerce service providers raised more than 1.45 billion Yuan, involving platforms including LianLian Digital, ZongTeng Group, E-commerce payment platform EMQ, PANEX, Xiaoman Technology, Lingxing, etc.

2. Financing of Internet financial services company

The ecosphere business development of cross-border E-commerce business has led to the growth of a number of emerging Internet financial services companies, such as Alibaba OneTouch, LianLian, PingPong, etc.

3. Financing of cross-border E-commerce platform

For small and medium-sized sellers, Alibaba, Amazon, eBay, Wish and other cross-border E-commerce platforms have additional financing assistance policies in some special periods, such as the epidemic situation, to ease the financial pressure of some entrepreneurs.

Alibaba enterprise finance can provide super L/C financing interest rate discount as low as 7.65% for businesses, and cooperate with China Construction Bank to

出口或进口业务向金融服务商获取资金支持。

1. 资本融资

自 2015 年该行业兴起，大型跨境电商企业融资一直受到资本市场青睐。2020 年，中国经过疫情考验，快速恢复经济，跨境电商蓬勃发展。根据网经社电子商务研究中心发布的《2020 年中国跨境电商融资数据榜》，网经社"电数宝"电商大数据库显示，2020 年中国跨境电商领域共有 33 家平台获得融资，融资总额超 70.9 亿元。进口跨境电商融资事件 9 起超 30.8 亿元，包括行云集团、KK 集团、豌豆公主、你好世界、洋码头等。出口跨境电商融资 9 起超 18.5 亿元，包括时尚跨境电商网站 SheIn、万拓科创、斯达领科、全速在线、澳鹏网络等。跨境电商服务商融资 10 起超 14.5 亿元，涉及的平台包括连连数字、纵腾集团、电商支付平台 EMQ、泛鼎国际、小满科技、领星等。

2. 互联网金融服务公司融资

跨境电商业务的生态圈业务发展带动一批新兴互联网金融服务公司的成长，比如阿里巴巴一达通、连连、乒乓等。

3. 跨境电商平台融资

对于中小型卖家，阿里巴巴国际站、亚马逊、易贝、Wish 等跨境电商平台在疫情等一些特殊时期都有额外融资帮扶的政策，以缓解部分创业者的资金压力。

阿里巴巴国际站企业金融可为商家提供低至 7.65% 的超级信用证融资利率优惠，并会同中国

Knowledge Extension: CBEC Financing Platforms

OneTouch financial services: OneTouch provides export, customs clearance, tax rebate, foreign exchange and other one-stop online services, covering the financing needs of all aspects of import and export. Bank of China took the lead in setting up a foreign exchange settlement network in the company to provide more convenient and efficient foreign exchange settlement services. Customers directly enjoy the A-level qualification of foreign exchange management, who can flexibly choose the time of foreign exchange settlement. And it can also provide foreign exchange hedging services for customers, so as to lock in the exchange rate cost of future foreign exchange settlement or purchase in advance and prevent the risk of exchange rate fluctuation. In addition, the company provides "OneTouch flow loan" products for customers who use Alibaba OneTouch's basic export services, and uses the export line to accumulate the credit line as a pure credit loan service without mortgage and guarantee. According to the needs of export enterprises in the use of L/C funds, package loans (before shipment) and post presentation loans (including buyout and financing after shipment) are introduced, which can be flexibly selected on demand.

LianLian financial services: LianLian provides online technical solutions for Order Treasure and Credit Treasure. Order Treasure and Credit Treasure have the advantages of full line operation and what you see is what you get. They help small and micro cross-border E-commerce sellers solve the financing difficulties and high financing costs in the process of capital turnover. Order Treasure is a financing product solution based on cross-border E-commerce seller's orders. Lianlian generates a credit line according to the seller's daily orders in transit. The maximum single credit line provided by financial institutions is 10 million Yuan, and the maximum borrowing period is 60 days. Credit Treasure is a financing product solution based on seller's digital credit. Through comprehensive evaluation of the seller's operation on the E-commerce platform, the seller will be granted a credit line of up to 2 million Yuan in advance, with interest

知识拓展：跨境电商融资平台

一达通金融服务：一达通提供出口、清关、退税、外汇等一站式线上服务，涵盖进出口各环节的融资需求。中国银行率先在该公司设立结汇网络，提供更加便捷、高效的结汇服务。客户直接享有A级外汇管理资质，可灵活选择结汇时间，并可为客户提供外汇对冲服务，锁定未来结汇或购汇的汇率成本，提前防范汇率波动风险。此外，公司提供"一达通流动贷"产品，面向使用阿里一达通基础出口服务的客户，使用出口额度累计授信额度为纯信用贷款服务，不需要抵押担保。根据出口企业使用信用证资金的需要，推出了打包贷款（装船前）和交单后贷款（包括买断和装船后融资），可按需灵活选择。

连连金融服务：连连为订单宝和信用宝提供在线技术解决方案。订单宝和信用宝具有全线运营优势，所见即所得。该公司帮助小微跨境电商卖家解决资金周转过程中的融资难、融资成本高等问题。订单宝是一款基于跨境电商卖家订单的融资产品解决方案。连连根据卖家日常在途订单生成信用额度，最大单笔授信额度为1 000万元，最长借款期限为60天。信用宝是基于卖家数字信用的融资产品解决方案。通过综合评估卖家在电商平台的经营情况，预给卖家最高200万元的授信额度，每日计息，接连偿还，

calculated daily and repayment with loan. The loan period is up to 90 days. The seller can enjoy pure credit and no mortgage online financing services within the credit line.

PingPong financial services: PingPong launched the "Light Year" series of advanced collection products to solve the problem of shortage of funds and financing difficulties for sellers. Under the "Light Year" series, there are currently "Accelerated Earning" and "Zhiri Da" products. Among them, "Accelerated Earning" is a short-term capital turnover product. "Zhiri Da" is a medium and long-term capital turnover product. "Light Year" series products are flexible in cash withdrawal, helping sellers to cross the longest 90 days' collection cycle, revitalize funds and solve financing difficulties.

贷款期限最长为 90 天。卖家可在授信额度内享受纯授信、无抵押网上融资服务。

乒乓金融服务：乒乓开启"光年"系列先进的收款产品，解决资金短缺问题及卖家的融资困难。在"光年"系列下，目前有"加速赚"和"指日达"产品。其中，"加速赚"是短期的资金周转产品，"指日达"是中长期资金周转产品。"光年"系列产品提现灵活，帮助卖家跨越最长 120 天收款周期，盘活资金，解决融资难问题。

reduce the e-tax loan interest rate, with the annualized interest rate reduced from 5% to 4.5%. From February 4, 2020, new customers could enjoy the discount within the validity period of the contract (12 months). From February 12, 2020, E-commerce banks could provide B2B businesses with a 12-month special assistance loan with a total amount of 10 billion Yuan, and a minimum loan interest rate of 20%.

The period from shipment to collection of cross-border E-commerce is relatively long. Some cross-border E-commerce retail platforms, such as Amazon, Wish, AliExpress and eBay provide financing services according to orders, and the seller can get advance collection. AliExpress's financing products are relatively mature, and Wish is also actively promoting its products.

4. Bank financing

Under the pressure of strong competition, traditional commercial banks implement financial reform and transform their offline business to online business. Through online banking, they collect information from cross-border E-commerce operators in order, production, logistics, delivery, payment and other aspects of the supply chain, provide real-time online electronic financial services, such as international

建设银行下调电子税贷款利率，年化利率由 5% 下调至 4.5%。自 2020 年 2 月 4 日起，新申请的客户在合同有效期（12 个月）内可享受优惠。自 2020 年 2 月 12 日起，网商银行为 B2B 商家提供为期 12 个月、总额为 100 亿元的特别扶助贷款，贷款利率最低 8 折。

跨境电商发货到收款周期比较长。亚马逊、Wish、速卖通、eBay 等一些跨境零售平台跨境电商提供按订单进行融资的服务，卖家可以获得预先收款。阿里速卖通融资产品做得较成熟，Wish 目前也在积极推行。

4. 银行融资

传统商业银行在强大竞争压力下实施金融改革，线下业务向线上转型。通过网上银行向跨境电商经营者集中采集供应链订单、生产、物流、交付、付款等各环节信息，提供实时在线的国际贸易融资、商业账款管理等综合服

trade financing, commercial account management and other comprehensive services, and realize the structural integration of the information of receivable, payable, prepaid and inventory in the supply chain.

务的电子化金融服务，实现对供应链中应收、应付、预付和存货等信息的结构性整合方案。

New words

1. payment and settlement 支付与结算
2. People's Bank of China 中国人民银行
3. bank card 银行卡
4. credit card 贷记卡
5. debit card 借记卡
6. China UnionPay 中国银联
7. search engine 搜索引擎
8. GMV（Gross Merchandise Volume）商品交易总额
9. SWIFT（Society for Worldwide Interbank Financial Telecommunication）code 环球银行间金融电信协会（每个成员银行拥有的特定）代码
10. foreign exchange（FEX）外汇
11. bank telegraphic transfer 银行电汇
12. settlement of foreign exchange（出口）结汇
13. foreign exchange purchase（进口）购汇
14. State Administration of Foreign Exchange（SAFE）国家外汇管理局
15. penalty provision 处罚规定

Chapter 8

Cross-Border E-Commerce Customer Service

跨境电商客户服务

Lead-in case

Xiaowei has known the main links of cross-border E-commerce, platforms, logistics, settlement, etc. She has already roughly known what cross-border E-commerce is. Now she is ready to start with the products she is familiar with, and starts to learn how to operate and sell. How does cross-border E-commerce do? Cross-border E-commerce customer service is the main link of product operation and sales. This chapter takes AliExpress and Shopee as examples. After studying this chapter, you will work with Xiaowei to get a preliminary understanding of how to conduct customer communication and provide service on cross-border E-commerce platform.

Learning objectives

1. Objectives of knowledge

(1) To master the customer service process of cross-border E-commerce.

(2) To grasp the characteristics of the customer service communication of the mainstream global cross-border E-commerce platform.

(3) To understand the requirements and career development direction of cross-border E-commerce customer service positions.

2. Objectives of skills

(1) To be able to communicate in foreign languages and use computer software to handle daily business correspondence and other documents.

(2) To respond to customer's enquiry quickly and to sort the information in time.

(3) To demonstrate the flexible communication skills during the commodity operation and selling processes according to the different characteristics of customers.

案例导入

小薇了解了跨境电商概况、平台、物流、结算等主要环节。她已经大致知道了跨境电商是什么。现在,她准备从自己熟悉的产品入手,开始学习如何运营和销售。跨境电商是怎么做的?跨境电商客户服务是产品运营销售的主要环节。本章内容以速卖通和Shopee平台为例,通过学习你将与小薇一起初步了解在跨境电商平台如何进行客户沟通和服务。

学习目标

1. 知识目标

(1)掌握跨境电商的客户服务流程。

(2)掌握全球跨境电商主流平台客服沟通的特点。

(3)了解跨境电商客服岗位的要求和职业发展方向。

2. 技能目标

(1)能用外语进行商务沟通,用计算机软件处理日常业务函电等文件。

(2)能迅速回应客户,并及时对信息进行分类整理。

(3)能根据客户的不同特点,在商品经营和销售环节展现灵活的沟通能力。

3．Objectives of qualities

(1) To have the professionalism of customer first, and find out the problems in the process of online and offline operation in advance.

(2) To have the psychological quality of rationally, calmly and objectively mobilizing resources and properly handling customer complaints.

(3) To have a lasting interest in learning new knowledge and new skills.

8.1 Pre-Sale Service of Cross-Border E-Commerce

8.1.1 Understanding the Process of Making Goods

Pre-sale service of cross-border E-commerce is the most inconspicuous but most important link for cross-border E-commerce platforms to conduct transactions. Understanding the production process of commodities is the prerequisite for analyzing the financial costs of commodities. The purpose of analyzing financial costs is to calculate the external quotations of commodities, finally understand the problems that customers may ask, and can deal with various problems that may arise in the process of customer service.

Take clothing as an example, which is the category cross-border E-commerce sells best, the first thing customer service needs to do is to know the material, color, basic workmanship, special size and processing technology of clothing; as to shoes, customer service needs to know the style of shoes, materials and colors, and the most important thing is to have an accurate understanding of the size units of shoes in different countries; as to electronic products and lightings, customer service should be familiar with the composition, accessories, functions and voltage of the product. There are also products that are relatively easy to operate in cross-border E-commerce, such as maternal and child products, jewelry, home furnishings, and luggage, customer service only needs to understand what the products are made of. Only by understanding the production process of the commodities, can customer service answer various questions raised by

8.1 跨境电商售前服务

8.1.1 了解商品制作过程

跨境电商售前服务是跨境电商平台达成交易的最不起眼但却最重要的环节。了解商品的制作过程是分析商品财务成本的前提。分析财务成本的目的是核算商品的对外报价，最终对客户可能提出的问题了然于心，可以应对在客户服务过程中出现的各种问题。

以跨境电商销售最多的类目服装为例，客服先要做到的就是知晓服装的材质、颜色、基本做工、特殊尺寸和加工工艺等；对于鞋类，客服在对鞋子的样式、材质和颜色了然于心的同时，最重要的是要对不同国家衡量鞋子的尺码单位都有精准的认识；对于电子产品和灯具，需要对商品的构成、配件、功能及电压等参数非常熟悉。对于母婴商品、珠宝首饰、家居用品、箱包等跨境电商比较容易经营的商品，客服只需要了解商品是由什么制成的即可。只有了解商品的制作过程，才能回答交易过程中客户提出的

customers during the transaction.

8.1.2   Analyzing Financial Costs of Commodities

The financial cost of a commodity generally refers to the purchase costs. Factors such as raw materials cost, production cost, sales cost, and the human resources cost of the commodity should be taken into account during the purchase. The "inquiry-quote" model in traditional foreign trade is equally applicable to cross-border E-commerce. Cross-border E-commerce customer service is equivalent to half of the salesperson in the traditional trade, which means they must learn to analyze the financial costs, and predict logistics costs and sales profits of goods exactly.

8.1.3   Accounting for External Quotation of Commodities

The premise of calculating the external quotation of goods is to analyze the financial cost of the goods, but also it needs to consider the quality and grade of the specific goods, the distance of transportation, the location and conditions of delivery, seasonal changes in demand, the sorting of transactions, the conditions of payment and the changes in exchange rate risk. For the same product, the quotations received by B2B customers on the cross-border E-commerce platform are definitely different from those received by B2C customers. The quotations received by B2B customers are not only lower than the quotations received by B2C, but also they have more choices. Because wholesale customers' inquiries are often sent to sellers in batches, after receiving multiple quotations, customers will compare the quotations and transportation service conditions horizontally. That is the reason why many quotations do not get replied. B2C customers are generally individuals, who receive retail prices, and B2C customers will also compare horizontally, but for the reason that the unit prices are similar, they tend to place orders as soon as possible. Therefore, the external quotations sent by the customer service for customers with different needs are different.

各种问题。

8.1.2   分析商品财务成本

商品财务成本一般指采购成本。采购时需要考虑商品的原材料成本、生产成本、销售成本、人力资源成本等因素。传统外贸中的"询盘—报价"的模式在跨境电商中一样适用。跨境电商客服相当于传统贸易中的半个业务员，即要学会分析商品的财务成本，对商品的成本、物流运输费用和销售利润的预算都有准确的预判。

8.1.3   核算商品对外报价

核算商品对外报价的前提是分析商品的财务成本，但也要考虑具体商品的质量、档次，运输距离，交货地点和条件，季节性需求变化，成交的梳理，支付的条件和汇率变动的风险。对于相同的商品，B2B 客户在跨境电商平台上收到的报价和 B2C 客户收到的报价肯定不同。B2B 客户收到的报价不但比 B2C 收到的报价更低且有更多的选择。因为批发客户的询盘往往是向卖家批量发出的，在收到多个报价后，客户会对报价及运输服务条件进行横向比较。这是很多批发价报出去之后石沉大海的原因。B2C 客户一般是接受零售价格的个人，B2C 客户也会进行横向比较，但因为单价相差不多，往往会尽快下单。因此，客服面对不同需求的客户采用的对外报价是不同的。

8.2 In-Sale Service of Cross-Border E-Commerce

8.2.1 Customer Counseling and Response

1. To be the leader of communication

As we all know, the main job of customer service is communication. In the business field, another layer of communication means negotiation. One of the necessary professional skills for customer service is to be the leader of negotiation, to control customers' perception of products and emotions towards transactions. Under normal circumstances, cross-border E-commerce customers will not contact the seller before placing an order. "Silent ordering" is a common situation of cross-border E-commerce, unless the customer is buying technology products or during B2B bulk wholesale, otherwise the role of customer service in the pre-sale consultation is not as obvious as during or after sales. Therefore, whenever customer service encounters a pre-sale consultation, it needs to answer questions about "products" or "services". Cross-border E-commerce has a huge variety of products, and there are huge differences in product specifications at home and abroad. When customers ask any questions about the products, the customer service must provide a complete answer, put forward a feasible plan, and be the leader of the communication.

Customer service is required to have two most basic qualities for consultation. The first is to have a full and in-depth understanding of the industries and products in which they operate. As mentioned in the previous section, if you are dealing in clothing and footwear industry, you need to have a full understanding of the definition of different size units in our country and abroad to help customers choose the right size; if you are dealing in electrical and electronic products, you must be familiar with the capacity, voltage, current, plug, etc., to ensure that the technical indicators of domestic and foreign products can be safely matched, so that customers can use them safely when they receive the goods.

8.2 跨境电商售中服务

8.2.1 客户咨询与回复

1. 做沟通的主导

众所周知，客服的主要工作是沟通。在生意场上，沟通的另一层意思就是谈判。做谈判的主导，控制客户对商品的认知和对交易的情绪，是客服必备的职业技能之一。一般情况下，跨境电商客户在下单购买之前是不会与卖家进行联系的。"静默式下单"是跨境电商常有的状态，除非客户正在购买技术类产品或是B2B大宗批发买卖，否则客服的作用在售前咨询这个环节体现的作用并不如售中或售后那么明显。因此，但凡客服遇到售前咨询，都需要客服解答或有关"产品"或有关"服务"的问题。跨境电商的商品种类庞杂，商品规格存在巨大的国内外差异。当客户提出任何关于商品的问题时，客服都要做出完整的解答，提出可行的方案，要做沟通的主导。

客服提供咨询需要两个最基本的素质。一是对所经营的行业与商品有充分和深入的了解。如上一节所述，若经营服装和鞋类，则要对国内外不同尺码单位界定要有充分的了解，以帮助客户选到适合身材或脚型的商品；若经营电器电子类产品，则要对商品的容量、电压、电流、插头等计量有换算的能力，保证国内外产品的技术指标安全匹配，让客户收到商品时可以安全使用。这些

These are the qualities that customer service needs first. The second is that the customer service must be familiar with the cntire cross-border E-commerce business process. It needs to clearly understand the production process of the product, cost accounting, logistics methods, and customs clearance policies of various countries, so as to occupy a leading position in the transaction communication process, promptly and effectively respond to customer doubts, so as to facilitate transactions.

2．To use reliable data

Due to the long distance and cumbersome process of cross-border transactions, coupled with differences in language and culture, these are all obstacles in cross-border transactions. Customers will inevitably not trust the seller during the purchase process. Therefore, whether it is pre-sale, in-sale or after-sale, customer service needs to provide real data that can convince customers. Especially in the in-sale link, when the customer service predicts that the order may be placed soon, it is necessary to provide the customer with detailed data to ensure the success of the transaction. For the product itself, the detailed pictures of the product, detailed instructions for how to use, video explaining the technical details of the product, customer praise rate, repurchase rate, etc., are all real data visible to the customers; for logistics and customs inspection issues that customers care about, the relevant parcel order number, logistics query tracking website, customs inspection certificate, etc., are also supporting data for customers to buy with reliance.

3．To take responsibility

In general, the party who made the "mistake" often needs to bear the "responsibility". However, in the field of E-commerce, especially cross-border E-commerce, when after-sales disputes arise, "responsibility" and "mistake" need to be distinguished temporarily. "Mistake" is the cause of the problem. One party does something unreasonable or irregular that leads to negative effects or undesirable consequences. "Responsibility" is the solution to the problem caused by "mistake", which is for one party to restore the negative impact or make up for the bad consequences of measures or

都是客服需要首先具备的素质。二是客服要熟悉整个跨境电商经营流程。对商品的制作过程、成本核算、物流方式、各国的清关政策等步骤，客服都需要清楚明白，这样才能在交易沟通过程中占据主导位置，及时有效地解答客户的疑虑，促成成交。

2．用可靠的数据

由于跨境交易距离远、流程烦琐，加上语言和文化的差异，所以这些都是跨境交易的障碍。客户在购买过程中不可避免地会对卖家不信任。因此，无论是售前、售中还是售后，客服都需要提供让客户信服的数据。尤其在售中环节，客服在预知可能马上就要谈妥下单时，需要给客户提供详尽的数据来确保交易的成功。对商品本身而言，商品的细节图片、详细的使用说明、说明商品的技术细节视频、客户的好评率、回购率等都是客户肉眼可见的真实数据；对于客户关心的物流和海关检验问题，相关的包裹订单号、物流查询追踪网址、海关检验通过的证明等，也是客户得以放心购买的支撑数据。

3．勇于承担责任

在一般情况下，犯"错误"的一方往往需要来承担"责任"。但在电商尤其是跨境电商领域，当产生售后纠纷时，需要暂时区分"责任"和"错误"。"错误"是出现问题的原因，一方做出不合情理或常规的事导致结果的负面影响或不良后果；"责任"是"错误"导致的问题的解决方案，是一方为了挽回负面影响或弥补不良后果做出的措

proposed solutions.

8.2.2 Encouraging Customers to Place Orders and Making Payments

Common communication skills are as follows:

1. Language using

It is not necessary for every position in the cross-border E-commerce industry to have superb foreign language skills, but for customer service, it is necessary to master the language of the most important customers. Customer service needs to continuously learn foreign languages and understand the culture of the target country, and especially need to accurately grasp the professional terms of the products sold. In terms of working attitude, customer service is also required to avoid spelling and grammatical errors. Correctly using the customer's mother tongue is not only to show respect to customers, but also to effectively improve customer trust.

2. Communication methods

The communication method of cross-border E-commerce customer service is often the way of real-time Q&A or message answer. The former needs to quickly understand what customers mean and respond quickly. When communicating in this way, pay attention to using short sentences with simple structure and plain words, so that customers can understand the meaning of the seller in the shortest time. The language used most by cross-border E-commerce platforms is English, but there may be customers who come from more than 220 countries and speak different languages. Many customers' native languages are not English, and customers often read customer service responses through softwares such as Google Translate. At this time, it is even more necessary for customer service to simplify language and improve communication efficiency.

The communication method of answering messages is more common in B2B cross-border trade. This kind of communication is often presented by mail. There are two points to pay attention in E-mail communication. The first is that there should be no capitalization in paragraphs. Using capital letters to highlight key information in E-mail can

施或提出的方案。

8.2.2　促成客户下单与付款

常用的沟通技巧如下：

1．语言运用

跨境电商行业并非需要每个岗位都具备高超的外语技能，但对于客服而言，必须熟练掌握最主要客户的语言。客服需要不断加深对外语及目标国家文化的学习和理解，特别需要准确掌握所售商品的专业用词。在工作态度上，也要求客服避免拼写和语法错误。正确使用客户的母语既是展示对客户的尊重，也能有效提高客户的信任度。

2．沟通方式

跨境电商客服的沟通方式往往是即时问答或留言回答的方式。前者需要快速理解客户的意思且迅速做出回应。在用这种方式沟通时要注意使用结构简单、用词平实的短句，使客户可以在最短时间内理解卖家所要表达的意思。跨境电商平台使用最多的语种是英语，但客户可能是来自220多个国家使用不同语言的客户。很多客户的母语不是英语，客户往往会通过Google翻译等软件来阅读客服的回复，这时更加需要客服用简练语言提高沟通效率。

回复留言的沟通方式在B2B的跨境贸易中更为常见。这种沟通方式往往采用电子邮件的方式来呈现。电子邮件沟通需要注意两点。一是不能有成段的大写。在电子邮件中使用大写符号突出

indeed allow customers to see the core content at a glance, but the side effect is that the use of capitalized paragraphs in English is often understood as expressions of anger and irritability, which is an impolite way of writing. The second is to pay attention to segmentation and blank lines. Normally, people read E-mails by "skimming" or "scanning" to speed up their reading. When composing E-mails, the customer service needs to divide the E-mails into reasonable paragraphs according to the transaction logic, and leave blank lines between the paragraphs, which are conducive to the customers to browse the important information quickly, and at the same time, it leaves the customers with a professional and well-organized good impression to enhance customers' trust.

3．Diversified reply methods

On cross-border E-commerce platforms, there are many products that are complicated to assemble, use or maintain. For these kinds of products, sellers often write a lot of product descriptions, and customer service tirelessly describes or explains technical parameters, usage methods, maintenance, etc. to customers, but this does not certainly solve their doubts. Even if customer service with a good language foundation or rich cross-cultural knowledge, it is difficult to explain complex issues in the written text because of insufficient knowledge in a certain area of the product. At this time, diversified communication methods are needed. For example, making installation flowcharts, shooting demonstration videos, finding suitable spokespersons to describe products in self-media such as YouTube, Twitter or Facebook (it's now called Meta), and leaving online voice or video contact information are all forms of diversified communication and response. Nowadays, the popular live streaming of E-commerce in China has gradually penetrated into the cross-border E-commerce field. Through real-time live broadcast explanation, customers can intuitively feel the performance and function of the product.

重点信息的确可以让客户一目了然地看到核心内容，但副作用是英语使用成段的大写往往会被理解为愤怒和暴躁的情绪表达，这是没有礼貌的书写方式。二是要注意分段和空行。通常，人们阅读电子邮件的习惯会采用"跳读"或"略读"的方式以加快阅读速度。客服在写电子邮件时需要按照交易的逻辑将邮件合理分段，在段与段之间加空行，有利于客户较快地浏览到重要信息，同时给客户留下专业、有条理的良好印象，以增强客户的信任度。

3．多样化的回复方式

在跨境电商平台上，有许多商品的组装或使用或后期的维护都比较复杂。卖家往往是通过撰写大量的产品描述，以及客服不厌其烦地向客户描述或解释技术参数、使用方法、维护保养等，但这并不一定能彻底解决客户的疑惑。即使是语言基础较好或跨文化知识较为丰富的客服，也会因为对商品相关的某一领域不够了解，使写出的文字难以解释复杂的问题。这时候，就需要采用多样化的沟通方式。制作安装流程图、拍摄演示视频、在 YouTube 或推特或 Facebook（现被称为 Meta）等自媒体中寻找合适的代言人描述商品，留下网络语音或视频的联系方式等，都是多样化沟通和回复的形式。现在，中国境内电商流行的直播带货也慢慢渗透到跨境电商领域。通过即时的直播讲解可以让客户直观地感受到商品的性能和功用。

8.3 After-Sale Service of Cross-Border E-Commerce

8.3.1 Understanding the Collection Channels of the Platform

Cross-border E-commerce platforms continue to connect with various payment channels, and generally support most mainstream payment methods in the world. At present, the most widely used payment method at home and abroad is still Visa and MasterCard, which can be seen everywhere online and offline. This payment method provides merchants all over the world with a safe and convenient instant payment online service. Cardholders can use Visa, MasterCard, JCB, AmericanExpress, and Diners Club International (Credit Card of Diners Club International) to pay, and easily complete online transactions. The payment amount is generally less than 50,000 US dollars. If a dispute occurs during the transaction that leads to a refund, the payment platform will complete the refund within 10-15 working days.

MasterCard is also a payment tool widely used in cross-border E-commerce. The payment limit of MasterCard is also under 50,000 US dollars. If there is a dispute in the transaction that leads to a refund, it will take 10-15 working days to complete the refund like Visa.

Western Union is currently recognized as the world's leading express money transfer company, with a history of 150 years. It has the largest and most advanced electronic remittance financial network in the world, with agency branches in 200 countries and regions around the world, and the payment amount is 20.01-50,000 US dollars. If a dispute occurs during the transaction that leads to a refund, the buyer can usually receive the refund within 7-10 working days.

Bank Transfer (TT payment) is a more traditional transaction method. The remitter pays a fixed amount of domestic currency to the domestic foreign exchange bank in exchange for a fixed amount of foreign exchange, and states the name and address of the beneficiary, and then the remittance

8.3 跨境电商售后服务

8.3.1 了解平台收款途径

跨境电商平台不断对接各种支付渠道,一般而言支持全球大部分主流的支付方式。目前,境内外使用最广泛的支付方式依旧是线上与线下随处可见的 Visa 和 MasterCard。该支付方式为全球商户提供了安全、便捷的即时到账在线支付服务。持卡人可用 Visa、MasterCard、JCB、AmericanExpress、Diners Club International(大莱俱乐部国际信用卡)来进行支付,轻松完成网上交易。支付额度一般在 50 000 美元以下。如果交易中产生纠纷导致退款,该支付平台会在 10 ~ 15 个工作日内完成退款。

MasterCard 也是在跨境电商领域应用较为广泛的支付工具。MasterCard 的支付额度也在 50 000 美元以下。如果交易中产生纠纷导致退款,和 Visa 一样也是在 10 ~ 15 个工作日内完成退款。

西联汇款是目前全球公认较为领先的特快汇款公司。它有 150 年的历史。它拥有全球最大和最先进的电子汇兑金融网络,代理网点遍布全球 200 个国家和地区,支付额度为 20.01 ~ 50 000 美元。如果交易中产生纠纷导致退款,买家通常可以在 7 ~ 10 个工作日内收到退款。

银行转账(TT 支付)是较为传统的交易方式。由汇款人以定额本国货币交于本国外汇银行换取定额外汇,并述明收款人的姓名与地址,再由承办银行即汇出

bank that is the undertaking bank converts and sends the telegram-style telegram, which is a remittance method that is passed to a branch or correspondent bank (remittance bank) in another country for instructions to settle the payment to the beneficiary. For this payment method, the bank generally takes 7 working days to confirm the buyer's payment and update it to the cross-border E-commerce platform.

QIWI Wallet is the largest third-party payment tool in Russia, similar to AliPay. Its maximum payment amount is below 5,000 US dollars. If it exceeds the amount, other payment methods will be needed to take its place. If a dispute occurs during the transaction that leads to a refund, the buyer can receive the refund within 10-15 working days.

Yandex.Money is a popular E-wallet in Russia, with 18 million active users, and its daily number of transaction reaches to 150,000, and the brand recognition in Russia is as high as 85%. AliExpress incorporated it into this younger payment channel through business evaluation.

WebMoney is a currency used for online shopping launched by the WebMoney company in Japan. It is presented in the form of a plastic card. The surface of the card is a password consisting of 16 uppercase and lowercase letters and numbers. There are two kinds of amounts, 2,000 Yen and 5,000 Yen. If a refund occurs, it can be received within 7-10 working days.

Boleto is a commonly used E-wallet payment method in Brazil, with a payment amount of 1-3,000 US dollars. The bank usually takes 7 working days to confirm the buyer's payment and update it to the cross-border E-commerce platform. If a dispute occurs during the transaction that leads to a refund, the cross-border E-commerce platform will refund via Ebanx, and buyers generally receive it within 7~10 working days.

MercadoPago is a payment company under eBay. Payment business is carried out in six countries: Argentina, Brazil, Chile, Colombia, Mexico, and Venezuela. AliExpress cooperates with MercadoPago. So buyers in Mexico can use

行折发加押电报式电传给另一国家的分行或代理行（汇入行）指示结付给收款人的一种汇款方式。对于该支付方式，银行一般需要 7 个工作日，以确认买家的付款并更新到跨境电商平台。

QIWI Wallet 是俄罗斯最大的第三方支付工具，类似于支付宝。它可以支持的最大支付额度在 5 000 美元以下。如果超额则需要更换其他支付方式。如果交易中产生纠纷导致退款，买家可以在 10 ～ 15 个工作日内收到退款。

Yandex.Money 是俄罗斯较为流行的电子钱包，拥有 1 800 万名活跃用户，日交易处理能力可以达到 15 万笔，在俄罗斯的品牌认可度高达 85%。速卖通通过商业评估将其介入了这个较为年轻的支付渠道。

WebMoney 是日本 WebMoney 公司推出的用于网上购物的货币。它以一张塑料卡的形式呈现。卡面是由 16 位大小写字母和数字构成的密码。额度有 2000 日元和 5000 日元两种。如果发生退款，可在 7 ～ 10 个工作日内到账。

Boleto 是巴西常用的电子钱包付费方式，支付额度为 1 ～ 3 000 美元。银行通常需要用 7 个工作日确认买家的付款并更新到跨境电商平台。如果交易中产生纠纷导致退款，跨境电商平台将通过 Ebanx 退款，买家一般在 7 ～ 10 个工作日内收到退款。

MercadoPago 是 eBay 的一家支付公司。在阿根廷、巴西、智利、哥伦比亚、墨西哥、委内瑞拉这六个国家都开展支付业务。

MercadoPago to shop directly on AliExpress. This is one of AliExpress' new payment methods in the South America market.

8.3.2 Mastering After-Sales Evaluation and Dispute Handling Rules

1. Evaluation

(1) Types of evaluation.

Evaluation is generally divided into credit evaluation and seller's itemized evaluation, which determine the seller's credit score and positive feedback rating respectively. Detail Seller Ratings (DSR) is a system that reflects the buyer's overall evaluation of the quality of the shop or product service.

Credit evaluation means that the buyer and seller of the transaction evaluate the credit status of the other party after the order transaction is over, which usually contains two parts: a five-point score and a comment.

The seller's itemized evaluation refers to the buyer's anonymous comment on the accuracy of the seller's item as described, communication quality and response speed, and the reasonableness of the item's delivery time. The evaluation is a single-direction evaluation of the buyer to the seller.

(2) Rules of evaluation time.

All orders shipped by sellers can be evaluated within a certain period of time after the transaction ends. For credit evaluation, if neither party has given an evaluation, the order will not have any evaluation record. If one party gives an evaluation, and the other party does not evaluate it, the system will not give the evaluation party a default evaluation.

(3) Rules of evaluation modification and deletion.

If the seller disagrees with the credit evaluation given by the buyer, he can contact the buyer within the validity period after the evaluation takes effect, and ask the buyer to modify the evaluation; the buyer can modify the evaluation

速卖通与MercadoPago合作，墨西哥的买家可以使用MercadoPago在速卖通上直接购物。这是速卖通在南美洲市场新增的支付方式之一。

8.3.2 掌握售后评价和纠纷处理规则

1. 评价

（1）评价的类别。

评价一般分为信用评价和卖家分项评价两种，分别决定了卖家信用积分和正反馈评级。卖家服务等级评分（DSR）是反映买家对店铺或商品服务质量的总体评价的系统。

信用评价是指交易的买卖双方在订单交易结束后对对方的信用状况进行评价，一般为五分制评分和评论两部分。

卖家分项评价是指买家在订单交易结束后以匿名的方式对卖家在交易中提供的商品描述的准确性、沟通质量及回应速度，物品运送时间合理性等方面做出的评价。这是买家对卖家的单向评分。

（2）评价时间规则。

买卖双方对所有卖家全部发货的订单在交易结束的一定期限内均可评价。对于信用评价，如果双方都未给评价，则订单不会有任何评价记录。若一方给出评价，另一方未评价，则系统也不会给评价方默认评价。

（3）评价修改、删除规则。

如果卖家对买家给出的信用评价有异议，可在评价生效后的有效期内联系买家，请买家对评价进行修改；买家可在有效期内

within the validity period to change the bad reviews to good ones, but the number of revisions is only once; similarly, if the buyer disagrees with the credit evaluation given by the seller, he can contact the seller within the validity period after the evaluation takes effect and ask the seller to modify the evaluation; the seller can modify evaluations within the validity period, and can change the bad reviews to good ones, but the revisions can only be made once. Buyers and sellers can also reply and explain the comments they have received. As for the buyer's shared evaluation, once the seller submits it, the evaluation takes effect immediately and cannot be modified. All cross-border E-commerce platforms reserve the right to change the credit system, including evaluation methods, calculation methods of praise rate, and various evaluation indicators.

2. Rules of dispute resolution

(1) Types of disputes.

① Do not receive the goods. Non-receipt of the goods is the most common type of dispute, including but not limited to the following situations: logistics information cannot be found; logistics shows that the goods have been delivered but the buyer complains that the goods have not been received; the goods are detained at the customs; the logistics shows that the goods are between the circumstance of "received and sent" and "delivered properly", such as leaving China, sending to a certain place, arriving at a post office, failing to deliver, etc.; the original goods are returned; the seller privately changes the logistics mode.

② The buyer refuses to sign. Buyers' refusal can be with or without reason. Reasonable refusal means that when the goods are delivered to the buyer, the buyer finds that the goods are damaged or are not in line with the order, such as damaged goods, short shipments, wrong goods, etc., under these circumstances, so the buyer refuses to sign on the spot. Refusal without reason is when the goods are delivered to the buyer, he refuses to sign for it without any reason.

对自己做出的评价进行修改，可以将差评改为好评，但修改次数只有一次；同样，如果买家对卖家给出的信用评价有异议，可在评价生效后的有效期内联系卖家，请卖家对评价进行修改；卖家可在有效期内对自己做出的评价进行修改，可以将差评改为好评，但修改次数只有一次。买卖双方也可以针对自己收到的评价进行回复解释。对于买家的分享评价，一旦卖家提交，评分即时生效且不能修改。所有的跨境电商平台都保有变更信用体系的权力，包括变更评价方法、好评率计算方法、各种评价指标等。

2．纠纷处理规则

（1）纠纷的种类。

① 未收到货。未收到货是最常见的纠纷种类，包含但不限于以下情况：查不到物流信息；物流显示已经妥投但买家仍投诉未收到货；货物在海关被扣留；物流显示货物介于"收寄"与"妥投"之间，比如离开中国、发往某地、到达某邮局、未妥投等；货物原件退回；卖家私自更改物流方式。

② 买家拒签。买家拒签包括有理由拒签和无理由拒签。有理由拒签是指货物递送至买家时，买家发现货物存在肉眼可见的损坏或与订单不符的情况，如货物破损、短装、货错等情况，买家当场拒绝签收。无理由拒签是指货物递送到买家时，买家无任何理由拒绝签收。

(2) Dispute settlement.

① Make a request. The prerequisite for the dispute must be done after the seller has shipped all the goods, otherwise the buyer cannot initiate the dispute. If the seller has not delivered the goods, the buyer can choose to cancel the order by himself, so there is no need to raise a dispute. The delivery time varies according to the promised delivery time set by the seller. Take AliExpress as an example, if the promised delivery time is less than 5 days, the buyer can file a dispute after the seller has shipped all the goods. If it is more than or equal to 5 days, the buyer can take up the dispute 5 days after the seller has shipped all the goods.

② Duration of dispute. Disputes rules on cross-border E-commerce platforms are constantly changing, and the time limit for filing disputes has become longer, which requires sellers to pay more attention to product quality and services. The increasing duration of dispute has a positive effect as well, which makes the buyers to be more willing to confirm that the goods have been received to some extent.

③ Number of dispute. Disputes on the AliExpress platform can only be raised by the buyer. Only after the two parties have reached a return agreement, the seller can raise the dispute at the receiving stage. The buyer can raise the dispute repeatedly before the order is sent to the platform until the two parties negotiate a solution, or wait the system to send it to the platform automatically.

④ Response time. Regardless of the reason, after the buyer submits or modifies the dispute, the seller must "accept" or "reject" the buyer's refund application within 5 days, otherwise the order will be executed according to the buyer's refund amount. At present, there are countless orders and sellers who have missed the 5-day response period, and this loss is hard to recover.

⑤ Platform ruling. If the buyer and seller cannot reach a consensus on the dispute, they can submit it to the platform for judgment. If the buyer raises a dispute and asks for refunds, as long as the seller refuses, he can upgrade to the

（2）纠纷处理。

①提起要求。纠纷提起的前提条件必须是卖家全部发货后，否则买家无法提起纠纷。如果卖家还未发货，买家可以选择自行取消订单，所以也不需要提起纠纷。交货时间根据卖家设置的承诺的交货时间而定。以速卖通为例，如果承诺的交货时间小于5天，则买家在卖家全部发货后就可以提起纠纷；若大于或等于5天，则买家在卖家全部发货后的5天后可以提起纠纷。

②提起时效。跨境电商平台纠纷规则不断变化，提起纠纷的时效相继变长，这就要求卖家更加注重产品的质量及服务。提起时效变长也有正面作用，在一定程度上使买家更愿意确认已收到货。

③提起次数。速卖通平台的纠纷只能由买家提出。只有双方达成退货协议后，卖家在收货阶段可以提起纠纷。买家在订单上送平台之前可以反复提起纠纷，直至双方协商出解决办法，或者等系统自动上送平台。

④响应时间。无论何种原因的纠纷，当买家提交或修改纠纷后，卖家必须在5天内"接受"或"拒绝"买家的退款申请，否则订单将根据买家提出的退款金额执行。目前，错过5天响应期的订单和卖家数不胜数，这种损失难以挽回。

⑤平台裁决。如果买卖双方无法就纠纷达成一致的处理意见，则可以提交到平台裁决。买家提起纠纷退款，只要卖家拒绝就可

platform for ruling; the seller can also submit a ruling to the platform for the return and refund agreement for unreceived goods within 30 days.

Online Dispute Resolution (ODR) mechanism could be also called online dispute resolution system, which is a platform or system providing online dispute resolution for buyers and sellers in the field of E-commerce, saving the communication cost of telephone or on-site transactions. In the current environment of cross-border E-commerce, the purpose of establishing an online dispute resolution mechanism is to build a low-cost, high-efficient, transparent and fair shopping environment for consumers.

8.3.3   Understanding the Punishment Regulations of the Platform

The most common punishment method for cross-border E-commerce platforms is to delete the illegal products and temporarily close the shop. This is the most common punishment method. The penalty of the violation of the customer's agreement is relatively not that serious, and the seller is directly judged to pay the liquidated damages. The most serious punishment is the permanent closure of the shop, which is definitely a punishment for serious violations. Generally, sellers dare not touch it. Intellectual property infringement, sales of prohibited and restricted goods, publication of prohibited information, fraud and other acts are not allowed on various cross-border e-commerce platforms. Take Shopee as an example, the punishment methods and rules are stipulated from three aspects, including the account usage, transaction behaviour, and the commodity itself.

以升级到平台裁决；卖家也可以就退货退款协议在 30 天内未收到货向平台提出裁决。

在线纠纷解决机制，也可称在线纠纷解决系统，就是为电商领域的买卖双方提供线上解决纠纷的平台或系统，节约了电话或实地交易的沟通成本。在当前跨境电商发展的大环境下，建立在线纠纷解决机制的目的是为消费者构筑低成本、高效率、透明公正的购物环境。

8.3.3   了解平台的处罚规定

跨境电商平台常见处罚手段是删除违规商品，并短暂封闭商铺。这是最常见的处罚方法。违反客户约定的处罚相对较轻，直接判定商家赔付违约金。最严重的惩罚是永久封闭店铺。这肯定是对严重违规的处罚。一般店铺是不敢触碰的。知识产权侵权、销售禁限售的商品、发布禁止发布的信息、欺诈等行为在各家跨境电商平台都是不允许的。以Shopee 为例，从账户使用和交易行为、商品本身三个方面规定了处罚方式和规则。

Knowledge Extension: Punishment Methods and Rules on Shopee

Account usage/transaction behavior: ① Fraud or affect transaction security; ② Order not made by oneself; ③ Fail to continuously contact with the verified mobile phone number; ④ Behavior that disrupts the platform or user; ⑤ Establish fake orders to sell and buy by oneself (e.g.

知识拓展：虾皮的处罚方式和规则

账户使用 / 交易行为：①诈骗或影响交易安全；②非本人下单；③经认证之手机号码持续联系未果；④扰乱平台或使用者之行为；⑤建立假订单自买自卖（例如，相

the act of opening an account with the same name, device, address, etc.)-revise reviews, sales or discount codes, credit card at random; ⑥ Abuse of shipping subsidies, discount codes, and Shopee coins.

Commodities: ① Major violation of regulations; ② Serious infringement of the intellectual property rights of third parties; ③ Avoidance of transaction fees (for example, setting unreasonable shipping charges).

Others: ① When using the services provided by Shopee, impersonate any person or entity, or falsely report the relationship with any person or entity; ② Seriously infringe the intellectual property rights of a third party; ③ Avoid transaction fees (for example, set unreasonable freight); ④ Preventive freezing-spam chat messages-establish false identity (used to deceive others) -use suspicious personal data to register multiple clone accounts; ⑤ It does not belong to the items as mentioned, but it has obviously harmed the interests of Shopee or violated the norms.

同姓名、装置、地址等开分身之行为）—洗评价、销量或者折扣码、信用卡红利；⑥滥用运费补助、折扣码、虾币。

商品：①重大违规商品；②严重侵犯第三人智慧财产权；③规避成交手续费（例如，设定不合常理的运费）。

其他：①使用虾皮提供的服务时，冒充任何人或实体，或虚报与任何人或实体之关系；②严重侵犯第三人智慧财产权；③规避成交手续费（例如，设定不合常理的运费）；④预防性冻结—滥发聊天信息—建立虚假身份（用于欺骗他人）—使用可疑的个人资料注册多个复制账号；⑤不属于上述项目，但已明显有损虾皮公司利益或使用规范之行为。

8.3.4 Learning Customer Relationship Development and Maintenance

1. Analysis of the purchase process of new and old customers

Customer management is the key to discover customers and retain customers to increase repurchase rate. It focuses on customer, includes collecting and analysing customer data, integrates marketing, management, data, and software together, and analyzes the purchase process of new and old customers.Moreover, it proactively and selectively establishes customer relationships and maintains good customer relationships, which is the driving force for profit generation. Compared with domestic E-commerce sales, buyers in cross-border E-commerce sales will have a higher dependence on a good shopping experience, especially there are many small wholesale customers (commonly known as B2 small B). With a guaranteed cross-border E-commerce platform, small

8.3.4 学习客户关系开发与维护

1. 新老客户的购买流程分析

客户管理是发掘客户和留住客户提升复购率的关键。它以客户为中心，包括对客户数据进行收集和分析，整合营销、管理、数据、软件等辅助，分析新老客户的购买流程。另外，它主动且有选择地建立客户关系，并良好地维系客户关系，这是产生利润的动力。相比境内电商销售，跨境电商销售买家会对良好的购物体验产生更高的依赖性，尤其是跨境电商中存在不少小额批发客户（俗称 B2 小 B）。通过有保障

wholesale customers will choose to bypass distributors in their home country to directly obtain high-quality goods at low prices.

New customers generally enter the shop or product page through keyword search, category browsing, or paid advertisements, and subjectively distinguish product styles, detailed descriptions, price discounts, shop reputation and evaluation conditions. As long as one link is not satisfied, they may exit the page, which is commonly known as bounce rate. If new customers are interested in goods, they will not place an order directly, instead, they will add to the shopping cart or favourites, and then decide to purchase after comparative consultation. After the transaction, there will be disputes due to negligence of services or logistics problems. Old customers will have an objective understanding of the product quality and services of the shop. If they have a good shopping experience, when they see the products they are interested in again, they will consult briefly or place an order directly. If there is a shortage of goods or logistics and other problems, it is easier to solve. After receiving the goods, they will be more inclined to perceptually evaluate the products. The rate of disputes is extremely low. They are also willing to share the goods they have purchased and experiences to gain friends' approval.

2．Analysis of potential value of old customers

Data shows that the maintenance cost of an old customer is 1/7-1/8 of the cost for developing a new customer. If you can maintain a good deal of customers and prompt them to purchase again and become an old customer, the old customer will become an important customer, then sellers can also operate more easily. The relationship of old customers can reduce marketing costs, increase profit margins, and can effectively and quickly optimize communication. With the help of the public praise from old customers, it is beneficial to the construction of commodity brands.

The completion of a transaction does not mean the end. The success of a transaction should be regarded as the beginning of communication again, to tap the potential value of customers and their circles, and to increase the

的跨境电商平台，小额批发客户会选择绕过本国的经销商直接以低廉的价格获得优质的商品。

新客户一般通过关键词搜索、类目浏览或付费广告进入店铺或商品页面，对商品的款式、详细描述、价格折扣、店铺信誉和评价情况等进行主观辨别。只要对一个环节不满意，他们就可能退出页面，这俗称跳失率。新客户如有感兴趣的商品，往往不会直接下单，而是加入购物车或收藏，比较咨询后才会决定购买。在成交后，还会因为服务疏忽或物流问题产生纠纷。老客户会对店铺的产品质量和服务有客观的认识，如果有良好的购物体验，当再次看到自己感兴趣的商品时，往往会简单咨询或直接下单购买。如果发生缺货或物流等问题，也较容易解决。在收到货后对产品更倾向于感性评价。纠纷提起率极低。他们还乐意分享自己购买的商品和经历，以获得朋友的认可。

2．老客户潜在价值分析

有数据显示，一个老客户的维护成本是开发一个新客户成本的 1/7 ～ 1/8。如果维系好成交的客户，促使其再次购买变成老客户，老客户就会变成重要客户，卖家也能较轻松运营。老客户的关系可以降低营销成本，提高利润率，可以有效与快捷地优化沟通。借助老客户的口碑力量，有利于商品品牌的建设。

一次交易的完成并不意味着结束。应把一次交易的成功看成再次沟通的开始，挖掘客户及客户圈的潜在价值，增加老客户的

number of transactions with old customers, which means to increase sales and profits. The opinions and suggestions of old customers on the products are more pertinent and credible, and the development of products that meet the needs of old customers can also seize market opportunities. The maintenance of old customers is also an important way to enhance customer stickiness. Sharing customers' praise will gain the trust of more buyers and gain brand promotion through the power of word of mouth.

3. Business strategy of customer relationship management

The repurchase rate is what every seller expects. Making customers who have bought multiple times to buy more is not only related to the product itself, but also related to the effort of the customer service. It is needed to form interaction with customers and enhance customer stickiness. When the customer has an order demand, they firstly think of the seller, which will build the customer's loyalty.

- In the communication of resolving after-sales disputes, simply admitting errors and proposing solutions such as direct refunds, reissues, etc., are often not professional or sincere solutions. By thinking in another way, cross-border E-commerce customers have waited for a few weeks to receive the goods which have problems. If you simply tell them to refund or resend, you may lost a repeat customer. Customers will not be willing to wait for the second long-term logistics. If the refund is made directly, the customer will no longer trust the quality of the goods or the professionalism of the seller.

Therefore, it is necessary to strengthen interactive communication and keep the communication method consistent with customers, which is like providing customers with door-to-door service. Initially, customer service and customers usually establish contact through website messages, order messages, etc. When ordinary customers become important customers, customer service needs to communicate with them by E-mail, phone or other communication tools such as Skype, Facebook, Twitter, etc.

- Paying attention to customer feedback is mainly

成交次数，意味着提升销量和增加利润。老客户对产品的意见和建议更为中肯与可信，开发符合老客户需求的商品也可以抢得市场先机。老客户的维系也是增强客户黏性的重要方式。分享客户的好评，将会获得更多买家的信任，通过口碑的力量获得品牌的宣传效应。

3. 客户关系管理的经营策略

复购率是每个卖家都期望的。让多次购买的客户买得更多，不仅与商品本身有关，更与客服的努力程度有关。需要与客户形成互动，增强客户黏性。当客户有下单需求时，第一时间想到的卖家就构建了良好的客户忠诚度。

- 在解决售后纠纷的沟通中，简单承认错误并提出直接退款、重发等解决方案，往往显得不够专业和诚恳。换位思考，跨境电商客户等了几周时间收到商品有问题。如果简单地告诉他们退款或重发，则可能失去了一个回头客。客户不会愿意等待第二次长周期的物流。如果直接退款，则客户不会再信任商品的质量和卖家的专业。

因此，要加强互动性沟通，沟通方式与客户保持一致，这好比为客户提供上门服务。最初，客服和客户一般通过站内信息、订单留言等建立联系。当普通客户变成重要客户后，客服就需要用邮件、电话或Skype、Facebook、Twitter等通信工具与客户进行沟通。

- 重视客户反馈主要是关注

concerned with customer reviews. Any bad reviews will affect the score of the product and the seller's service level, thereby affecting the ranking and sales of the product. It is also difficult to negotiate with customers to change the evaluation after the bad review occurs. For various reasons, it is difficult for sellers to make customers 100% satisfied, but we must pay attention to the feedback of important customers, and actively ask for opinions and suggestions, such as whether the packaging is deformed, what are the shortcomings of the product design, and whether the customer service is satisfied etc., for collecting this information is to enable customers to have a better shopping experience.

Facing customers' doubts and complaints, sellers must find a reasonable and acceptable reason for customers. Commodity disputes caused by force majeure of a third party are the best choice for customer psychology. Finding a reasonable explanation is not to pass the buck, instead, it is easier for customers to accept the solution proposed by the seller. Shift the "mistake" to a third party reasonably, and at the same time show that even if the mistake is not the seller's, the seller is still willing to solve the problem wholeheartedly for the customer, so that it is easier to calm the customer's dissatisfaction and accept the seller's plan more smoothly.

The key point of after-sales dispute resolution is whether the solution can satisfy customers. Therefore, professional customer service should be the one who proactively proposes solutions and provides at least two solutions for customers to choose from. Only in this way can the cost and difficulty of solving the problem be reduced. Multiple alternatives can make customers feel sincerity and professionalism, and can also prevent customers from unilaterally raising disputes or leaving negative comments on the platform when they do not accept the main recommendation.

- Forecasting customer needs is a prerequisite for improving goods and services. Sellers need to have a

客户的评价。任何一个差评都会影响商品的得分和卖家的服务等级，从而影响商品的排名和销量。差评产生以后与客户协商更改评价也很困难。出于各种原因，卖家很难让客户100%满意，但是一定要重视重要客户的反馈，积极主动询问意见和建议，比如包装是否变形、商品设计有什么不足之处、客户服务是否满意等，收集这些信息是为了让客户有更好的购物体验。

面对客户的质疑和投诉，卖家要为客户找到一个合理的能够接受的理由。由第三方的不可抗力导致的商品纠纷是照顾客户心理的最佳选择。寻找一个合理的解释不是推卸责任的表现，而是让客户更容易接受卖家提出的解决方案。把"错误"合理地推给第三方，同时表明即使错误不在卖家，卖家仍愿意全心全意地为客户解决问题，这样更容易平息客户的不满情绪，更顺利地接受卖家的方案。

售后纠纷解决的关键点在解决方案是否能让客户满意。因此，专业的客服应该是主动提出解决方案的一方，并且要提供至少两种以上解决方案供客户选择。这样才能降低解决问题的成本和难度。多方案的备选能让客户感受到诚意和专业，也可以防止客户在不接受主推方案时单方面向平台提起纠纷或留下差评。

- 预测客户需求是改进商品和服务的前提。卖家需要

full understanding of customers' customs and habits, geography, climate conditions, etc., and obtain the categories and purchasing power of the products frequently purchased by customers based on their hidden information, and through daily communication to understand major customers' distribution channels and objects, as well as the current popular elements, actively provide merchandise sales and services that match customers' needs, and enhance their loyalty.

In the long run, only by treating customers as friends, treating each other with sincerity, and solving after-sales problems in the quickest and most thorough way, can we accumulate customer trust in practice time after time. Problems and contradictions are not necessarily a bad thing. As long as we can make customers feel sincerity and solve problems to recover their losses, we can make customers easier to convert into long-term ones.

对客户的风俗习惯，地理概况，气候状况等有充分的了解，根据客户的隐性信息获取客户经常购买的商品类别和购买能力，通过日常沟通了解大客户的分销渠道和对象，以及当前的流行元素，主动提供与客户需求相匹配的商品销售和服务，提升客户的忠诚度。

从长远来看，只有把客户当成朋友，以诚相待，以最快捷、最彻底的方式解决售后问题，才能在一次次实践中积累客户的信任。出现问题、有了矛盾不一定是坏事，只要能够让客户感受到诚意，并解决问题挽回客户损失，才能让客户更容易转化为长期客户。

New words

1. consulting 咨询
2. dispute resolving 解决纠纷
3. selling pushing 促进销售
4. managing monitor 管理监督
5. Detail Seller Ratings（DSR）卖家服务等级评分
6. Online Disputes Resolution（ODR）在线纠纷解决
7. credit score 信用积分
8. long-term customer 长期客户
9. bad review 差评
10. good review 好评
11. communication tool 通信工具
12. customer stickiness 客户黏性
13. repurchase rate 复购率
14. silent ordering 静默式下单